CHINA AND
THE GLOBAL
ECONOMIC CRISIS

Series on Contemporary China　　　(ISSN: 1793-0847)

Series Editors: Joseph Fewsmith *(Boston University)*
Zheng Yongnian *(East Asian Institute, National University of Singapore)*

Published*

*To view the complete list of the published volumes in the series, please visit:
http://www.worldscibooks.com/series/scc_series.shtml

Series on Contemporary China – Vol. 22

CHINA AND THE GLOBAL ECONOMIC CRISIS

edited by

Zheng Yongnian & Sarah Y Tong

(East Asian Institute, National University of Singapore, Singapore)

World Scientific

NEW JERSEY · LONDON · SINGAPORE · BEIJING · SHANGHAI · HONG KONG · TAIPEI · CHENNAI

Published by

World Scientific Publishing Co. Pte. Ltd.

5 Toh Tuck Link, Singapore 596224

USA office: 27 Warren Street, Suite 401-402, Hackensack, NJ 07601

UK office: 57 Shelton Street, Covent Garden, London WC2H 9HE

British Library Cataloguing-in-Publication Data
A catalogue record for this book is available from the British Library.

CHINA AND THE GLOBAL ECONOMIC CRISIS
Series on Contemporary China — Vol. 22

ISBN-13 978-981-4287-70-8
ISBN-10 981-4287-70-9

Typeset by Stallion Press
Email: enquiries@stallionpress.com

Printed in Singapore by B & Jo Enterprise Pte Ltd

Contents

v

List of Contributors

BO Zhiyue is a Senior Research Fellow at the East Asian Institute of the National University of Singapore. He obtained his Bachelor of Law and Master of Law from Peking University and Ph.D. from the University of Chicago. He taught at Beijing University, Roosevelt University, the University of Chicago, American University, St. John Fisher College, Tarleton State University, and the Chinese University of Hong Kong. He is a recipient of the *Trustees' Distinguished Scholar Award* at St. John Fisher College and the inaugural holder of the *Joe and Theresa Long Endowed Chair in Social Science* at Tarleton State University. His research interests include China's elite politics, Chinese provincial leaders, central–local relations, and cross-strait relations. He is the author of a trilogy on China's political elites and elite politics, namely, *Chinese Provincial Leaders: Economic Performance and Political Mobility since 1949* (Armonk, NY: M. E. Sharpe, 2002), *China's Elite Politics: Political Transition and Power Balancing* (Singapore: World Scientific, 2007), and *China's Elite Politics: Governance and Democratization* (Singapore: World Scientific, 2009).

CHEN Gang is a Research Fellow at the East Asian Institute of the National University of Singapore. He studied international relations and obtained his Ph.D. degree from the China Foreign Affairs University. He is the author of *Politics of China's Environmental*

Protection: Problems and Progress (Singapore: World Scientific, 2009) and *The Kyoto Protocol and International Cooperation against Climate Change* (Beijing: Xinhua Press, 2008). His research papers have appeared in refereed journals such as *China: An International Journal, East Asian Policy, Twenty-First Century, The Chinese Journal of International Politics, The Journal of East Asian Affairs, American Studies Quarterly, Journal of China Foreign Affairs University* and *the International Forum.* His research interests include China's domestic politics and foreign policy, environmental governance, international relations, and transnational cooperation against climate change.

CHEN Shaofeng specialises in energy and environmental studies, Chinese political economy, and international political economy. He completed his PhD studies at the National University of Singapore in August 2008 and worked at the East Asian Institute (EAI) as a Research Officer and Visiting Research Fellow from October 2007 to April 2009. He has conducted his own research on China's approach to energy security against the backdrop of its integration into the world economy in his stay at EAI. He also has over two years' experience in a consulting company, as well as further academic experience at the Beijing Foreign Studies University where he taught at the undergraduate level. He has authored more than 10 articles and book chapters.

CHONG Siew Keng is a Research Assistant at the East Asian Institute, National University of Singapore. She obtained her Master of Arts (Contemporary China) from Nanyang Technological University, Singapore. Her research interest includes ASEAN and China relations — politics and economy, cross-Strait relations, and North-East Asian economy and development.

HUANG Yanjie obtained his Bachelor of Social Sciences in economics with Honours from the National University of Singapore in July 2008. His honours thesis deals with the evolution of China's dualist economy and its policy implications. His current research interests cover a broad range of issues related to China's economic development. While focusing on the economic aspect of China's development, he also takes deep interest in other aspects of the ongoing modernisation programme, such as political development, international relations, social changes, and institutional evolution in mainland China. A multi-linguist, Huang aspires to work on comparative political economy and other related fields of studies.

Fung KWAN, Assistant Professor of Economics at the University of Macau, is also on the Board of Directors of the US Chinese Economists Society (2008–2009). He was visiting fellow at Clare Hall, Cambridge and Official Visitor of the Faculty of Economics of the University of Cambridge from February to July 2008. His research interests include development economics and macroeconomics. Currently, his research is on the rural labour market and productivity growth of China. His most recent article is "Agricultural Labour and the Incidence of Surplus Labour: Experience from China during Reform" in the *Journal of Chinese Economic and Business Studies* (forthcoming).

LIM Tin Seng is a Research Officer at the East Asian Institute in the National University of Singapore. He received his M.A. in History from the National University of Singapore. His research focuses on the regional impact of China's economic development and China's foreign relations with developing countries. He is the co-editor of *Harmony and Development: ASEAN–China Relations* (World Scientific, 2007) and *China's New Social Policy: Initiatives for A Harmonious Society* (World Scientific, 2009).

LYE Liang Fook is a Research Fellow at the East Asian Institute of the National University of Singapore. His research interests include China's central–local relations, the mass media, leadership changes, and political legitimacy in China. He has also written extensively on Singapore's relations with China including flagship cooperative projects like the Suzhou Industrial Park and China-Singapore Tianjin Eco-city Project. Besides his academic work, he manages the Secretariat of Singapore's Network of East Asian Think-Tanks

(NEAT), a Track 2 body to foster ASEAN plus Three cooperation. Before joining the academia, he was a Foreign Service Officer with Singapore's Ministry of Foreign Affairs.

Sarah Y. TONG is an Assistant Professor of the Economics Department and Research Fellow at the East Asian Institute. She obtained her Ph.D. in Economics from the University of California at San Diego. Her research interests include Chinese economy, international trade, foreign direct investment, economic reforms, and industrial restructuring. Her publications have appeared in international journals such as *Journal of International Economics, China Economic Review, Review of Development Economics, China: An International Journal, China and the World Economy,* and *Global Economic Review.*

John WONG is a Research Director at the East Asian Institute (EAI) of the National University of Singapore (NUS). He was formerly Director of the Institute of East Asian Political Economy (IEAPE), Singapore (1990–1996).

Prior to this, he taught Economics in the University of Hong Kong (1966–1971) and then the NUS (1971–1990). He also taught briefly in Florida State University as a Fulbright Visiting Professor in 1979. He had visiting appointments with Harvard's Fairbank Centre, Yale's Economic Growth Centre, Oxford's St. Antony College, and Stanford University. In 1996, he held the Chair of ASEAN Studies in the University of Toronto.

He has done consultancy work for the Singapore government and many international organisations, including UN ESCAP, ADB, UNIDO, and APO. He serves on the editorial board of many learned journals on Asian studies and economic development.

He has written and edited 28 books, and published over 400 articles and papers on the development of China and other East Asian economies, including ASEAN.

He obtained his Ph.D. in Economics from London in 1966.

YANG Mu is a Senior Research Fellow and Co-ordinator of the China Cooperation Programme at the East Asia Institute, National

University of Singapore. He was previously a CEO and Executive President of several companies in Hong Kong and China. In the 1980s, he was Deputy Director and Senior Research Fellow of the Institute of Industrial Economics, Chinese Academy of Social Sciences and had participated in China's central government policy formulation in industrial development, the reform of SOEs and others. He is the author of China's first academic book on "产业政策研究" (Industrial Policy Research). In 1988, he was awarded Sun Ye Fang's Economic Prize for his article on the *People's Daily* (人民日报). Now, his research focuses on world financial crisis, China's macroeconomic policy, China's industrial development, and Chinese companies' M&A abroad.

YU Hong obtained his PhD in economic geography from the University of Sheffield. His research interests lie in the field of regional economy. He has particular interest in the sources of regional economic growth and spatial inequality that can affect long-run development and human welfare improvement. He also has a parallel interest in the areas of industrial development and political economy of China. He has presented four refereed papers at a number of international conferences and workshops in regional economic growth and spatial inequality. Currently, he is revising his doctoral thesis, titled Regional Inequality in Guangdong Province.

ZHANG Yang is an Assistant Professor at the Faculty of Business Administration, University of Macau. She obtained her Ph.D. in Economics from Nanyang Technological University, Singapore. Her research interests include applied econometrics, nonlinear dynamics, the Chinese economy, and regional economics. Her articles have appeared in *Journal of Economic Behaviour and Organization*, *Issues & Studies* and *China: an International Journal* among others.

ZHAO Hong is a visiting senior research fellow at the East Asian Institute, National University of Singapore. His research interests are on China–ASEAN economic integration, cross-Strait economic relations, and East Asian economic community.

ZHAO Litao is a Research Fellow at the East Asian Institute, National University of Singapore. He obtained his PhD degree in sociology from Stanford University. His research interests include social stratification and mobility, sociology of education, organisational analysis, and China's social policy. His research has appeared in *China Quarterly, Research in Social Stratification and Mobility, International Journal of Educational Development, Social Sciences in China, Built Environment, China: An International Journal,* and *Frontiers of Education in China.* He is the author of *Paths to Private Entrepreneurship: Markets and Mobility in Rural China* (VDM Verlag, 2008) and a co-editor of *China's Reforms at 30: Challenges and Prospects* (World Scientific, 2009).

ZHENG Yongnian is a Professor and Director of East Asian Institute, National University of Singapore. He is an Editor of Series on Contemporary China (World Scientific Publishing) and Editor of China Policy Series (Routledge). He is also the editor of *China: An International Journal.*

Professor Zheng has studied both China's transformation and its external relations. His papers have appeared in journals such as *Comparative Political Studies, Political Science Quarterly, Third World Quarterly,* and *China Quarterly.* He is the author of 13 books, including *Technological Empowerment, De Facto Federalism in China, Discovering Chinese Nationalism in China* and *Globalization and State Transformation in China,* and co-editor of 11 books on China's politics and society including the latest volume *China and the New International Order* (2008).

Besides his research work, Professor Zheng has been an academic activist. He served as a consultant to United Nation Development Programme on China's rural development and democracy. In addition, he has been a columnist for *Xinbao* (Hong Kong) and *Zaobao* (Singapore) for many years, writing numerous commentaries on China's domestic and international affairs.

Professor Zheng received his B.A. and M.A. degrees from Beijing University, and his Ph.D. at Princeton University. He was a recipient of Social Science Research Council — MacArthur Foundation

Fellowship (1995–1997) and John D. and Catherine T. MacArthur Foundation Fellowship (2003–2004). He was a Professor and founding Research Director of the China Policy Institute, the University of Nottingham, United Kingdom (2005–2008).

ZHOU Shengqi is a visiting scholar at East Asian Institute, National University of Singapore and professor in economics at Qingdao University, China, where he lectures on international trade and economics. He is also the head of the Research Institute of Yellow Sea Economic Rim, director of International Trade and Economics Department in Qingdao University, and a member of Consultative Committee of Qingdao City. His research interests include international trade, foreign direct investment, ecological economy, and sustainable development. He received his M.A. in political economics from Shandong University, and Ph.D. in agricultural economics at the Shandong Agriculture University.

Introduction

ZHENG Yongnian and Sarah Y. TONG*

Since late 2008, the financial crisis-turned-economic crisis has spread widely across the globe. Like many countries in both the developed and developing world, China has been affected extensively. To a large extent, this is due to China's growing integration with and rising dependence on the rest of the world. Consequently, the global economic crisis, currently still unfolding, is expected to have profound and lasting implications for China in both its internal conditions and its changing role in the wider world.

Initially, the evidence of a serious economic downturn was not clear due to the measures implemented by the Chinese government to rein in an overheating economy and to improve the environment ahead of the Olympic Games in August 2008. By the fourth quarter of 2008 though, it became evident that the Chinese economy had suffered a sharp decline as a result of the sudden disappearance of export demand from the United States and the European Union.

* In putting this volume together, we are indebted to John Wong, Research Director of the East Asian Institute for going over the early drafts of many of the papers included in this volume; and Jessica Loon, for copyediting the chapters. We are also grateful to our contributors for their timely submissions.

1

Year-on-year gross domestic production (GDP) growth slowed to only 6.6% in the last quarter of 2008, from 11.5% in the last quarter of 2007. For the whole year of 2008, the economy registered a 9% growth, ending China's five years of double-digit growth since 2003.

While the figures themselves may look quite decent, especially when compared to the performance of other major economies which have registered negative growth, the quick deceleration caused grave political and social concerns in Beijing. For a large developing country like China which is undergoing rapid economic and social transformation, sustaining a healthy growth is crucial to generating employment and maintaining social stability. Often, the government considers an annual GDP growth of 8% as the minimal level to generate sufficient job opportunities to absorb the number of new entrants to the labour market as well as those moving from the rural to the non-agricultural sector.

Recognising that the economy is facing unprecedented difficulties and a deterioration in growth prospects, the Chinese government responded quickly in November 2008 with a series of strong and decisive measures. These include policy initiatives to prop up domestic demand in both consumption and investment as well as measures to assist export firms. While numerous policy initiatives have been announced and discussed at the national and local levels, such as the loosening of monetary policy, subsidising rural consumption of various home appliances and increasing tax rebates for exports successively, the government's ambitious stimulus package of four trillion RMB has attracted the most attention, domestically and internationally.

Many important questions may be asked regarding the Chinese government's various efforts to reinvigorate the economy. One set of questions concerns the immediate or short-run implications of these efforts. As domestic demand has played the dominant role in advancing China's economic growth over the past decades, there are good reasons to believe that the aggressive stimulus package which placed great emphasis on massive investment, as well as other policy measures, will be able to prevent the economy from sliding further down and that the target of 8% economic growth for 2009 is achievable.

Indeed, we have already see signs of economic recovery as shown by recent economic figures. In the second quarter of 2009, GDP grew by 7.9% on a yearly basis, not far off from the 8% target for the whole year and a significant improvement over the 6.1% in the first quarter of 2009.

The more essential and difficult question, however, is whether this economic recovery or growth is sustainable in the medium to long term. The current global economic crisis has served to expose various weaknesses in the world economy, including the expanding global imbalances among economies. Similarly, the grave impact suffered by the Chinese economy during the current crisis has made it more evident that the country needs to reflect on its growth experience and contemplate its way forward to achieve lasting development.

Over the last three decades, the Chinese economy's average annual real growth of close to 10% had been remarkable. Such attainment has been built upon two main pillars: economic liberalisation and integration with the world economy. Domestically, marketisation and decentralisation have jointly re-energised and intensified competition among firms and among localities. Equipped with a young and relatively well-educated labour force and a high saving rate, China has invested heavily and thus industrialised rapidly. Indeed, domestic investment and the resulting industrialisation are the main engines of China's growth.

Externally, China has benefited from various favourable economic conditions. China's economic opening since the late 1970s coincided with the industrial restructuring in much of East Asia when export-oriented manufacturing sectors in these economies were forced to relocate in search of lower production cost and a more favourable policy environment. China has become one of the most favoured designations for direct investment. China's accession to the World Trade Organisation in late 2001 propelled a new wave of inward foreign direct investment to China as it is formally included in the global trading system.

Not only did China rapidly expand its trade to become intensely integrated with the world economy, it has also developed into a centre of regional production network in Asia. Essentially, China imports various inputs, including raw materials as well as parts and components, from neighbouring economies. After further processing and assembling, China shipped the finished products to the world markets, mainly the United States and the European Union. Thus, what might have appeared to be "made in China" is quite likely a product "made in Asia".

This has a number of implications for China's external economic relations. First, China's trade expansion, or more accurately export expansion, depends crucially on the growth of the consumer markets in the West such as the US and the EU. As this current economic crisis has shown, such consumer expansion is not sustainable. Further, the large and increasing trade deficits these economies have with China may also lead to protectionist policies. Second, as the centre of the regional production network, changes in China's export markets would lead to even greater fluctuations in its trade with neighbouring economies, where many have large trade surplus with China. To alleviate such perils, Asian countries may step up efforts to establish a formal regional trade bloc by pushing forward negotiations for various free trade agreements.

Indeed, China's neighbouring economies, including Korea, Taiwan, Hong Kong, Macao and members of ASEAN, are without exception affected by the global economic crisis as well as by China's declining trade with them. Each has taken measures to stimulate its economy while strengthening its trade relations with China and among themselves. These include efforts by the Ma administration of Taiwan to normalise and strengthen economic ties with the Mainland and to initiate talks on a possible trade pact across the Taiwan Strait.

Domestically, China's rising dependence on trade for growth has also led to several consequences. First, the economy is more vulnerable to external shocks than many have believed. Although domestic investment and consumption has contributed more than four-fifths of China's total GDP in recent years, trade and foreign investment are hugely important for the economy, for example, to generate employment and improve productivity through technology transfer and intense competition. Moreover, the problem of trade decline has hit most severely the regions that have been the most dynamic and prosperous, including the Pearl River Delta and the Yangtze River Delta regions. The regions, already struggling with rising costs, have to accelerate their efforts to re-structure and re-innovate their economies. Furthermore, among different groups of people, migrant workers from inland areas working in the export sector in coastal regions have been the first and the most seriously affected. This has caused grave concerns about human grievances as well as societal stability and social cohesion.

Running in tandem is a new round of ideology debates on development and progress highlighted by the criticism of the Washington Consensus and neoliberalism, both emphasising private entrepreneurship and market. Inside China, this is represented by the ascending voices of the New Left who advocate strongly the role of the government in redressing the problems of injustice, inequality, pollution and other negative effects of liberalisation and globalisation advocated by the West. Such ideological debates may push government policy making to shift from the growth-above-all-else mantra towards one that combines market with social concerns such as social security, equity, and strong environment protection.

There is little doubt that after 30 years of reform and opening to the world, China has achieved remarkable economic progress. At the same time, however, the country is facing growing challenges including huge and rising trade imbalances, over-dependence on investment and inadequate consumption, rising income inequality, insufficient job creation, and environmental degradation. Such problems are further exasperated by the current global financial and economic crisis.

In this edited volume, we present 13 chapters that examine various aspects of the problems engendered by the current global economic crisis on China and some of its neighbours. The first three chapters examine broadly China's economic conditions since 2008 as well as government's policy response to counter the negative impact of the global economic crisis. In Chapter 1, John Wong provides an overview of China's economic performance and the country's economic outlook for 2009. He reckons that the sharp slowdown in China's growth in late 2008 was due to both domestic policies to prevent overheating and the sudden negative external shocks. He believes that the government's stimulus package will be able to pull the economy out of the downturn while China's growth pattern of a heavy reliance on domestic investment and foreign trade will remain unchanged. Such confidence in the resilience of China's economy is also reflected in Chapter 2. Yang Mu and Lim Tin Seng believe that domestic demand remains the main source of China's growth. Consequently, China's strong fiscal position and its accommodative monetary policy will ensure its growth in 2009 and that the country is in a pole position to recover. However, the authors also express caution that a strong and lasting resurgence has to wait till the world's economic condition improves. Chapter 3 by Sarah Y. Tong focusses on the Chinese government's policy measures in response to the crisis, both at the central as well as various local levels. While the policy initiatives cover a broad range of areas, including spending on investment, stimulating domestic consumption, accelerating the development of the social safety net, and revitalising industries, the paramount emphasis remains on investment. While the policies are believed to be pragmatic to restore economic momentum, Tong warns that they may slow China's pursuance of a more balanced development in the longer term.

The next two chapters take a regional approach to examining the impact and implications of the economic crisis. Chapter 4 by Huang Yanjie and Chen Shaofeng looks at the Pearl River Delta region in southern China, which has served as the forefront of China's economic reform over the past three decades and is China's most export-oriented region. Consequently, the region is most severely affected by the sudden drop in export demand and the subsequent economic and social difficulties, including mass plant closures and layoffs of migrant workers. The local leadership, determined to invigorate the economy, initiated various policy measures to accelerate industrial upgrading. While it might still be early to evaluate the outcome, such exercise will offer important lessons for China's economic development in the long term. Chapter 5 by Yu Hong compares Yangtze River Delta region with the Pearl River Delta region in their economic performance during the current economic crisis. These two regions accounted for more than a third of China's total GDP and are two of China's most dynamic regions. While both are highly export-oriented, there exist distinct differences between the two, such as their industrial structures, and export compositions. Yu examines the differences and the relative strengths and weaknesses of the two regions to show how they might learn from each other.

Chapters 6–8 examine the three neighbouring economies of Taiwan, Hong Kong, and Macao, respectively. Chapter 6 by Zhao Hong discusses the grave impact of the global economic crisis on Taiwan and the government's efforts to stabilise the economy. Such efforts focus on two aspects: stimulating domestic economic activities in investment and consumption and strengthening economic ties with mainland China. In the long-term, as Zhao argues, Taiwan's economic vigour depends on its ability to restructure the economy into one that is domestic demand-driven and more tightly integrated with economies in East and Southeast Asia. In Chapter 7, Zhang Yang highlights the downward spiral of Hong Kong's economy during the crisis due to slackening exports, weaker domestic demand, and withering investment. While the Hong Kong government responded swiftly by putting forward measures to stabilise the financial market, support enterprise and create employment, Zhang maintains that Hong Kong's economy is expected to shrink modestly by around 6% in 2009. This is attributable to its close economic relations with a growing hinterland in mainland China. Chapter 8, by Zhang Yang and Fung Kwan, discusses the economy of Macao, which has suffered gravely during the current economic crisis due in part to its over-dependency on the gambling industry. While the Macao government has long been convinced that the long-term prosperity of the territory's economy lies in its diversification, Zhang and Kwan believe the current crisis and the break in the gambling and tourism-led boom may serve as an additional force to facilitate economic diversification, where a more diversified tourism with leisure and business conventions is likely to be the focal point.

Chapters 9 and 10 examine two of China's important trade relations, one with ASEAN and the other with South Korea. In Chapter 9, Sarah Y. Tong and Chong Siew Keng explain how a sharp slowdown in China's trade expansion has led to an even greater decline in its trade with many of its neighbours including ASEAN, due to a highly inter-dependent regional production network in the region. Tong and Chong believe that, with the looming danger of trade protectionism across the world, economies in Asia need to reaffirm their commitment to free trade and economic integration in both intra-regional and extra-regional perspectives. The region needs also to develop its own consumer market to ensure long-term growth and prosperity. In Chapter 10, Zhou Shengqi examines Sino-South Korean bilateral trade relations, which have developed strongly since the early 1990s but have encountered growing challenges in recent years, especially during the current economic crisis. While the two economies continue to demonstrate complementarity in many trade goods, there is increasing competition between "made-in-China" and "made-in-Korea" products both at home and overseas markets. Zhou assumes that a bilateral Free Trade Agreement will bring benefits to both countries by expanding the market and facilitating industrial restructuring.

The remaining three chapters, Chapters 11 to 13, look at the impact of the crisis on ideological, social as well as foreign relations aspects. In Chapter 11, Bo Zhiyue and Chen Gang examine the current ideological debate spurred by the current economic crisis and the ascendance of China's New Left, who criticise Anglo-Saxon Neoliberalism and advocate "state capacity". The aspiration of the New Left is to use state power to redress the problems of injustice, inequality, pollution and other negative effects of privatisation, marketisation and globalisation. Bo and Chen argue that the New Left may already have affected Chinese government policy making as seen in the shift towards social security, equity and environment protection.

Chapter 12, by Zhao Litao and Huang Yanjie, discusses the implications of the current economic crisis on China's social stability. In particular, Zhao and Huang examine two groups of people — retrenched migrant workers and newly graduated college students — who are having difficulties in finding a desirable job. Overall, the authors believe they will not pose serious challenges to social stability. While the number of retrenched migrant workers is huge, Zhao and Huang argue that the retrenched are too disorganised and segregated to launch large-scale protests in urban areas. They also believe that college students, with the resources to organise protests, are likely to lower their expectations than resort to collective action. The possibility of social unrest may further be reduced as the government is acting to pre-empt a potential crisis by increasing employment and addressing the grievances of disgruntled social groups.

Chapter 13, by Zheng Yongnian and Lye Liang Fook, examines China's external response in the global economic crisis. Since late 2008, China has been inadvertently thrust into the political limelight as the world's largest holder of foreign reserves. While China has been perceived as a "saviour" and expected to act more assertively to stabilise the international financial system, China's response has been cautious and calibrated, according to Zheng and Lye. As the Chinese government stated, its primary preoccupation is getting its own house in order. Zheng and Lye believe that China is ready and willing to work with other countries and international institutions to restore world growth and be regarded as a responsible and constructive player. They also argue that China should not take a leadership role in bringing the world out of its economic doldrums as it is not in its interest to do so.

Chapter 1

China's Economy 2008 and Outlook for 2009: Crisis of a Sharp Slowdown

John WONG

China's economy ended 2008 with 9.0% growth, after sustaining double-digit growth for five years. Starting with an over-heated economy but ending with global recession, the Chinese leadership was forced to make a full swing its economic policy from deflationary to stimulus measures. Faced with the crisis, the Chinese government is committed to implement a 4 trillion *yuan* fiscal stimulus package over two years. With the combined efforts of an expansionary fiscal policy, easy monetary policies and export subsidies, the government is determined to reach a target growth rate of 8% for the year 2009. However, the more daunting task will be the unemployment problem for migrant labourers and college graduates.

With growth in the first three quarters of 2008 already at 9.9% (above the 30-year growth trend of 9.8%), the Chinese economy ended the year with a 9% growth[1] (Figure 1). Though it was a marked decline

---

[1] "National Statistical Bulletin on Economic and Social Development 2008, PR China (中华人民共和国2008年国民经济和社会发展统计公报)", National Bureau of Statistics, 26 February 2009, http://www.stats.gov.cn.

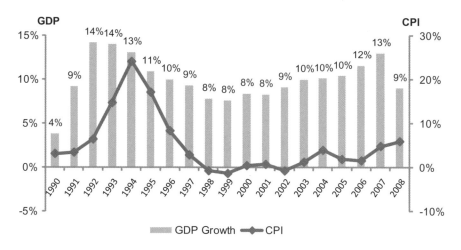

Source: China Statistical Yearbook 2008; NBS Database.

Fig. 1.   China's economic growth and inflation, 1990–2008.

from the 13% growth of 2007, the 2008 growth rate would still rank China as the best performing economy in the world based on the estimated global average growth of only 2.1%.[2] All eyes, both inside and outside China, are now on its potential growth for 2009, which has been variously estimated to be around 7–8%, or possibly lower. But should China's economic growth plunge to 5–6% in 2009, there would probably not be much growth at all in the global economy, which is projected to be negative by IMF.

China started 2008 with an overheated economy that was also threatened by rising inflation, after having chalked up double-digit rates of growth for five years in a row. To rein in the runaway economic growth, the government had to introduce tight macroeconomic control measures in the first half of 2008 in the hope of steering the economy to a soft landing. Towards the end of 2008, however, as major economic indicators suddenly plummeted, the government was caught in a completely different macroeconomic scenario underpinned

---

[2] Note: global GDP growth is based on market exchange rate. (Source: *World Economic Outlook Database, April 2009*, http://www.imf.org.)

by the spectre of a severe economic downturn or even a deflation. Seldom has the Chinese leadership experienced such a radical reversion of economic fortunes in a short span of just a few months, from the euphoria of high growth to the worry of a sharp downturn.

Indeed, in early October 2008 when the third quarter GDP figures came out with only 9% growth, the government appeared to be unaware of the strong growth deceleration momentum. It was apparently still thinking of the downturn as merely a consequence of its ongoing macroeconomic policy to cool overheating and the temporary effects of production disruptions due to the Sichuan earthquakes and the Beijing Olympics (shutting down many factories to facilitate this event).

China's economic downturn started to surface in October as production and exports came down rapidly. Worse still, the November and December figures really took a tumble as industrial production grew only at 5.4% (compared to 8.2% for October), the lowest since 1999 while exports fell by 2.2% (compared to 19% growth for October), the first contraction in seven years.[3] By this time, the government had no doubt whatsoever that the economy was heading for a sharp and severe slowdown. In response, the government hastily put together a huge fiscal stimulus package of four trillion *yuan* (US$590 billion) designed to boost economic growth for the next two years.

In the initial phases of the global financial crisis, many Chinese economists and policy makers believed that China could be "decoupled" from its negative impact on account of China's strong internal and external balances (its huge foreign reserves) plus the existence of capital control measures, even though the Shanghai Stock Exchange had plunged more than 60% by mid-2008. Subsequently, as the global financial tsunami deepened, throwing the US and Japan into recession, China was still optimistic that its "real economy" (production and exports) could somehow escape from such a severe external impact. It is commonly assumed that China's economic growth, technically speaking, is mainly driven by domestic demand, particularly domestic investment.

---

[3] In December 2008, growth of industrial production remained weak at 5.7%, while export contracted further by 2.8% on year-to-year basis.

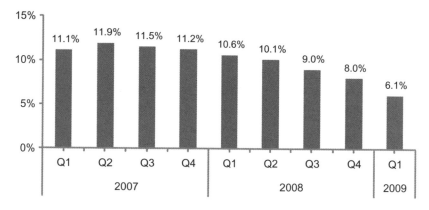

Source: NBS Database.

Fig. 2.   China quarterly GDP, 2007–2009.

Why was there such an abrupt about-turn in the government's economic mood? It seems that the government had initially misread or simply ignored, long before the crunch in the final quarter of 2008, several telltale signs of the downward growth momentum as manifested in the growing bankruptcy of many small and medium enterprises and production cutbacks in many key industrial items like electricity, steel and metal products, cement, automobile, petrochemicals and so on. As shown in Figure 2, China's quarterly GDP growth had started to decline from its peak of 12% in Q-2 of 2007 to the 9% in Q-3 of 2008, partly as a result of the tightening of macroeconomic policies. Initially, the government might have taken the downward trends as part of the normal process of industrial restructuring caused by such policies as the new labour protection law.

Subsequently as the situation rapidly deteriorated, the government was alarmed by the swiftness and ferocity of the sudden economic downturn. This explains why, in addition to the fiscal stimulus package, the government has also applied other direct policy intervention measures aimed at stimulating exports (e.g. raise the rate of tax rebates) and promoting rural consumption (through direct subsidies for the purchase of home appliances) as well as adopting a loose monetary policy (with inflation now being a nonconcern) and even mulling over the possibility of devaluating the *Renminbi* (RMB) to promote exports. In fact, almost all available government policy instruments have been utilised for the single-minded objective of boosting economic growth in 2009.

Initially, the World Bank projected a 7.5% growth for 2009, and later adjusted it downward to 6.5%.[4] But it is likely that the Chinese government would push growth to 8% as 2009 is an important year for China politically, being the 60th anniversary of the founding of the People's Republic of China. Apart from the political need for high growth, it is also socially imperative for China to maintain 8% growth (保八), commonly regarded as the required minimum growth rate to generate reasonable employment. The double-digit rates of growth of the past five years had, on average, created 17 million new jobs a year. With about five million new entrants to the labour force every year, any sharp economic slowdown would bring about serious unemployment, which is unacceptable to a government much in fear of social instability.

With all available fiscal and monetary ammunitions at its disposal and with strong external reserves and a comfortable fiscal position, the Chinese government is thus institutionally and economically capable of achieving the 8% growth target for 2009, even against the background of a weak external demand for its exports. In the long run, a lot of infrastructure investment will expand the future growth capacity of the economy. In the short run, however, the problems of inefficiency and wastage arising from investment duplication or lack of proper coordination are bound to arise when growth is rammed through such a set of hastily packaged stimulus policies. For long-term benefits, the government should make proper use of the stimulus measures to rebalance the economy for a more sustainable growth.

PATTERN OF GROWTH REMAINS

The pattern of economic growth for 2008 was pretty much the same as that of 2007, despite the slowdown. The supply-side aspect of

---

[4] The World Bank, "China Quarterly Update, March 2009", http://web.worldbank.org.

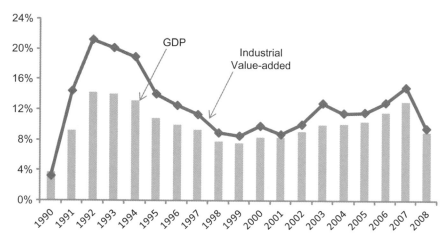

Source: NB: China Statistical Yearbook 2008; NBS Database.

Fig. 3.   Growth of GDP and industrial value-added GDP, 1998–2008.

growth is focussed primarily on the productivity growth of its major sectors. Manufacturing is a large sector in China, accounting for 43% of its GDP in 2007 (only slightly smaller than the 49% accounted for by the service sector), and it also grows much faster than other sectors. China's economy is basically pulled along by its rapid industrial growth. As shown in Figure 3, industrial growth follows GDP growth closely. Since 2002, industrial value-added has been growing at an average annual rate of 13%, which gave rise to over 10% GDP growth for this period. For 2008, growth of industrial production came down sharply to about 9.5% compared to 14.9% for 2007, hence a much lower GDP growth for 2008. As noted earlier, industrial production for November and December 2008 plummeted even further to 5.4% and 5.7%, respectively, and that certainly augurs ill for 2009.

For the demand-side source of growth, increases in GDP stem from the rise in both domestic demand (domestic investment and consumption) and external demand (net exports). China's economic growth, as shown in Figure 4, was basically fuelled by domestic demand, particularly domestic investment. Of the 13% GDP growth in 2007, investment contributed 5.3% and consumption 5.1% while net

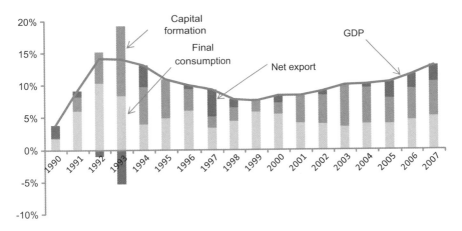

Source: China Statistical Yearbook 2008; NBS Database.

Fig. 4. Contribution of final consumption, gross capital formation, and net export China's GDP growth, 1990–2007.

exports accounted for only 2.6%.[5] This also explains why the current government's expansionary fiscal policy of boosting growth is heavily concentrated on investment.

In 2008, fixed investment grew at 25.5% in nominal term (slightly higher than in 2007). For consumption, as measured by total retail sale, growth also held up strongly at 21.6% for 2008, compared to 16.8% in 2007. Export held up reasonably well despite the revaluation of the RMB, as it still grew at 17.2% for the whole year, though down from the 25.5% of 2007. Weaker demand for Chinese exports from the developed economies had been partially compensated by China's greater market shares in the emerging economies. All in all, this translates to lower GDP growth for 2008. But it should be noted that export growth started to decline to 19% in October and nosedived to −2.2% in November. In a way, the

---

[5] GDP growth for 2007 was adjusted upward, from 11.9% (in China's Statistical Yearbook 2008) to 13.0% (National Statistical Bulletin on Economic and Social Development 2008, PR China 中华人民共和国2008年国民经济和社会发展统计公报). The assumption here is that the contribution shares remain the same as those in the China's Statistical Yearbook.

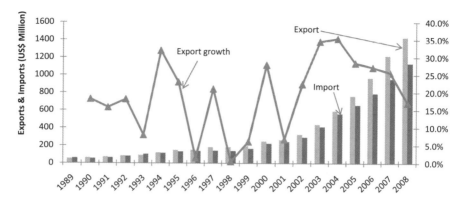

Source: China Statistical Yearbook 2008, China Custom Statistics, December 2008.

Fig. 5.   China's trade and growth, 1990–2008.

slump in exports this time was the signal of the general economic slowdown (Figure 5).

The importance of external demand in China's overall growth, expressed as "net exports", can be misleading. As clearly shown in Fig. 4, the contribution of net exports to overall growth, particularly prior to 2005, has been mostly marginal or even negative. This is mainly because China has been a huge "export processing zone" for the world — nearly 60% of China's exports are done by foreign enterprises. China has to import a lot (raw materials, intermediate products, and machinery) before it can export. In other words, China's exports initially generated only a small proportion of domestic value-added, thus making a small contribution to GDP growth. Since 2005, the share of net exports has increased, and its contribution to GDP growth has also increased, currently at about 20% to overall GDP growth.

Still, such a simple demand analysis as shown earlier has grossly underestimated the actual economic importance of exports in China's economy, because it has missed out a great deal of highly important "indirect" economic activities that are connected with the export sector. A large export-oriented industry creates many supporting local service activities as well as investment in upstream and downstream industries, not to mention the multiplier effect on the broader economy generated by its employees. Not surprisingly, the loss of growth momentum in exports in the second half of 2008 (which has also brought down domestic consumption) prompted the government to take action to cope with the economic downturn.

China's total trade for 2008 rose by 17.8% to US$2.6 trillion, yielding a total trade surplus of US$295 billion, up 11.2% from 2007. China has had a sizable trade surplus since the early 2000s, largely because about half of China's exports are processing trade, which by its very nature will inevitably yield China a trade surplus as domestic value-added (for the service performed). This, along with the large annual inflow of foreign direct investment (which amounted to US$84 billion in 2007 and US$92 billion in 2008), constitutes China's "twin surpluses" (also the "twin engines" of China's export-led growth). The sustained growth of surplus led to the rapid build-up of China's foreign reserves standing at US$2.1 trillion by the end of 2008.

China's swelling external surplus has actually aggravated its macro-economic imbalance towards over-production and over-investment, and put pressure on the revaluation of the RMB. Through 2008, the RMB had appreciated 8.1% year-on-year against the US dollar, 20.3% against the Euro, and 32.1% against the British pound while depreciating 7.6% against the yen. From July 2005 to September 2008 (before the outbreak of the global financial turmoil), the RMB's REER (real effective exchange rate) had appreciated 21.8%. The rising RMB has been one of the contributing factors for the export decline.

Figure 6 brings out China's unique pattern of trade balances with its major trade partners. For many years, China has been incurring trade deficits with neighbouring economies in Asia, which are making use of China's vast domestic markets (for both manufactured goods, intermediate products and raw materials) for their own economic growth. China turns around by running trade surplus with the EU and USA — in a way, implying that China is a proxy holder of trade surplus for Japan, Korea and Taiwan in these two markets. Such a trade pattern also reflects the pivotal role of China in the global trade balances. For 2009, as the EU and US economies sink deeper into recession, trade frictions are expected to intensify.

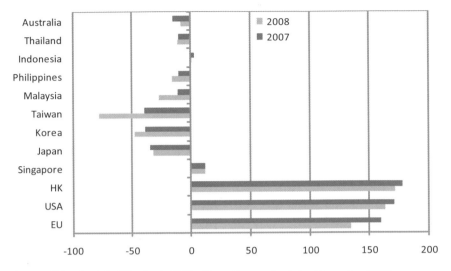

Source: China Statistical Yearbook 2008, China Custom Statistics, December 2008.

Fig. 6.   China's trade balance with selected countries, 2007–2008 (US$ billion).

HOW WILL THE ECONOMIC TONIC WORK?

Towards the end of every year, China holds the Central Economic Work Conference to map out policies for the following year. For 2008, the focus was naturally on shoring up economic growth for 2009. Coming out of this meeting, top leaders like Hu Jintao all pledged strong efforts to ensure a "stable and relatively faster" economic growth by boosting domestic demand and restructuring the economy at the same time. The economic growth objective mainly relies on the stimulus package targeting at infrastructure investment. Apart from restoring economic growth, the next emphasis is on employment creation, which requires spending in social areas such as rural development, education, healthcare and those directly related to "improving the people's livelihood".

During the 1997 Asian financial crisis, Premier Zhu Rongji had also had to boost China's sagging economic growth with expansionary fiscal policies; Zhu's task at that time was much more daunting due to chronic fiscal deficits and an ailing banking system. This time round, Premier Wen Jiabao is obviously facing much less challenges, thanks to China's comfortable fiscal surplus, strong external balance, and well-capitalised state banks. Hence, on 9 November 2008, the government was able to promptly put up a pro-active fiscal stimulus package.

The main areas for government spending cover (a) public housing for low-income groups; (b) rural infrastructure such as water supply and conservation, rural roads and power grid; (c) transport infrastructure such as highways, railways and airports; (d) healthcare and education; (e) ecological and environmental projects; (f) innovation and R&D, and industrial upgrading; and (g) the Sichuan earthquake reconstruction. The costs of these projects for the first two years were estimated to be four trillion *yuan* or about 15% of China's 2007 GDP. The central government has already committed 1.18 trillion *yuan*, with the rest to be jointly financed by local governments through various means including bank loans and debt issues.

While mega projects like railways clearly belong to the central government, a lot of other smaller ones, particularly related to the social service areas, will largely depend on local initiatives. Many local governments are heavily in debt, and they are not permitted to issue debt. But the rich provinces can do a lot, not only for activities in education, healthcare, and public housing, but also in many large-scale projects such as urban mass transit, water supply, and environmental protection. Shortly after the announcement of the four trillion *yuan* stimulus package, several rich provinces like Guangdong, Jiangsu, and Shandong put up their own trillion *yuan* worth of development programmes, totalling over 14 trillion *yuan*! Clearly, the success of the stimulus package depends critically on local initiatives.

To complement this Keynesian-type fiscal policy, other supporting measures have been introduced. The most important is the easy monetary policy. On 23 December 2008, the People's Bank of China announced another interest rate cut of 23 basis points, not long after the massive cut of 103 basis points in November. The series of rates cut along with the lowering of reserves requirement for banks are designed to inject more liquidity into the economy in order to help the business sector and the housing market.

Table 1.   China's economic growth and employment, 2003–2007.

Year	GDP growth (%)	Total labor force (million)	Yearly increase in labor force (million)	Yearly employment creation (million)	Percentage increase in employment (%)	GDP-employment elasticity
2003	10	744	6.9	10.2	1.38	0.138
2004	10.1	752	7.7	20.5	2.75	0.272
2005	10.4	758	6.3	19.2	2.56	0.246
2006	11.6	764	5.8	19.8	2.62	0.226
2007	11.9	770	5.9	17.1	2.23	0.187
Average 2003–2007	**10.8**	**758**	**6.5**	**17.4**	**2.53**	**0.189**

Note: Percentage increase in employment is calculated as the ratio between employment creation in the present year and total labour force in the previous year, i.e. $E = (Dt/Bt - 1) \times 100\%$.

Source: China Statistical Yearbook, 2008.

With all these vigorous pro-growth fiscal and monetary policies in operation, the government is probably able to prop up GDP growth in 2009 to 8%, though much still depends on the state of the global economy. Beijing has already made clear that the government would do more should the global economic environment worsen. But employment remains a big challenge.

Expansionary fiscal and monetary policies may successfully pump-prime the economy with short-term GDP increases, but they are ineffective in resolving the unemployment problem. As can be seen from Table 1, China's double-digit rates of economic growth since 2002 have on average created about 17.4 million new jobs a year, giving rise to an average growth-employment elasticity of 0.189, i.e. every 1% of economic growth generates about three million new jobs, and vice versa for more unemployment. With the expected lower growth in 2009, there will certainly be many more millions of unemployed.

Even more serious will be the problem of the "educated unemployed", as at least one-third of China's six million or so new university graduates in 2009 will not be able to find a job. Hence, the big economic challenge for the Chinese leadership in 2009 lies not so much in maintaining the 8% growth as in coping with the rising unemployment problem.

Chapter 2

Recession Averted? China's Domestic Response to the Global Financial Crisis

YANG Mu and LIM Tin Seng

China is optimistic that its economy will continue to grow in 2009. Unlike its neighbours, domestic demand rather than external demand is the main source of China's growth. China also has a strong fiscal position and an accommodative monetary policy. However, China would not be able to fully recover if the global economic situation remains weak. Given China's strong economic fundamentals, it is in a pole position to recover.

The global financial crisis has had a devastating effect on the world's economy. Not only has it raised high levels of doubt on the fundamentals and sustainability of the world's current financial system, it has also wiped out the euphoria that came with the strong growth posted by most economies in 2007 and early 2008. China is one good example. Prior to the outbreak of the crisis in the third quarter of 2008, China's economy had been expanding at a spectacular pace, registering double-digit growth since 2005. At one point, China's stellar economy even seemed to be overheating, prompting Beijing to introduce a series of measures to constrict economic growth. However, the onset of the financial crisis turned the tide as plunging world demand sent China's all powerful economy into a downward spiral. Initially, the damage seemed to be quite extensive but it somewhat subsided as 2009 progressed. By end-May 2009, green shoots of recovery seemed to be sprouting in China's economy. Whether these are real signs of recovery remain to be seen, but they reveal the resilience of China's economy.

The objective of this chapter is to explain the state of the Chinese economy amid the global financial crisis. It argues that the Chinese economy seems to be holding up despite being badly embattled by the financial crisis. The resilience that the Chinese economy is showing is to a large extent due to its sound fundamentals. Despite having able to successfully adopt an export-oriented approach for economic growth, the Chinese economy is also fuelled by its huge domestic demand. As a result, by increasing domestic demand through government spending, China is able to cushion the full impact of the financial crisis.

EFFECTS OF THE GLOBAL FINANCIAL CRISIS ON CHINA'S ECONOMY

China's red-hot economy has slowed considerably as a result of the global financial crisis. In the final quarter of 2008, the Chinese economy registered one of its slowest growths of 6.8%. This pulled down economic growth for the whole of 2008 to 9%, ending China's nearly four years of double-digit growth (Figure 1). As 2009 progresses, there is still a high level of uncertainty in China on whether the economy will be able to register the crucial growth of 8% for 2009, a level commonly regarded as the minimum growth rate to generate sufficient employment.

Initially, the stakes appear to be stacked against China. In January 2009, China's exports declined for the third consecutive month by 17.5% in value from a year ago as global demand for electronics, cell phones, steel products, and other goods made or assembled in

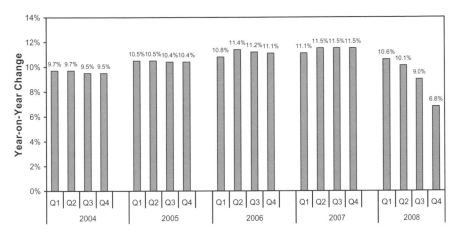

Fig. 1. China's quarterly GDP growth, 2004–2008.

China plunged (Figure 2).[1] The fall in January 2009 has been China's largest since October 1998. But above all it indicated troubles ahead for China's all-powerful industrial sector. However, after January 2009's massive drop, China's exports seemed to have recovered slightly and remained stable in the first quarter of 2009. This could well indicate that the Chinese economy could have already bottomed out and recovery is on the cards.

However, it is still too early to judge whether or not the Chinese economy has bottomed out. Global demand is still weak and this could spell more trouble for China's exports in the coming months especially when a continuation of weak exports could force more Chinese factories to close down. Indeed, it has been reported that at least 67,000 small- and medium-sized companies across China were forced to shut down in 2008 due to inflationary pressure in the first half of 2008 followed by the retreat of global demand in the later part.[2] For instance, in 2008 China's toy industry started with more

[1] "China's January Exports Fall 17.5% from a Year Ago", *Los Angeles Times*, 12 Feb. 2009.
[2] "Factories Shut, China Workers are Suffering", *New York Times*, 13 Nov. 2008.

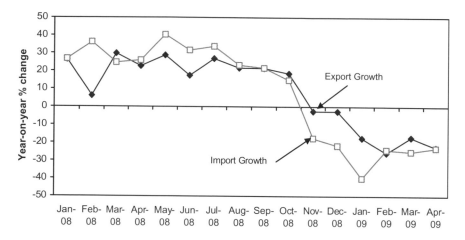

Source: Various compilations by authors.

Fig. 2.   China's trade growth, January 2008–April 2009.

than 8,600 factories producing and exporting 70% of the world's toys. But by the end of 2008, only about 4,400 remained.[3]

The closure of Chinese factories has had adverse effects on China and the global economy. In China, the rate of factory closures is driving the country's unemployment upwards for the first time since China began its double-digit growth in 2005. For instance, in February 2009, the Central Rural Work Leading Group stated that more than 20 million migrant workers lost their jobs during the final months of 2008.[4] This was about 15% of the total migrant labour pool. According to the Ministry of Human Resources and Social Security, China's unemployment rate hit 4.2% at the end of January 2009, up from 4% in 2008. By the end of 2009, the Ministry estimated China's unemployment rate would reach 4.6%, the highest since the 1980s.[5] But this could be an understatement as China's labour market has to prepare for the entry of the largest pool of Chinese university graduates in June 2009.

---

[3] "Half of China's Toy Factories Close after Exports Slump", *The Times*, 10 Feb. 2009.
[4] "Chinese Migrant Job Losses Mount", *BBC News*, 2 Feb. 2009.
[5] "China's Unemployment Rate Climbs", *China Daily*, 21 Jan. 2009.

According to *Beijing Evening News,* China would witness the graduation of 6.1 million students in 2009, the largest in history and nearly six times as many as in 2000. The figure is expected to increase to about eight million in 2010 and nine million in 2011. Beijing has implemented a number of measures to cushion the blow for unemployed graduates such as providing loans for them to start their own business, encouraging them to take up government posts in rural areas, and absorbing them into the Communist Party. However, these measures are still not generating enough employment opportunities due to the overwhelming number of graduates.[6]

For the global economy, the slowing down of China's industrial sector has led to a sharp decrease in Chinese demand for global supply of equipment, machines, and commodities such as crude oil and metals. In January 2009, China's imports slumped over 40% in value from a year ago. This has resulted in the swelling of China's trade surplus to a record of US$39.1 billion, adding tension to the already delicate state of China's trade relations with industrialised economies such as the United States and the European Union.

OPTIMISM AMID SLOWDOWN

Despite the bleak economic outlook, Beijing remains optimistic. During his "trip of confidence" to Europe in late January 2009, Chinese Premier Wen Jiabao stated in his speech at the World Economic Forum that the Chinese economy can continue to grow amid the global downturn.[7] Premier Wen's upbeat outlook falls in line with views that China will be the first to recover from the current financial crisis once global demand recovers.

Indeed, in comparison with other Asian economies, China's economy seems to be holding up despite being badly hit by the financial crisis. Although China's GDP declined from 9% in the third quarter of 2008 to 6.8% in the fourth quarter of 2008, China's overall economic

---

[6] "Where Will All the Students Go?", *The Economist,* 8 Apr. 2009.

[7] "Chinese Premier Upbeat About China Growth, Stresses Confidence in Addressing Crisis", *Xinhua News Agency,* 29 Jan. 2009.

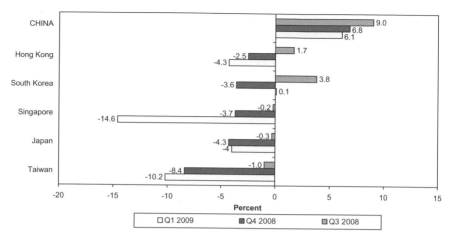

Source: EIU.

Fig. 3.   Quarterly GDP growth of China, Japan, and the NIEs (Q3 2008–Q1 2009).

performance is still much better than its neighbours after the global financial crisis struck (Figure 3). Furthermore, China's GDP remains relatively healthier than its Asian counterparts in the first quarter of 2009 as it grew 6.1% as compared to that of Singapore, Hong Kong, and Japan which shrank 14.6%, 4.3% and 4%, respectively. Besides, the decline of China's rate of exports is considerably smaller when compared to Japan's and the NIEs' (newly industrialised economies). In the third quarter of 2008 and first quarter of 2009, the decline of Chinese exports was considerably smaller than the year-on-year change in the exports of Japan and the NIEs during the same period (Figure 4).

DOMESTIC DEMAND AS A SOURCE OF GROWTH

China is in a better position to recover from the global downturn compared to its neighbours because its fundamentals are sound. Unlike most Asian economies, China's economic growth is not solely driven by external demand. Rather, domestic demand, comprising consumption and fixed-asset investment, is the main source of growth for China. As a result, this has limited China's exposure to the current global financial crisis.

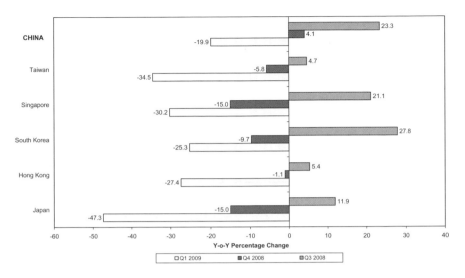

Source: EIU.

Fig. 4. Exports change of China, Japan, and the NIEs (Q3 2008–Q1 2009).

China's reliance on its domestic demand for growth is not a surprise as the country is a huge continental economy comprising one-fifth of the world's population. Furthermore, China is still in the process of industrialisation and urbanisation. In fact, China's urban population only amounts to about 43% of the country's total population. This means that there is still plenty of room for China's domestic demand to grow through infrastructure and other urban expansion projects. However, China's domestic demand is often overlooked by many Western scholars and media as they often cite the decline in China's exports as the end of its economic growth.[8]

As shown in Figure 5, domestic demand is the mainstay of China's total demand. From the 1980s through the 1990s, the share of domestic demand within China's total demand accounted for an average of more than 90%. Even after a surge in China's external trade

---

[8] See "Dire Indian and Malaysian Data Fuel Asian Fears", *Financial Times*, 1 Mar. 2009 and "China's Stimulus Challenge", *The Wall Street Journal*, 2 Mar. 2009 for alternative views.

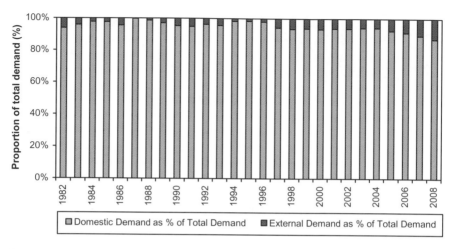

Source: EIU.

Fig. 5.   China's sources of economic growth, 1982–2008.

following its accession to the World Trade Organisation in 2002, domestic demand still constitutes about 85% of China's total demand.

A study on the fluctuation of China's past economic growth with the components of domestic demand shows that fixed investment has always been the major source of China's growth. In fact, the numerous "business cycles" (or variation of economy growth) that China experienced over the past three decades tended to swing with the ups and downs of fixed-assets investment (Figure 6). This relationship also indicates that the central government uses fixed investment as the fiscal instrument to expand the economy when domestic deflation sets in or to curb growth when the economy is overheating.

Indeed, local governments' enthusiasm to develop their economies increased following Deng Xiaoping's *nanxun* in 1992 that led to a surge in domestic investment which in turn resulted in a sharp rise in economic growth. This subsequently caused the economy to overheat. To address this, former Premier Zhu Rongji cut fixed investment in the mid-1990s, allowing China's economy to achieve a "soft landing" in 1996. Fixed investment was then adjusted upwards in the late 1990s to offset the effects of the Asian financial crisis

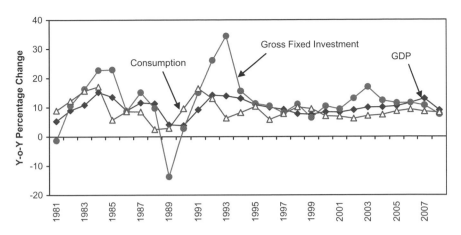

Source: EIU.

Fig. 6.   China's domestic demand and economic growth performance, 1981–2008.

and more recently downwards to cool the economy in late 2007 and early 2008.

The stimulus package unveiled by Beijing in November 2008 is a continuation of the central government's practice to peg China's economic growth to the level of fixed investment. In fact, the package is meticulously prepared to boost domestic demand for economic growth. The main areas of government spending include (1) public housing for low-income groups; (2) rural infrastructure such as water supply and conservation, rural roads and power grids; (3) transport infrastructure such as high-speed railways, mass transit systems, highways and airports; (4) healthcare and education; (5) ecological and environmental projects; (6) innovation and R&D, and industrial upgrading; and (7) the Sichuan earthquake reconstruction (Figure 7).

The estimated cost for the first two years of these projects is about US$586 billion (four trillion *yuan*) which is around 15% of China's GDP in 2007. On a global scale, China's stimulus package is the second largest in the world after the United States' US$780 billion "American Recovery and Reinvestment Plan" stimulus package which was passed in February 2009 (Figure 8). It is, however, the largest

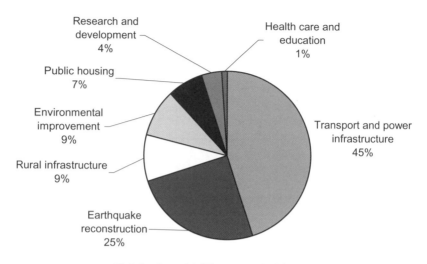

Total value: 4 trillion yuan (US$586 billion)

Source: NDRC.

Fig. 7.   Areas of spending in China's stimulus package (%).

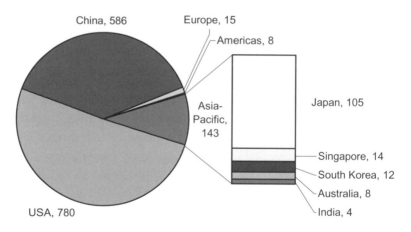

Source: Asian Wall Street Journal.

Fig. 8.   Economic stimulus packages worldwide (US$ billions).

among the stimulus package unveiled by Asian and European economies.

Although Beijing's response to the global downturn is focussed on boosting domestic demand, this does not mean that it is disregarding its external trade. In fact, Premier Wen urged major economies to continue to maintain a liberalised trading environment and made it clear that Beijing is against taking on any protectionist measures. The Chinese Premier also admitted that China would not be able to fully recover from the current global recession if global demand remains weak. Overall, it shows that China still views external demand as playing a key supporting role in inducing growth in the economy.

In addition, although China's external demand constitutes only a small share of its GDP growth, it has been rising in recent years especially after China's accession to the World Trade Organization in 2002. As Figure 9 illustrates, the share of net exports in China's GDP growth had been growing for the past decade from about 6% in 1998 to over 11% by the end of 2008. This rising trend indicates that external demand is set to play a more important supporting role for China's economic growth in the future.

In particular, industries in Guangdong's Pearl River Delta, China's manufacturing and export hub, and other coastal areas are highly dependent on external demand. Therefore, it is crucial for the external situation to improve before these regions can recover from the effects of the global financial crisis. These regions of mostly foreign-funded firms were badly hit by the crisis. In fact,

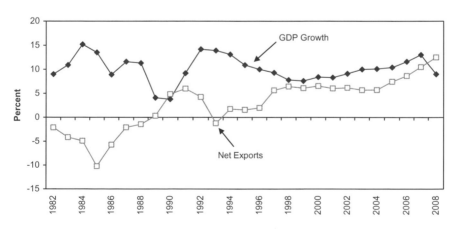

Source: EIU.

Fig. 9.   Contribution of China's net exports to GDP, 1982–2008.

Huang Yunlong, vice governor of Guangdong province, termed 2008 as "the most difficult year after the 1998 Asian financial crisis".

Huang's remark was not an understatement. According to the Guangdong Statistics Bureau, 100,600 new firms were established in 2008 but by the end of the year, more than 62,400 had been eliminated. This alarming closure rate has also resulted in massive job loss. In fact, the Statistics Bureau reported that an estimated 600,000 migrants lost their jobs in 2008.[9]

For this financial crisis, however, the Chinese leadership is more concerned with stimulating domestic demand than external demand as it is aware that the weakening global demand is beyond the control of the Chinese government. Nonetheless, it is important to note that most of the measures taken to stimulate the domestic market such as the stimulus projects are also aimed at creating jobs.

CHINA'S STRONG FISCAL POSITION

China's fiscal health explains why it is possible for the Chinese economy to rebound from its current slump faster than regional and Western economies. First, China's budget deficit has been decreasing rapidly in recent years. From 2000 to the end of 2007, China's fiscal balance increased from a deficit of nearly 3% of GDP to a surplus of 0.7% of GDP. On the other hand, most developed economies, particularly the United States, have been experiencing growing budget deficit and rising public debt. For instance, the United States' budget balance dropped from a surplus of 2.4% of GDP in 2000 to a deficit of 3.2% of GDP by the end of 2008 (Figure 10). Because of the massive fiscal stimulus package, China's budget deficit is expected to increase quite significantly in 2009. In March 2009, Premier Wen Jiabao projected China's fiscal deficit budget to hit 950 billion *yuan* (US$139 billion) which will be the highest in six decades. Despite the deficit surge, China's constant deficit drops in previous years provide room for issuing more bonds in 2009.[10]

---

[9] "600,000 Migrant Workers Leave Guangdong Amid Financial Crisis", *Xinhua News Agency*, 9 Jan. 2009.

[10] "China Budgets $139b Fiscal Deficit in Crisis Fight", *China Daily*, 5 Mar. 2009.

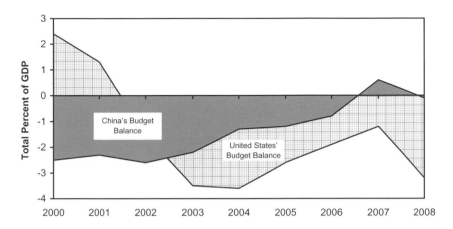

Source: EIU.

Fig. 10. China's and the United States' budget balance, 2000–2008 (% of total GDP).

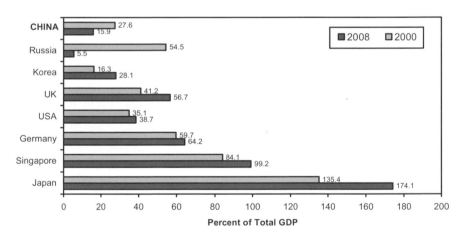

Source: EIU.

Fig. 11. China's public debt, 2000 and 2008.

In addition, China's public debt is declining. This allows Beijing to flex its fiscal muscle to fight the recession. From 2003 to 2007, China's public debt decreased from nearly 30% of GDP to only about 18% of GDP. In comparison, the United States' public debt increased from 35% of total GDP to nearly 40% of GDP during the same period (Figure 11).

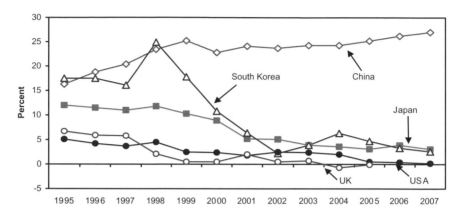

Source: China Bureau Statistics; OECD.

Fig. 12.   Household savings rate in China and selected economies, 1995–2007.

Besides, China's savings rate is very high. On average, a Chinese household saves about 26% of total disposable income. This is considerably higher than the savings rate of most developed economies (Figure 12). For instance, United States' savings rate was less than 0.5% of total disposable income in 2007.[11]

China's banks are also well capitalised. In fact, three out of the world's top 10 cash-rich companies are Chinese banks (Table 1). Furthermore, the three Chinese banks in the list, namely Bank of China, Industrial and Commercial Bank of China (ICBC), and China Construction Bank, have a total net cash of US$272 billion which is nearly 55% of the total net cash of all the top 10 companies.

LOOSENING MONETARY POLICIES

To fight the recession, Beijing also made important adjustments to loosen its monetary conditions. Some of these measures include cutting interest rates and lifting lending limits on commercial banks. As Figure 13 shows, China's central bank had adjusted lending rates quite

---

[11] "Consumers Are Saving More and Spending Less", *The New York Times*, 2 Feb. 2009.

Table 1. Top ten cash-rich companies as at end of 2008.

	Companies	Net cash (US$ billion)
1	Berkshire Hathaway	106
2	Bank of China	101
3	ICBC	89
4	China construction bank	82
5	ExxonMobil	28
6	China mobile	26
7	Apple	25
8	Cisco systems	20
9	Microsoft	19
10	Google	14
	Total net cash	540

Source: Bloomberg.

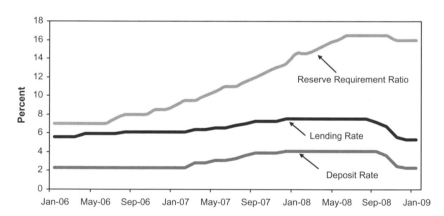

Source: EIU.

Fig. 13. China's lending rate, deposit rate, and bank reserve requirement ratio, Jan. 2006–Jan. 2009.

significantly downwards in recent months from 7.2% to 5.6% from August 2008 to November 2008. Lending rate was further revised to 5.3% in December 2008. Similarly, the central bank also cut half a percentage point on the reserve requirement ratio for banks from an all-time high of 16.5% to 16% in December 2008.

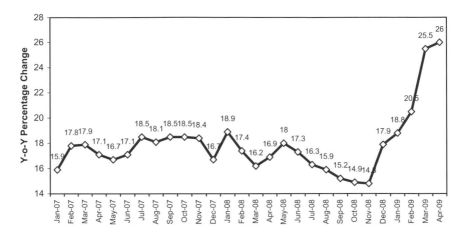

Source: EIU.

Fig. 14.   China's money supply (M2) growth, Jan. 2007–April 2009 (%).

As part of the blueprint to ease the country's monetary conditions, the central bank has also started to increase China's money supply. As shown in Figure 14, China's money supply in December 2008 and January 2009 had registered its highest year-on-year percentage change since May 2008 of 17.9% and 18.8%, respectively. This continued well into 2009 reaching 20.5%, 25.5% and 26% in February, March and April respectively. According to the State Council, China will continue to maintain a high level of money supply growth of around 17% in 2009.

With the stabilisation of the country's runaway inflation in the second half of 2008, the central government should be able to continue relaxing the country's monetary conditions in 2009. The massive foreign reserves and favourable trade surplus also allow China to maintain the stability of its currency, both of which are important monetary factors for China to maintain the competitiveness of its economy and its attractiveness to FDI inflow.

CHINA'S BUSINESS CYCLE

Unlike developed economies, particularly the United States, China's current economic slump does not originate from the meltdown of its financial sector. Instead, the slowdown started as part of the process of its economic fluctuation or "business cycle".

In the later part of 2007 and early 2008, the Chinese economy was in danger of overheating. The country's economic growth was clocking double-digit growths and investment and inflation growth have gone beyond the government's comfort zone. For instance, China's Consumer Price Index was averaging nearly 8% from the fourth quarter of 2007 through the second quarter of 2008 (Figure 15).

To fight inflation and cool the overheating economy, Chinese policy makers introduced various tightening measures to slow down the economy. Since domestic demand plays an important role in inducing growth, one of the main strategies was to cut government spending. Indeed, government spending dropped quite significantly between 2006 and 2008 from 11.6% of total GDP in 2006 to 10.7% of total GDP in 2007 and to 7.6% of total GDP in 2008, respectively.

The Chinese authorities have also administered policies to tighten the monetary conditions. These included raising interest rates and increasing the banks' reserve requirement ratio. From January 2006 through September 2008, China readjusted the requirement ratio upwards about 15 times. Similarly, lending rates were also raised more than 10 times during the same period.

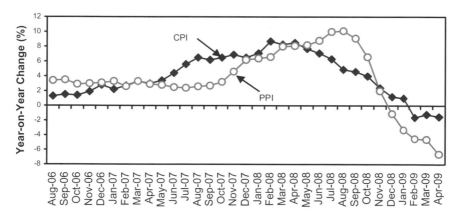

Source: National Bureau of Statistics of China.

Fig. 15. China's consumer price index and producer price index rate, Aug. 2006–Apr. 2009.

The central government also implemented a series of measures to slow the growth of industries and to curb overinvestment. These included tightening land supply for industrial use and taking steps to restrict the inflow of FDI. Incentives were also removed from labour-intensive industries and environmental fees were slapped on polluting industries.

To a certain extent, China's current economic slowdown also stemmed from a whole string of events that disrupted production in the country. These ranged from the snowstorm in early 2008 to the Sichuan earthquake in mid-2008 as well as the Olympics in August 2008.

EARLY SIGNS OF RECOVERY AND THE ROAD AHEAD

It is still too early to conclude if the policies undertaken by Beijing to boost the economy are effective, but there are some encouraging signs to show that the steps taken are yielding results. First, China's Purchasing Management Index (PMI) which measures new orders made by the manufacturing sector registered an increase of 41% in December 2008. This has put to a stop the slide of the country's PMI for the first time since May 2008 (Figure 16). Although the PMI in

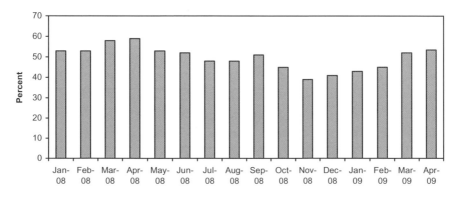

Source: RCIF.

Fig. 16.   China's purchasing management index, Jan. 2008–Apr. 2009.

December 2008 was still below 50%, indicating that the economy is still in decline, the index is creeping upwards. Indeed, by March 2009, China's PMI broke the 50% barrier by reaching 52% and then 54% in April 2009.

Second, China's credit problem seems to be easing. For instance, bank loans made in China in January amounted to 1.62 trillion *yuan* (US$237 billion), a year-on-year increase of over 800 billion *yuan* or 104% (Figure 17). The massive growth in bank loans signals that banks are lining up to provide funds to developers for the stimulus-package projects. This could be a blessing for cash-strapped domestic enterprises trying to stay afloat amid shrinking overseas demand and waning consumer confidence.

Overall, it is still too early to determine whether the early signs of recovery are sustainable. But there are definitely indications that the Chinese economy is reacting positively to the central government's measures. This should place China firmly in pole position to recover from the current global downturn once the global economic conditions stabilize. However, as soon as China's recovery gains momentum, it is important for Beijing to introduce measures to reverse the effects of emergency actions taken to free credit markets and boost demands.

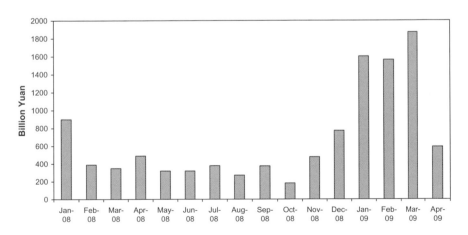

Source: PBOC.

Fig. 17.   Bank loans made in China, Jan. 2008–Apr. 2009.

The emergency actions taken by the global economies, particularly the United States, to free credit markets and boost demands are likely to bring a second round of inflation.[12] In fact, signs of inflationary pressure could be seen in the recent spike of oil prices from about US$40 per barrel in March 2009 to over US$70 per barrel by mid-June 2009 as well as the 20% increase of raw material prices and the surge of gold futures to over US$1000 during the same period. Furthermore, signs of a weakening dollar can already be seen with yields of the 10-year Treasury bill jumping from around 2% at the end of 2008 to almost 4% by early June 2009.[13] Exchange rates of the Euro as well as other international currencies have also strengthened considerably against the US dollar in recent months.

In order to cushion itself from the imminent round of inflation, China has to prepare to tighten its loose monetary policy by increasing the interest rate and reducing money supply once China's economy stabilises. This, however, has to be done through a coordinated effort with other economies so as to prevent derailing the recovery process of the global economy. The central government should also reduce government spending in order to maintain a sizeable deficit thereby keeping the country's fiscal position in check and mitigating the burden of cost on the people.

More importantly, as it is almost certain that the global financial system will take on a different shape once the recession is over, China has to reassess its role in the global economy. This may require Beijing to step up efforts to liberalise its financial and capital markets. So far, Beijing seems to be aware of this developing trend with its announcement of internationalising the Chinese currency and turning Shanghai into an international financial centre.[14] China is also showing more willingness to take on a bigger leadership role in a post-recession global economy. For instance, Beijing has become a leading voice

---

[12] "The Biggest Bill in History", *The Economist*, 13 Jun. 2009.
[13] "This Way Out", *The Economist*, 6 Jun. 2009.
[14] Lan Xinzhen, "Rebranding Shanghai", *Beijing Review*, 14 May 2009.

in supporting calls for less dependency on the US dollar. In recent months, it has suggested the establishment of a super-sovereign reserve currency and spearheading efforts with BRIC (Brazil, Russia, India, and China) countries in purchasing IMF instead of US Treasury bonds.[15] Besides, China has concluded a number of currency swap agreements with its trading partners and is exploring the idea of conducting bilateral trade using the Chinese *yuan* and the respective trading partner's currency.[16] All in all, these developing events are clear indications that the world economy may progress into a new system where China would have a more important role to play.

---

[15] "BRIC Building Road to Global Economic Recovery", *China Daily*, 18 Jun. 2009.
[16] "Malaysia, China Consider Ending Trade in Dollars", *The Wall Street Journal*, 4 Jun. 2009.

Chapter 3

China's Decisive Response to the Economic Crisis Bears Fruits

Sarah Y. TONG

China has responded vigorously to the impact of the global economic downturn on its economy. Besides a four trillion RMB stimulus package, policies include additional spending on health care, an industry revitalisation plan and an extension of rural household subsidy for home appliances and measures to create employment. Local governments have acted proactively to propose investment projects, boost consumption and promote exports. The stimulus policies are pragmatic enough to restore economic momentum, but may slow China's pursuit of a more balanced development in the long term.

Since late 2008, the global financial-turned-economic crisis has spread widely across the world. Like many of its neighbours in Asia, China has been affected significantly due largely to its growing integration with and rising dependency on the rest of the world. As early as November 2008, the government already announced strong stimulus measures, recognising that the economy is facing unprecedented difficulties and challenges.

The National People's Congress (NPC) meeting in March 2009 attracted much international attention as a result of the global economic crisis and the growing influence of China's economy. Ways to cope with the sudden deteriorating economic conditions amid the global financial crisis top the agenda of this annual event of China's parliament. While no new stimulus programme was announced, as some had speculated, Premier Wen reiterated 2009's target of 8% economic growth, which is considered essential by the leadership for the country to "generate employment for both urban and rural residents, raise people's incomes, and ensure social stability".

In late 2008, as signs of economic distress became evident, and recognising the potential ramifications of a dramatic economic slowdown, the government responded swiftly and vigorously by putting in place a series of quick and decisive stimulating policies. The central piece of the policy initiatives was an eye-popping multi-dimensional and multi-phase Keynesian-type stimulus package of four trillion RMB by 2010, announced in November 2008.

During the NPC annual meeting in March 2009, measures to promote employment were also announced, with the priority on finding jobs for university graduates and retrenched migrant workers. The government pledged to allocate 42 billion RMB for a proactive employment policy and aimed to provide nine million new urban jobs in 2009 to keep its registered jobless rate at below 4.6%.

A probable consequence of this series of fiscal programmes is a change in the official stance on the national budget. In Premier Wen Jiabao's NPC report, an aggressive fiscal deficit budget of 950 billion RMB (US$139 billion) has been set aside, including 200 billion worth of government bonds to be issued for local governments through the Ministry of Finance. This deficit, a record high in six decades and a massive rise from the 180 billion RMB for 2008, is about 3% of GDP, up from a much smaller deficit of 0.4% in 2008[1] and a surplus of 0.6% of GDP in 2007.

Details of the government stimulus plan suggest that strong emphasis is being placed on investment, especially in infrastructure

---

[1] "Factbox: Selected figuers from China's 2009 budget", *Reuters*, 5 Mar. 2009, http://www.reuters.com.

spending. While it is considered necessary to prevent a sharp decline of the economy, heavily investment-centred stimulus programmes may risk skewing the economy too much towards investment at the expense of consumption and therefore is inconsistent with China's long-term pursuit of a more balanced development model. In response to such concerns, the government seems to have moderated the composition of the RMB four trillion package, although few details were available. In the newly released report by the National Development and Reform Commission (NDRC) in early March 2009, the percentage of spending for healthcare, education and affordable housing has been raised by about six percentage points compared to the figure revealed in November 2008, while those for investment on transport, infrastructure, and environment have been reduced.

With the aggressive stimulus package and massive investment, the target of about 8% economic growth in 2009 seems to be within the reach of China. There are already signs of early recovery as recent figures indicated. For example, GDP grew by 6.1% in the first quarter of 2009 and 79% in the second quarter of 2009, compared to a year ago. While significantly lower than the 10.6% in the first quarter of 2008, it is not too much lower than the government target of 8% for the year. Export decline has also stabilised. In late 2008, China's total export growth turned negative, from 19% in October to −2% in November and December. It dropped further to contract by 18% and 24% on a year-to-year basis in January and February 2009, respectively. Such freefalling has been stabilised to maintain at around 25% in the following three months. Indeed, the World Bank has recently adjusted upward its prediction for China's growth in 2009, from 6.5% to 7.2%.

The objective of maintaining unemployment rate below 4.6%, however, remains a harder task to actualise as employment generation usually takes place after the economic turnaround. Government support for the service and labour-intensive manufacturing sectors, especially for small and medium enterprises, would be needed to create more jobs and ease unemployment pressure.

CENTRAL GOVERNMENT'S POLICY INITIATIVES

When first released in November 2008, the central government's four trillion RMB package was very much a preliminary and rough number. This reflects the urgency felt by the leadership to act speedily as a way to boost confidence when economic conditions deteriorated. The breakdown of the stimulus package was unveiled later in the year by the government, and later modified in March 2009 (see Figure 1). As shown, the largest portion of the spending goes to transport and

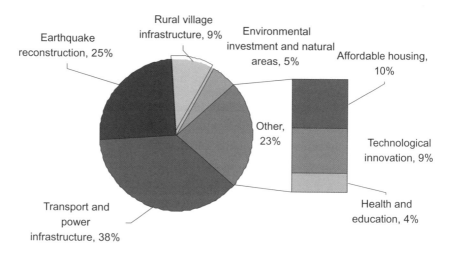

Source: National Development and Reform Commission. http://www.ndrc.gov.cn/xwfb/t20090306_264929.htm, accessed on 7 March 2009.

Fig. 1.   Composition of RMB 4 trillion stimulus package.[2]

---

[2] In an earlier version of the plan ("NDRC Details Four Trillion Stimulus Package", *Caijing Online*, 1 Dec. 2008; accessed on 20 Feb. 2009), the spending on transport and power infrastructure accounted for a larger portion of the total (45%), while that on healthcare and education made up only 1%. Figure 1 reflects the revised figures that are released by the National Development and Reform Commission on 6 March. In the current breakdown, the shares for affordable housing, technological innovation, healthcare and education in total spending have been raised, while those of spending on transport and power infrastructure and investment on environment and natural resources have been reduced.

power infrastructure, accounting for 38% of the total. Spending on earthquake reconstruction comes second, taking up another 25% of the total, followed by rural village infrastructure and investment for environmental protection, each accounting for 9% and 5% of the total respectively.

It is clear that the paramount emphasis of this stimulus package is on investment, especially on infrastructure projects. Spending in this broad category, including those on transport and power generation infrastructure, earthquake reconstruction, and rural infrastructure, may comprise almost three quarters of the total.

A second area of emphasis is on nurturing sectors important for sustainable development. This is reflected in the planned spending of about 14% of the total to strengthen environmental protection, conservation of natural resources, and technological capacity. Third, the package also attempts to address a number of social issues, such as providing affordable housing for low-income households and increasing spending on healthcare and education, which accounted for approximately 10% and 4% of the total package respectively.

In the fourth quarter of 2008, the central government allocated 100 billion RMB (US$15 billion) of the total four trillion RMB package to rural infrastructure[3] (see Table 1), taking up a third of the total. Following this spending, another batch of investment totalling 130 billion RMB (US$19 billion) was announced on 3 February 2009.[4] This instalment too is expected to focus primarily on infrastructure investment.

Along with the four trillion RMB package, the central government also introduced a number of complementary policies to stimulate the economy, including loosening credit policies, modifying value-added tax regime, and abolishing credit ceiling for commercial banks.[5] For example, in November 2008, the government raised the

---

[3] "China's Stimulus Package: Energy & the Environment", *China Economic Review*, 19 Nov. 2008, http://www.chinaenvironmentallaw.com.

[4] "China to spend $19 billion in second stimulus tranche", *Reuters*, 23 Feb. 2009, http://www.reuters.com.

[5] "China seeks stimulation", *The Economist*, 10 Nov. 2008, http://www.economist.com.

Table 1.   Central government's investment plan of 100 billion for November and December, 2008.

Sector	Amount (billion RMB)
Total	100
Rural infrastructure, methane, water and roads	34
Major transport infrastructure	25
Health and education	13
Urban water, sewage and energy conservation	12
Affordable housing and slum clearance	10
Technology	6

Source: National Development and Reform Commission (NDRC).

rate of value-added tax rebates for 3,770 export items. The increase varies across items, with the rate on tyres raised from 5% to 9%, glassware 5% to 11%, and various labour-intensive products from 11% to 13%.[6] This initial adjustment was later followed by another round of tax rebate rate rise for textile and garment exports from 14% to 15% announced in February 2009.

In addition to the four trillion RMB package, the State Council announced on 21 January 2009 another spending plan of 850 billion RMB (US$123 billion), including 331.8 billion RMB from the central government.[7] The plan aims to improve health care and provide universal health care coverage within three years.[8] According to this long awaited reform, measures will be undertaken to provide basic medical coverage to both urban and rural residents, improve the quality of medical services and make medical services more accessible and affordable for the ordinary people.

In addition, there is a new emphasis on identifying and developing key industries to enhance China's overall technological as well as industrial capacity. By 26 February 2009, the government had

---

[6] "China lifts tax rebates to boost export", *China International*, 18 Nov. 2008, http://en.ec.com.cn.

[7] "China to boost spending on welfare, education, health care", *Xinhua net*, 5 Mar. 2009, http://www.chinadaily.com.cn.

[8] "China to provide $123B for universal medical care", *China Daily*, 21 Jan. 2009, http://www.chinadaily.com.cn.

designated 10 sectors for its industry revitalisation plan, including mostly capital-intensive industries such as steel, automobile, shipbuilding, petrochemical, nonferrous metal and equipment manufacturing, as well as a number of other industries such as textile, light industry, information technology and logistics.

As summarised in Table 2, the plan highlights various policies such as tax incentives, government subsidies and bank loans to

Table 2. The state council's revitalisation plans for 10 industries.

Industry	Key elements	Date of announcement
Automobile	Lower purchase tax on cars under 1.6 litres, from 10% to 5% for the period of 20 Jan. to 31 Dec.; allocate five billion RMB (US$730 million) to provide one-off allowances to farmers to upgrade their three-wheeled vehicles and low-speed trucks to mini-trucks or purchase new mini-vans under 1.3 litres for the period of 1 March to 31 Dec.; increase subsidies for people who scrap their old cars and lift regulations that restrict car purchase; and urge improvements to the credit system for car loans. In the following three years, earmark 10 billion RMB to support auto companies to upgrade technologies, and develop new engines that use alternative energies.	14 Jan. 2009
Steel	Special funds to be allocated from the central government's budget to promote technological advancement of the sector, readjustment of products mix, and improvement in product quality.	14 Jan. 2009
Textile	Increase the rate of tax rebates from 14% to 15% for exporting firms of textile and garment; to set up a special fund to help in upgrading technology; encourage old factories to relocate to inland provinces and western regions; encourage financial institutions to support the growth and consolidation of local textile firms.	5 Feb. 2009

(*Continued*)

Table 2.   (*Continued*)

Industry	Key elements	Date of announcement
Machinery	Reduce reliance on imported parts; promote integration of research institutions; and encourage machinery exports and imports of key technologies and machinery parts by implementing tax policies.	5 Feb. 2009
Ship building	Increase credit support by an unspecified amount for ship builders; extend existing financial support policies for oceangoing vessels until 2012; provide tax rebates on key imported components for domestically owned oceangoing ships.	11 Feb. 2009
Electronics and information	Modify criteria for high-tech enterprises and adjust tax rebates for exporters of electronics and information products.	18 Feb. 2009
Light industry	Lift restrictions on processing trade; raise rates of export rebates: extend fiscal and credit support to SMEs: add microwave ovens and cookers to the list of appliance purchase subsidy programme.	19 Feb. 2009[9]
Petrochemical	Guarantee the supply of input materials for farming, such as fertilisers; promote technological innovation and the construction of major petrochemical projects; accelerate the building of reserves for oil products, and provide better tax policies and more credit access for firms.	19 Feb. 2009
Nonferrous metals	Promote company restructuring and provide subsidised loans for technical innovations of the sector; adjust the rate of export rebate for exporters of nonferrous products; eliminate technically undeveloped producers; and avoid excessive output capacity.	25 Feb. 2009

(*Continued*)

---

[9] "China unveils stimulus package for light industry, petrochemical sector", *Xinhua News Agency*, 19 Feb. 2009, http://news.xinhuanet.com.

Table 2. (*Continued*)

Industry	Key elements	Date of announcement
Logistics	Increase supply of necessary equipment and set an industry standard and establish an information platform; build a special region for logistics development; boost urban delivery, wholesale, and rural logistics; encourage mergers and restructuring of companies to nurture the emergence of internationally competitive large and modern logistics companies; encourage the development of logistics for energy, mining, automobile, and medical industries as well as for agricultural products; allocate 100 billion *yuan* (by central and local governments) within two years to promote the application of innovative products.	25 Feb. 2009

Source: Compiled by author with information from Xinhua net.

support these chosen industries. For industries like textile, the more immediate objective is to assist firms which are struggling to survive the sudden drop in external demand. For others, such as equipment manufacturing, the policies aim to strengthen technological capacity to enhance the firms' long-term competitiveness.

In addition to direct assistance to industries, the government has put in place measures to facilitate domestic consumption, especially those of rural residents. In 2007, the government kick-started a pilot scheme of rural household purchasing subsidy for home appliances. Under the scheme, each rural household is eligible to claim at their local township government finance agencies a subsidy of 13% for purchases of up to two items of three products, including colour TV sets, refrigerators and mobile phones from designated brands.[10]

---

[10] The claim should be made within 15 working days following the purchase.

The pilot scheme, which covered three agricultural provinces of Shandong, Henan and Sichuan, was extended to all rural residents nationwide on 1 February 2009, and four more products were added, including motorcycles, personal computers, water heaters and air conditioners.[11] The 13% subsidy was jointly funded by the central and local governments according to an 80-20 formula. The scheme is expected to help cushion the sudden drop in external demand for consumer electronics.

Several new measures were announced to achieve multiple objectives including revitalising certain industries, promoting domestic consumption and advancing energy efficiency. On 19 May 2009, the "Implementation Plan to Encourage Trade-in Purchase Scheme of Automobile and Home Appliances" was approved by the State Council. This is the government's newest measure, following the schemes to subsidise purchases of automobile, motorcycles and home appliances by rural households. The measure aims to further expand domestic consumption as well as to raise energy and resource efficiency.[12]

Also in May, the government embarked on new incentives to promote the production and consumption of home appliances and other electronic products that have achieved high energy efficiency. Ten products are included in the new scheme, such as air conditioners, refrigerators and television sets. Depending on the items, producers of such high energy standard products may receive government subsidies of several hundred RMB for each set.[13]

With rising job losses sparking fears of social unrest, the State Council issued a circular in February 2009 announcing measures to

---

[11] "China boosts rural consumption with household appliance subsidy program", *People's Daily*, 2 Feb. 2009, http://english.peopledaily.com.cn.

[12] "Standing Committee Meeting approves the Implementation Plan for Trade-in Purchase Scheme for Home Appliances (国务院常务会议审议通过家电以旧换新实施方案)", National Development and Reform Commission, 22 May 2009, http://www.ndrc.gov.cn.

[13] "Official Launch of Promoting Energy Conserving Product to Benefit Consumers (节能产品惠民工程正式启动)", National Development of Reform Commission, 21 May 2009, http://www.ndrc.gov.cn.

encourage the placement of university graduates. These include providing subsidies and social insurance to those who are willing to work in villages and local communities, and helping those who work in remote areas or join the Army to settle their student loans. A graduate trainee programme for up to one million unemployed college graduates will be launched within three years, while local governments and various organisations are expected to subsidise the trainees for their living expenses. The State Council also announced economic incentives for private companies to recruit more graduates and workers as well as disincentives for enterprises' job-cut.[14]

Although Premier Wen did not reveal any stimulus plans beyond the four trillion RMB package during his speech at the NPC session in March 2009, he did highlight some spending plans for 2009 in several areas. As shown in Figure 2, 293 billion RMB will be spent on improving the social safety net to expand coverage and benefits of

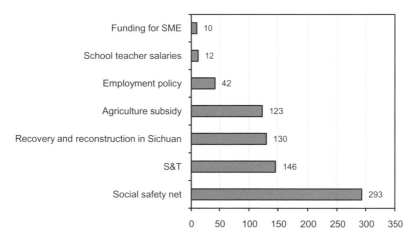

Source: "Key figures in government work report by Premier Wen", *Xinhua*, 5 March 2009, http://www.chinadaily.com.cn.

Fig. 2. Selected central government's spending plan in 2009 (RMB billion).

---

[14] One example of disincentives for enterprises' job-cut is that "a report needs to be filed with the local trade union when a firm is planning to lay off more than 20 workers or over 10% of the entire staff, unless the workers are notified 30 days in advance".

social security programmes; 146 billion RMB to the science and technology sector, and 130 billion RMB for earthquake reconstruction.

Since the second half of 2008, moderately loose monetary policies have been implemented to complement the fiscal stimulus programme to cope with the economic slowdown. The People's Bank of China (PBOC) lowered interest rates on 16 September 2008 and the benchmark one-year lending rate fell by 0.27% point to 7.2%, the first rate cut in over six years.[15] A complete reversal of monetary policy from its June orientation took place in October 2008 with several more rounds of interest rates cut and reserve requirement relaxation, as depicted in Figure 3.

The central government's grand fiscal spending programmes are expected to be followed by those of the local governments. Indeed, these initiatives have quickly given rise to many notable and innovative responses from governments at provincial and lower levels.

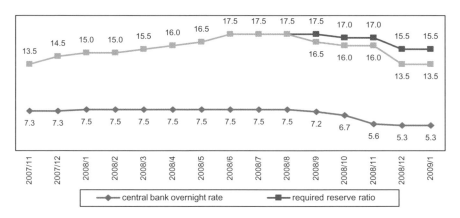

Source: People's Bank of China (PBOC).

Note: Since September 2008, the required reserve ratio has been different for financial institutions of different sizes. The ratio for relatively large financial institutions, including the big four state commercial banks, the Bank of Communication and China Postal Saving Bank is higher than that of smaller financial institutions. This is indicated by the gap of the top two curves in the above figure.

Fig. 3.   Interest rate and reserve ratio movements.

---

[15] "China cuts interest rates as Wall Street wobbles", *China Economic Review*, 16 Sept. 2008, http://www.chinaeconomicreview.com.

THE LOCAL GOVERNMENTS' RESPONSES

When the central government announced its ambitious stimulus programme in November 2008, it was stipulated that 1.18 trillion RMB out of the four trillion, less than a third, will be funded by the central government's fiscal budget. The remaining is expected to come from local governments' budgets, state-owned enterprises, and governmental ministries.[16] Not surprisingly, local governments responded positively to the initiative and acted proactively by drawing up and publicising plans to boost investment, export and consumption to tackle problems at their localities.

Various local governments have devoted much effort to proposing investment projects and seeking approval as well as subsequent partial funding by the central government. This is natural, given the national stimulus package's paramount emphasis on infrastructure investment. In fact, soon after the announcement of the central government's stimulus package, local governments proposed numerous projects, totalling an impressive 18 trillion RMB worth of investment.[17]

Overall, local governments have identified areas in which to focus their investment expenditure, depending on the relative importance of the projects to the localities. Table 3 lists the policy initiatives by governments of some provinces and municipalities.

Governments at various localities have also announced measures to shore up consumption, which is in fact consistent with the government's long-term objective of reducing the economy's reliance on investment and external demand. One measure that has been experimented by several regions is the issuing of coupons to spur local consumption. Table 4 documents a number of specific policies implemented by some provincial or city-level governments.

Many of the shopping vouchers are in the form of tourism coupons that are redeemable at designated travel agencies. The period

---

[16] "China details 4 trillion RMB stimulus package", *China Assistor*, 14 Nov. 2008, http://news.chinaassistor.com.
[17] "Local finances to struggle with 18 trillion yuan plan", *China Daily*, 26 Nov. 2008, http://www.chinadaily.com.cn.

Table 3.   Investment projects at local level.

Regions	Policy initiatives	Amount (million RMB)
Shaanxi	Project of Safe Drinking Water in Rural Areas, by 2012	800
Jiangsu	Transport and infrastructure, 2009	81,000
Wuhan of Hubei	Infrastructure for cultural activities, 2009	1,321
Hulunbuir of Inner Mongolia	Sandy Land Reclamation, 2009	150
Baotou of Inner Mongolia	Energy conservation and resources utilisation, 2009	Over 6,000
TEDA of Tianjin	Fix assets formation, 2009	21,000
Shanghai	EXPO-related investment projects, 2009	155,000
Guangxi	Fix assets formation, 2009	600,000
Anhui	Real estate development and investment, 2009	150,000–180,000
Ningxia	Fix assets formation, 2009	107,200
Jiangxi	Agricultural products, 2009	130
Tianjin	Agriculture, 2009	10,000
Hunan	Projects for people's livelihood	35,000
Guangdong	Transport infrastructure, 2009	97,600
	Energy security, 2009	75,300
	Modern manufacturing, 2009	28,900
	Modern agriculture and irrigation, 2009	20,400
	High-tech industry, 2009	16,600
Xinjiang	School building renovation	770
Sichuan	Infrastructure, industry and projects for people's livelihood and social work	280,000

Source: Compiled by author from various sources.

of validity of the coupons varies from one to three months. These coupons are expected to encourage more travel-related consumption such as in retail, food and beverage and accommodation.

In addition to directly issuing tourism and shopping coupons, some local governments experimented with alternative measures to boost consumption. One example is the issuing of coupons as part of employees' bonus or salary. In Hangzhou, Zhejiang province, civil servants receive coupons as part of their salary. In Shenzhen,

Table 4. Coupons issued by provincial and municipal governments (as of May 2009).

Region	Policy	Amount (million RMB)
Zhenjiang of Jiangsu	Tourism coupons to residents in the city and neighbouring cities	80
Nanjing of Jiangsu	Tourism coupons to local residents	20
Ningbo of Zhejiang	Tourism coupons to local residents	8
Hangzhou of Zhejiang	Tourism coupons	10
	Shopping coupons for low-income families	100
Chengdu of Sichuan	Shopping coupons to low income residents	37[18]
Guangdong	Tourism coupons for people age 55 and above	20
Guangdong	200,000 travel coupons to rural residents	At least 13% discount on airfares and hotels
Zhongshan and Zhaoqing of Guangdong	400,000 coupons to residents of Guangzhou	
Shanghai	Travel coupons will be sent to Citibank's credit card customers in Singapore, South Korea and other countries	200

Source: Compiled by author from various sources.

Guangdong province, instead of cash subsidies, the municipal government handed out coupons to pensioners. Such measures discourage savings, thus stimulating higher consumption.

The sudden drop in external demand is especially damaging to regions heavily dependent on export for growth, such as Guangdong. Dismal export perspectives prompted the local governments to implement additional stimulating policies aimed particularly at promoting export. At the beginning of 2009, Guangdong unveiled eight

---

[18] "Chengdu coupons working well", *CCTV*, 21 Jan. 2009, http://www.cctv.com.

favourable tax policies to reduce local exporters' tax burden of up to three billion RMB for the year. It also plans to earmark 1.9 billion RMB to support the industrial upgrade of the manufacturing sector and to restructure the export and import portfolios.

Meanwhile, local governments also put up plans to address employment problems of both migrant workers and college graduates. Guangdong province has pledged to spend six billion RMB between 2009 and 2012 to help establish several industrial parks in less developed regions within the province to accommodate enterprises relocating from the Pearl River Delta region and to provide employment to 379,000 migrant workers.

Guangzhou has pledged to considerably reduce unemployment insurance premiums from January 2009 to alleviate the burden of enterprises engaging in labour-intensive production. The Changchun municipal government in Jilin province recently passed policies to reduce sales tax and provide government financial assistance in terms of bank loans to university graduates who intend to start their own businesses.

EFFECTIVENESS OF THE STIMULUS MEASURES

Widely hailed at home and abroad as a giant step in the right direction, the announcement of the four trillion RMB package by the central government marked a determined effort to boost public confidence and forestall a sharp decline in market sentiments. Following the initial announcement, more details of the stimulus package were announced, along with numerous supplementary plans by the central government, including its ministries and local governments at various levels. It is evident that the overriding emphasis, by both central and local leaders, is the large expenditure on infrastructure, generally believed as the surest way to pump up China's economy.

While the government is loaded with a multi-target task, the immediate concern is business failures and loss of employment triggered by the economic slowdown. The government has acted quickly and decisively over the past several months with numerous plans, which encompass a variety of measures and large sums of funding commitment covering a wide range of sectors.

On close examination, however, this four trillion RMB package spread over two years will lead to an additional fiscal spending of 600 billion RMB a year by the central government, equivalent to about 2% of GDP in 2007. This figure is less substantial than what many first assumed, considering that the central government's fiscal spending in 2007 accounted for approximately 12% of GDP. [19]

What is more, the size of the plan is believed by some to be overstated as some of the investment projects announced in the package like rail network extension and earthquake reconstruction have already been earmarked earlier and thus cannot be classified as additional spending or incremental investment or "new" money. Some projects planned over the next five years are now brought forward and therefore will lead to higher infrastructure spending in the next two years.

Despite the Chinese economy's excessive dependence on investment and export demand, or perhaps partly because of it, over three quarters of the rescue package are for investment projects. This emphasis has been the subject of criticism; the fear is that this may perpetuate the economy's over-dependence on investment at the expense of consumption and therefore is inconsistent with China's long-term objective of pursuing a more balanced development model. Figure 4 shows that household consumption accounted for around 50% of China's GDP in the late 1970s; in the 1990s, it began to decline, especially after 2000 to hit a historical low of 35% in 2006, much lower than other major economies such as the US where 70% of GDP comes from household consumption. In addition, the contribution of the Chinese government spending has remained consistent but rather modest.

Consequently, policies directed at spurring consumption through income-tax cuts may not be able to offset the current downdraft as

---

[19] "Report on the Implementation of the Central and Local Budgets for 2007 and on the Draft Central and Local Budgets for 2008", *China.org.cn*, 18 Mar. 2008, Nethttp://www.china.org.cn.

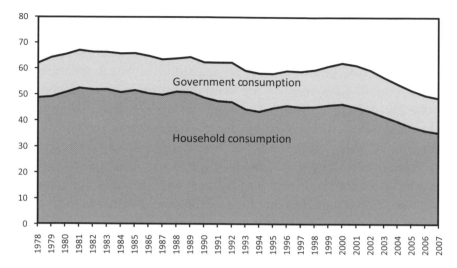

Source: China Statistical Yearbook, 2007.

Fig. 4.   Household and government consumption as share of GDP.

quickly as is desired. In fact, household savings rate increased over the past decade, from around 15% in 1995 to over 25% in 2007, compared to less than 5% in Japan and Korea. Thus, tax cuts or welfare benefits are more likely to be saved rather than spent, especially when individuals are facing economic uncertainty. As a result, the government has adopted an investment-centred stimulus programme to quickly restore economic growth momentum and prevent a hard landing.

Given the urgency to rescue the economy and the large sum of government planned funding injection, many are concerned about the quality of the projects and the possible misuse of the funding. For example, some investment projects, formerly not qualified for bank lending, may now be able to obtain loans. Indeed, bank lending jumped in November 2008 at the fastest annual rate in nearly five years. In January 2009 alone the banks extended new loans of 1,620 billion RMB, twice as high as that a year ago. Insurers were recently given the authority to lend to infrastructure projects. While it is conceivable that China will be able to achieve the 8% GDP growth in 2009, it may come at the price of low returns and a possible piling up of new nonperforming loans.

Since the bulk of the package focusses on investment expenditure and only a small portion deals with issues like social security, pension and healthcare, questions remain as to whether a more direct injection of funding into the social safety net should command more attention. In fact, with investment as a top priority, local governments and businesses may be much less interested in issues like worker safety, medical insurance and environmental protection. More importantly, without a comprehensive social safety net, the effectiveness of various consumption promoting plans would be limited. Worse, the rather scattered initiatives on consumption promotion may lead to a new round of local protectionism along provincial borders.

In general, the scale and magnitude of the stimulus plans from both central and local governments inevitably invite scepticism on efficiency and highlight issues of potential waste, suboptimal planning, unnecessary or meaningless projects and even corruption. Government-led lending could add to excess capacity in some sectors and even create new bad loans for banks.

Consequently, the full effect of boosting the economy to a great extent hinges on not only policy initiatives stipulated in the various stimulus programmes, but also the implementation, much of which remains unclear. Indeed, it takes time to get projects started and hence no overnight magic could be expected. To correct the structural imbalance of China's economic development, a more fundamental economic reorientation may be necessary in the long term.

Chapter 4

Pearl River Delta in a Crisis of Industrialisation

HUANG Yanjie and CHEN Shaofeng

The Pearl River Delta region (PRD), representing 80% of the economy of Guangdong, is suffering from a sharp decline in export demand, large-scale closures of small and medium enterprises and massive lay-offs of migrant worker. The crisis in this region is a combined result of global economic slowdown and structural problems inherent in the model of industrial development centring on the once booming labour-intensive export process sectors. The Guangdong leadership has endeavoured to cope with the crisis in the short run, while promoting industrial restructuring in the long run. The crisis and the response it elicits shall bring about major changes in the economic landscape of the PRD, and its experience can offer important lessons for China's economic development.

China's double-digit growth came to an abrupt halt in the month of October 2008 when the world began to feel the effects of the sub-prime induced financial crisis in the US. After a glorious and rousing Olympics Games in September, no one would have expected that the year 2008 would prove to be a tough year for China's economic development. This is especially true with regard to the Pearl River Delta[1] (PRD) region. The external shock waves triggered by the global financial crisis have combined forces with the ongoing industrial restructuring, causing dire economic consequences such as rising unemployment, slowdown in economic growth and massive bankruptcy of small and medium enterprises (SMEs).

As early as late 2007, when the global financial crisis had not yet affected the real economy, it was reported that a quarter of the shoe and textile factories in the region was already facing severe financial difficulties. With the onset of the financial crisis, large-scale closures of processing factories and laying off of migrant workers became a daily phenomenon in the course of 2008. While complete official statistics are still unavailable, it is estimated that more than 7,100 firms had closed in the PRD region.[2] The situation has worsened in the first quarter of 2009, with export-oriented SMEs facing tremendous pressure from plummeting overseas orders, forcing job and pay cuts.[3]

Reports of labour-related disputes multiplied. In 2008, the Shenzhen People's Court received a surge of 243% in labour-related cases compared with the year 2007, mostly concerning unpaid wages and compensation for lay-offs.[4] In another dramatic development in mid-September 2008, the largest toy manufacturer, Smart Union toy

---

[1] By the term Pearl River Delta region (珠江三角洲) we refer to the nine municipalities including Guangzhou, Shenzhen, Zhuhai, Dongguan, Zhongshan, Foshan, Huizhou, Jiangmen, and Zhaoqing in Guangdong province. Sometimes scholars also include the special administrative regions (SARs) of Hong Kong and Macau to form the "Larger PRD" and the neighbouring provinces of Guangdong to form the "Pan-PRD". Since the SARs and provinces are rather different from Guangdong in terms of their economic development and industrial structure, they are outside the scope of this discussion.

[2] Investigating the rumor of the close-down wave, http://news.dayoo.com/guangdong/200812/15/53873_4805971.htm.

[3] http://www.gd.chinanews.com.cn/2009/2009-04-11/2/13983.shtml, 6 Jun. 2009.

[4] http://www.zaobao.com/zg/zg081213_502.shtml, 18 Jan. 2009.

factory (合俊玩具厂), closed its doors due to mounting costs and plummeting overseas orders, resulting in 7,000 migrant workers losing their jobs without receiving their last month's wages and related compensation. The situation developed into large-scale protests which lasted for almost a week until the government intervened to settle the dispute.

Recent trends suggest a cold winter ahead for the export sector, as Guangdong's export in November 2008 registered an unprecedented 12.2% drop from that of the previous year, followed by a milder decline of 6.8% in December. The first quarter of 2009 again saw export decline by 17.8% and industrial output increase by a mere 1% from the previous year.[5] This led to the massive return of migrant workers to their homeland. For instance, in Dongguan, a hub for processing goods for export, 40% of migrant workers were already heading for hometown just after the New Year, ahead of their usual schedules.[6] Many of them may not be required to return after the Chinese New Year and have to find new work in their hometown in the rural area. The crisis of industrialisation in the PRD will thus have a spill-over effect on the inland provinces as well.

While the current crisis is largely generated by global economic conditions, other important causes need to be understood from a historic perspective. The labour-intensive, export-oriented development strategy has had its period of boom when the PRD, then an economically backward region, started to take off after reorientating itself to overseas market and opening itself to foreign capital and investments. As the region developed, the old model began to face constraints in rising land costs, labour wages and governmental environment protection initiatives. Many economists agree that even without the financial crisis, the industrial sector in the PRD region is expected to

---

[5] It is possible that industrial output in fact suffered a moderate fall or there has been a sharp change in industrial structure, since industrial electricity use experienced a sharp fall of 14.6%.

[6] 40% Migrant Workers Heading for Home Ahead of Schedule, http:www.mingpaonews.com/20090108/ccb1.htm, 17 Jan. 2009.

undergo a process of gradual structural change, often termed as "industrial restructuring",[7] just like the Asian Tigers have been experiencing during the last 20 years.

Looking back to the history of Guangdong's economic development in the reform era, although the government has essentially adhered to market principles, it has also played a decisive role whenever the economy was in crisis or at a crossroads. Both the provincial government of Guangdong and the central government are acutely aware of the ongoing crisis and are determined to act decisively. While certain voices in the government talked about radical approaches to the problem, such as "squeezing out" inefficient industries, the call for a more incremental and comprehensive approach clearly has taken precedence in view of the possible social consequences of the current crisis. Just as the government is committed to spend heavily in areas such as major development projects for niche industries, regional research and development (R&D) capacity and the creation of business environment conducive for industrial restructuring, policy initiatives are also taken to ease the plight of SMEs and reach out to the most affected social groups such as migrant workers.

In a general assessment, the crisis has both a short-run aspect closely associated with the global slowdown and long-run aspects contingent on other structural problems. In the short run, labour-intensive, export-oriented SMEs have absorbed most of the shocks; regions with a high concentration of such industries suffer proportionally more than other regions. In the long run, the lack of domestic demand and relatively low level of education and indigenous R&D capacity will pose serious challenges to the restructuring process. Although the government has strong fiscal resources to address the

---

[7] "Industrial restructuring" is a technical term in industrial economics referring to structural changes in the composition of the industrial sectors in terms of level and type of products, technological intensity and market orientations. Here it means the transformation of the export-oriented, labour-intensive, low-tech and low value-added industries in the Pearl River Delta region into more domestically oriented, relatively high value-added and high-tech industries.

crisis, the structural constraints built up during the past decades may require a long period of time to remove.

CAUSES OF THE CRISIS: INDUSTRIAL DEVELOPMENT IN PRD IN RETROSPECT

In the last 20 years, the PRD model is a model *par excellence* for China's export-oriented economic growth. The strength of the model lies in the rapid development of the labour-intensive export-oriented industrial sector that specialises in the production of various consumer goods, household durables and business equipment. A typical manufacturing firm in the PRD specialises in processing imported semi-finished goods and raw materials based on foreign patented technology before exporting the finished products to overseas markets.[8]

The PRD region enjoys numerous competitive advantages: unlimited supply of cheap migrant labour from inland provinces, abundant foreign investment especially through Hong Kong, favourable government tax and trade policies and a strategic location at the entrance of the South China Sea and the Pacific Ocean. "Made-in-China", or more precisely, "Made-in-Guangdong" products have made successful inroads into world markets of cheap consumer goods. By the end of 2008, Guangdong's international trade increased from merely US$21 billion to US$684 billion, representing about 28% of China's total trade. Moreover, the region's processing trade accounts for 42% of China's total processing trade. The rapid growth of Guangdong's trade is illustrated in Figure 1.

The PRD model could be best exemplified by the spectacular development of Dongguan (东莞), a city-level municipality located

---

[8] Since all imported semi-finished products and raw materials are counted as import items in statistical yearbooks, the PRD region has one of the highest import-to-GDP ratios as well as trade-to-GDP ratios. Moreover, processing trade is the most important type of trade for the region, representing about 63% of total trade. See Table 1 for the case of a typical city in the region (Dongguan) for reference.

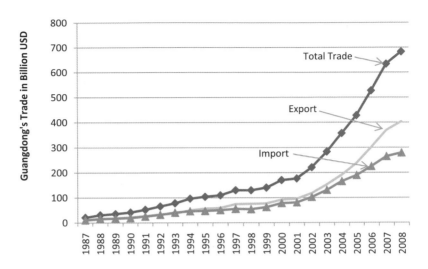

Source: Guangdong Statistical Bureau.

Fig. 1.   Guangdong's trade from 1987 to 2008.

strategically between Guangdong and Shenzhen. Dongguan has presented a rare growth rate of about 20% for the last 20 years, with its total trade skyrocketing from virtually zero to US$107 billion in 20 years' time and at an annual growth rate of 40% (Table 1).

The Dongguan miracle is attributed to the very factors of success shared by all cities in the region: huge inflow of migrant workers, reliance on foreign capital and technology, and access to overseas market. As in 2007, more than 70% of the 10 million residents in Dongguan are migrant workers. Textiles, shoes, consumer electronics and toys are among the key products of this city produced mostly by privately owned SMEs.[9]

Over the years, the PRD model encapsulated in the Dongguan miracle has also brought about serious problems as well, the most serious of which is its unsustainable development pattern, both in terms of resources and environment. Positioned in the low-value chain, some industries under this model typically require high energy

---

[9] For a closer look at the Dongguan miracle, see Table 1 in the appendix.

consumption and high labour input while producing high pollution and low value-added per unit output. As a result, this has posed daunting challenges for the sustainable development of Guangdong and China as a whole.

The second problem is with the PRD's vulnerability to foreign volatility due to its high dependence on foreign markets. This development model is now facing a grim test as prospects of export and economic growth look gloomier than ever. Even before the crisis, during the first three quarters of 2008, Guangdong's export experienced a modest 13% increase, a sharp fall from 21% in 2007 and a rather unsatisfactory performance compared with the national average growth of 22%. The crisis simply worsened the economic situation, causing export to grow negatively followed by a severe decline of 18.4% in the fourth quarter of 2008 and the first quarter of 2009, respectively. As the global economic crisis deepens, it is foreseeable that both trade and growth figures will decline even further.[10]

The shoes and toy manufacturers in Dongguan are already suffering a 50% decrease in overseas orders.[11] The downward pressure on demand for China's export has further been aggravated by the gradual appreciation of RMB by nearly 20% since July 2005, making "Made-in-China" products more expensive to foreign buyers. Looking beyond 2008, the global financial crisis is bound to bring about further decrease in orders and cause more factory closures and unemployment.

Prior to the financial crisis, many SMEs in processing trade in the region are already confronted with rising production costs, giving

---

[10] Export and growth data are from the Statistical Bureau of Guangdong province. According to most recent data on trade, November saw the sharpest decrease in China's trade with the world (a moderate fall of 2% compared with 2007), with Guangdong's external trade volume falling to −13% from the November 2007 level. Reports also indicate that half of the manufacturers of low value-added textiles and toys registered zero export for that particular month.

[11] Che Xiaohui, Liang Siqi, "Foreign enterprise moving out, the pain of transition for Pearl Delta River Region", *Xinhua News Agency*, http://news.xinhuanet.com/newscenter/2008-02/27/content_7676546.htm, 21 Jan. 2009.

greater urgency for upgrading. The root cause of price inflation could be attributed to the spiral increase in global oil prices since 2005, which led to price increases of oil-related products and other major raw materials such as minerals, coal, fibre, paper and imported plastic. State-owned power companies have adjusted electricity prices upwards several times from 2005 in response to rising fuel cost and structural shortage in power supply. Strict government regulations made extra land use scarce and costly.[12]

In general, the input price hike has aggravated the financial situations for most SMEs whose selling prices grow only moderately against raw materials and general consumer prices (Figure 2).[13] The combined effect of the increasing cost of key factor inputs has considerably narrowed the modest profit margin originally enjoyed by imported product processing firms in the region (Table 2).

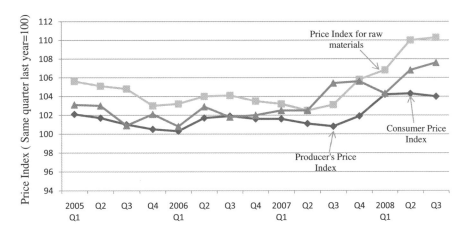

Source: Guangdong Statistical Bureau.

Fig. 2.   Price index for Guangdong prior to the crisis.

---

[12] Zhang Rui, "Small- and medium sized firms in the Pearl River Delta: the pain of restructuring and the road to transformation", *Journal of Guangdong Economy*, 2008:12.

[13] CPI (Consumer Price Index) refers to the index of average price of consumer goods and services; PPI (Producer's Product Index) refers to the index of average selling price of industrial goods received by the firms; Price Index for Raw Materials measures the price of raw materials and industrial inputs such as fuel, ore and energy among others.

For labour-intensive small- and medium-sized manufacturers, rising labour cost is another serious concern. During the period of rapid industrialisation and massive inflow of migrant workers, firms in the PRD region generally offer very low wages for unskilled labour. With hidden unemployment in the rural sector amounting to tens of millions, the region enjoyed an abundant reserve of cheap labour from the rural area without worrying about unit labour cost.

The situation has gradually changed thanks to increasing pressures from the government and, most decisively, the introduction of the new labour law in January 2008, which restricted employer's bargaining power and legalised mandatory social security and over-time payment for workers. With the new labour law taking effect, most firms in the region have experienced rising labour cost by up to 25%.[14] The labour cost in Shenzhen, for instance, has been rising steadily from 2005, with the first quarter of 2008 registering the sharpest wage hike in recent years.[15]

The crisis is also a result of a government policy shift in response to mounting social costs associated with the old model of economic growth. The government's heightening concern about environmental pollution, energy use inefficiency and provision for worker's safety and welfare, as evidenced by the new labour law and newly formulated environmental regulations for water and air pollution, has put pressure on firms to upgrade their businesses. Another example is the adjustment of the export tax rebate scheme introduced in 2006, which stipulated that most low-tech and low value-added exports will receive a much less tax rebate than before.[16]

---

[14] Oxford Analytica, "China: Guangdong faces restructuring test", *International Herald Tribune*, 19 Nov. 2008.

[15] While wage increases, the labour force has taken a tougher stand in demanding for more nonwage compensation for injury, over-time work, poor work environment, and welfare provisions.

[16] From 2006 to early 2008, the Ministry of Finance and General Custom Office lowered export tax rebate rate for low-value added products in general, and cancelled the rebate for products with high per-value added energy consumption and pollution. However, most recently, the rebate for textiles and toys has been raised in view of external shocks generated by the financial crisis. For details, refer to the Custom Duty Department of the Ministry of Finance website at http://www.mof.gov.cn/guanshuisi.

GOVERNMENT POLICIES VIS-À-VIS THE CURRENT CRISIS

Given the greater urgency for industrial upgrading, Wang Yang, party secretary of Guangdong, sees the financial crisis as a rare opportunity. He argued that Guangdong would face more difficulties and take a longer time to achieve the goals of industrial upgrading and establish a modern industrial system without the current grim economic situation. The provincial government thus appears very resolved to push forward its double restructuring programme[17] notwithstanding the ongoing economic hardship and rising number of factory shutdowns and unemployment in the PRD.

This programme aims to transfer rural labour in the less developed agricultural sector to industrial and service sectors and to transform the labour-intensive, export-oriented, low value-added processing industry into high-tech and high value-added industries and services. To that end, the Guangdong government will spend 50 billion RMB in the next five years for its industrial restructuring. The basic idea of the strategy, often referred to as "emptying the cage and changing the bird" (teng long huan niao, 腾笼换鸟), is to create an environment suitable for a high-tech and high value-added new economy to gradually replace the labour-intensive processing industry.[18]

The core of the government restructuring programme focusses strongly on the necessary infrastructure and business environment

---

[17] "Double restructuring" refers to two ongoing processes. The first process is industrialization of the relatively poor regions of Guangdong (outside PRD), based partially on relocation of labor-intensive industry from PRD to other parts of Guangdong. The second process is the industrial restructuring of PRD which is the main theme of this policy paper.

[18] In a recent government policy edict, the phrase "teng long huan niao" is used to generalise the policy package tailored for the more developed PRD region; the government coined another term "creating the forests to welcome the phoenix" (zao lin yin feng, 造林引凤) to generalise its strategy towards the less developed regions in the province, which in a nutshell calls for creating better business environment to facilitate the transfer of the labour-intensive processing industries to the poor regions within the province.

for industrial upgrading. In the coming five years (2009–2013), the government is expected to build more industrial parks specialising in new growth areas such as information technology (IT), bio-medicine, high-tech electronics, industrial waste processing, heavy chemicals and specialised business equipment. The most important elements of the industrial policy include government's direct investment in industrial infrastructure, R&D facilities, and special incentive packages aimed at helping SMEs to engage in R&D and climb up the value chain.

There will also be favourable tax policies, urban development projects and various incentives specifically tailored to encourage the inflow of high value-added capital investment and highly educated labour. Meanwhile, the government is committed to setting tougher standards on energy consumption and environment pollution, applying stricter criteria for tax rebate and requiring compulsory minimum wage and welfare provision for migrant workers for the labour-intensive low value-added industries in an effort to squeeze out some of the least efficient firms from the region with minimal economic and social costs.

Guangdong's determination to push forward industrial upgrading, however, has attracted a good deal of criticism because it showed indifference to large-scale SME bankruptcies and job losses. Wang Yang described these bankruptcies as "obsolete productivity forces" which were "discarded by the cycling fluctuation of the market" and as such "the government should not salvage them".[19]

As those losing jobs are mainly migrant workers from regions outside Guangdong, other provinces have to shoulder most of the social burden resulting from the sudden surge in unemployed migrant workers. There were numerous complaints about Guangdong's "selfish" behaviour. The central government is aware of the risk of shutdowns and surging job losses in the PRD to social stability. In his tour to PRD from 14 to 15 November, Premier Wen Jiabao

---

[19] Hu Jiang and Yue Zong, "Government Cannot Salvage Backward Productivity Force", *Nanfang Dushi Bao*, 14 Nov. 2008, AA10, 17 Jan. 2009.

requested local governments to support SMEs in order to help them weather through the difficulties.[20]

Obviously, the potential social consequence of large-scale unemployment is a major source of concern. With the lessons of the Smart Union toy factory incident still fresh in memory, the government is clearly aware that the crisis may easily engender massive collective incidents and endanger social stability. While this very short crisis has been resolved successfully, more serious social consequences of unemployment could be lurking in the corner.

In response to both the deteriorating economic situation and the pressure from the central government and the public, the Guangdong leadership decided to eventually change its previous policy of turning a blind eye to the shutdown wave while striving hard to implement its double restructuring programme. It has adopted measures to buttress the development of SMEs and assist those unemployed, such as annually allocating 180 million RMB in the following three years to facilitate loans to SMEs, setting up a provincial re-insurance company with one billion capital, reducing enterprise taxes and fees, speeding up infrastructure construction, launching extensive training programmes for the unemployed and helping to relocate the labour force.[21]

Meanwhile, the central government also participates actively in charting economic development, in particular, industrial restructuring of the PRD region in the far future. In a recently released outline by the Commission for Reform and Development (CRD), the CRD stated clearly that the central government has high expectations of the PRD model as a leading model for economic reform, openness and development. The outline stresses creativity and economy of scale as the key elements in the new economy, whereas the modern service sector, heavy industries, high-tech sectors and large multinational

---

[20] Li Bin, "Wen Jiabao emphasises that vigorous support should be provided to the development of SMEs in his investigation in Guangdong", *Xinhuanet*, 17 Jan. 2009.
[21] Chen Ji, "Investigating the truth of SMEs closedowns in the PRD", *Xinhua News Agency*, 25 Nov. 2008. http://news.xinhuanet.com/fortune/2008-11/25/content_10411916.htm.

firms are designated as key "growth areas".[22] Through the outline, the central government has set out a very comprehensive plan with high demands and expectations for the next 5–12 years, in areas like restructuring of traditional sectors, enhancing regional cooperation, promoting investment in infrastructure and human resources and the developing of innovative and competitive new industries; all efforts point towards a new grand development strategy. It can be expected that the provincial government, with limited resources and exigency of the ongoing crisis, will be much more cautious in its policy evaluation and execution.

ASSESSMENT OF EXTERNAL SHOCKS

In the short run, Guangdong's industrial upgrading plan has encountered grave challenges from the economic slowdown and surging unemployment. The Chinese Academy of Social Sciences (CASS) predicts that the Chinese economy will be sapped by withering trade, and actual unemployment rate would be over 9.4% in 2009.[23] The Chinese government has given priority to ensuring 8% GDP growth and creating more job opportunities in 2009. Guangdong's double restructuring programme is subject to this priority. This means that the restructuring process should not be conducted in a drastic manner which would lead to large-scale factory shutdowns and massive unemployment.

The first major concern of the PRD is that labour outflow would have a strong impact on the urban area as the economy undergoes restructuring. Since the whole idea of restructuring is about the general shift towards a less labour-intensive and more capital- and technological-intensive industrial structure, more migrant workers are bound to leave the PRD region in search of opportunities in other

---

[22] Outline of the planned reform and development in PRD region, Reform and Development Commission, 8 Jan. 2009.

[23] Han Fudong, "*Social Bluebook*: Income growth rate drops and unemployment rises", *Nanfang Dushi Bao*, 16 Dec. 2008, http://finance.southcn.com/jrdd/content/2008-12/16/content_4772342.htm.

regions in the long run, initiating significant changes in the population structure. The local residents, many deriving their livelihood from offering house rentals and other services for the migrant population, are already experiencing the consequences of the economic slowdown and stand to lose more from the restructuring. The government is likely to have a hard time formulating necessary policy packages to avoid the negative social consequences of de-industrialisation and urban decay.

Likewise, rural income will be directly affected by the present wave of migrant worker retrenchment in the region, with negative impact on the country as whole. A survey by China's Ministry of Agriculture finds that the number of employed workers in coastal regions by the end of October had declined by 6.5% compared with that of last year.[24] As 50% of rural income comes from the nonagricultural sector, particularly from migrant workers' remittances, and pay increment of the latter constitutes above 70% of peasants' income growth,[25] large-scale unemployment of migrant workers not only creates tensions in the existing tight job market, but also results in a sharp decline in peasants' income.

Regionally, the impact of the economic crisis on regions and sectors differs. In terms of export, apart from the industrial sector of Dongguan which appears to be the worst hit among major cities in the region, other industrial centres have suffered much less in terms of export and employment for the first 10 months; the industrial sector in some cities, like Foshan (佛山), where the industrialisation process have been initiated later and high-tech industrial parks built only in recent years with a view to industrial upgrading, are still moving on the track of rapid growth and expansion.

There are clear differences between the performances of different sectors as well. While toy and shoe manufacturers are having a bitter

---

[24] "Jobless migrant workers dramatically increase, central leadership investigate the development of SMEs in four provinces", *Xinhua News Agency*, 19 Nov. 2008.

[25] Chen Shanzhe, "7.8 million migrant workers returned home in advance, the State Council takes six measures to promote employment", *21 Shiji Jingji Baodao*, 18 Dec. 2008.

time, most firms with independent brand and core technological patent have weathered the crisis well despite far-reaching repercussions of the global financial crisis. A few Shenzhen firms suffice to serve as examples. Television manufacturer Konka (康佳彩电), consumer electronics maker Coship Electronics (同舟电子), and a global leading producer of environmentally friendly cars with petrol-electrical dynamos, Bydauto (比亚迪), have all seen their profits rising by 20–30% in the first three quarters of 2008. All success stories entail similar components: mastery of internationally competitive core technology, domestically oriented marketing and product design, and consistent investment in R&D.[26]

From an industry wide perspective, although the export-oriented labour-intensive industry still rules much of the economy, structural changes have already been highlighted by recent growth in high value-added and high-tech industries. Despite the financial crisis, the value-added of relatively high-tech sectors such as specialised equipment and electronics have increased or retreated much less in value-added growth compared with labour-intensive low-tech sectors like wood processing and textiles (Figure 3).

LONG-TERM PROSPECTS FOR INDUSTRIAL RESTRUCTURING

In the long run, the whole regional economy will have to go through a test of a critical nature. The restructuring plan requires the economy to become more domestically oriented. However, the domestic markets in Guangdong and China are still relatively underdeveloped and poorly integrated in contrast to world class productive capacity built during the years of export-oriented development. Meanwhile, growth in per-capita income and effective domestic purchasing power in China trail far behind its double-digit growth in trade and GDP.

The problem is demonstrated clearly by comparing domestic retail and sale and international trade of the PRD region. As shown by

---

[26] "Reliance on Self-innovation and Brand Creation", *Economic Daily*, 17 Jan. 2009.

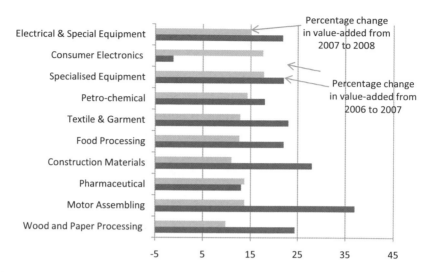

Source: Guangdong Statistical Bureau Database.

Fig. 3. Percentage change in value-added for the nine major industrial sectors of Guangdong.

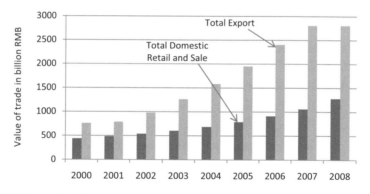

Source: Calculation based on Guangdong Statistical Yearbook, 2008.

Fig. 4. Guangdong's domestic and foreign trade, 2000–2008.

the latest figures (Figure 4) for 2008, although a strong RMB and the financial crisis have curbed the growth in value of exports in RMB and somewhat made the difference smaller, total domestic sale and retail of the region has been much smaller in volume and more modest in rate of growth than foreign trade for the past few years. It is unlikely that in the near future domestic demand will make up for the short-fall in foreign trade, which is expected to fall sharply. Since much of the excess productive capacity has to resort to domestic market to avoid a severe slowdown and unemployment, the industrial restructuring and economic growth of the PRD will be highly contingent on growth prospects of domestic demand.

This concern is to some extent mitigated by a general structural change in the Chinese economy. In the first 10 months of 2008, domestic consumption in China experienced a rise of 22% over 2007, or 14% considering the effect of inflation. In the following few years, domestic consumption is expected to rise in response to government incentive packages designed to sharply increase urban wages and rural income.[27] Riding on this opportunity, firms in the PRD region which survive the crisis with a competitive edge will benefit greatly and possibly lead the restructuring process.

Another serious concern is associated with the lack of human capital and R&D resources for restructuring. Compared with other regions in China, such as the Yangtze River Delta (YRD), the PRD region is not as well equipped in terms of an educated labour force, investment in educational infrastructure and R&D capacity. Tables 3 and 4 put the problem into perspective by comparing the level of education and R&D capacity in PRD with those of Beijing, Shanghai and Jiangsu. As human capital and R&D capacity are pre-requisites for successful restructuring, the region may face severe constraints in the competition for market and investments. Although Guangdong is already making use of its fiscal prowess to remedy the shortfall, it takes time and a more comprehensive strategy is needed.

Although external shocks have placed new urgency on the restructuring programme, which offers an ideal way out of the current crisis, long-run and short-run policy objectives may still clash in view of the daunting agenda vis-à-vis the rapidly deteriorating trade and growth prospects.

---

[27] *Weekly Economic Observation*, National Development Research Centre, Vol. 48, 2008.

Take the most urgent issue of employment creation and reemployment of laid-off migrant workers for example. On the one hand, as labour-intensive SMEs are the major employers of three quarters of the labour force in the region, a harsh programme of restructuring to squeeze out inefficient firms will naturally aggravate the employment situation and bring about serious social consequences to Guangdong and elsewhere. On the other hand, if the government overreacts to the current crisis and withdraws much of its proposed restructuring efforts, economic growth in the long run will be compromised. Since the government has only limited resources, the painful trade-off between long-run and short-run objectives still remains to be addressed.

In conclusion, while the situation is so far largely under control, prospects are less encouraging. In the short run, the sharp fall in export will inevitably lead to more severe reduction in growth and employment as the restructuring is still at an early stage; in the long run, structural problems such as lack of domestic demand and high-quality human resources may pose a real threat to the restructuring process.[28] While the government has been acutely aware of the situation and is quite timely in its response, addressing structural problems demands tremendous efforts in aligning short-term stimulus packages to cushion external shocks with long-term strategies to tackle the internal sources.

With the turn of events, restructuring is most likely to take place as business environment changes. The government is likely to play a key role in the process, given the determination and resources of the

---

[28] In early November, the Bureau of Small and Medium Firms in Guangdong province publically refuted the idea that a systemic crisis was occurring among the small and medium firms in the PRD, attributing large-scale factory closedown to individual specific reasons and natural consequences of industrial restructuring. Of the firm closures, 90% were labour-intensive manufacturers who were unable to survive or in search of other favourable sites. However, recently published statistics suggest that the aftermath of the financial crisis is worse than expected with regard to its adverse effect on at least some parts of the heavily export-oriented PRD, such as Dongguan, Zhuhai and Shantou.

Chinese local, provincial and central governments and past history of rather successful reform initiatives. However, depending on the evolution of the global economic downturn and its impact on China, the social and economic costs of the crisis of industrialisation in terms of lower growth and rising unemployment will inevitably undermine the region's harmonious development at least for the next few years.

APPENDIX

Table 1. Indicator of Dongguan's economic performance.

Year	GDP in billion RMB[29]	Total export in billion USD	Total import in billion USD	GDP growth (%)	Migrant labor in 10,000	Local residents in 10,000	FDI in billion USD
1999	67.2	7.8	7.6	27.40	127	144	5.2
2000	82.0	17.2	14.9	19.70	245	153	13.4
2001	99.2	19.0	15.5	19.90	450	154	15.4
2002	118.7	23.7	20.5	20.50	426	156	17.8
2003	145.3	28.0	24.1	20.50	433	159	20.5
2004	180.6	35.2	29.3	21.00	473	162	23.9
2005	218.1	40.9	33.4	19.40	553	166	28.1
2006	262.7	47.4	36.8	19.20	567	168	33.1
2007	315.2	60.2	46.4	18.20	533	173	30.3
2008	370.2	65.5	47.8	14.00	520	175	25.9

Sources: Dongguan Statistical Report, Dongguan Bureau of Statistics.

---

[29] Please note that the output here is measured in RMB. The trade dependency ratio of the economy of Dongguan, though seldom published officially, is extremely high. A rough estimate can put it at about 150%, more than twice the national level of 70%. The ratio is measured as the ratio between total trade and GDP in USD.

Table 2. General indicator of Guangdong's external economy and industrial sector.[30]

Month	Total trade (billion USD)	Total export (billion US$)	Total import (billion US$)	Total industrial value-added (billion RMB)
Jan. 2008	53.2 (18.3)	31.6 (26.3)	21.5 (8.1)	112 (13.4)
Feb.	48.49 (7.5)	23.4 (4.1)	18.7 (16.1)	92 (12.1)
Mar.	54.7 (28.5)	31.8 (16.4)	22.9 (12.4)	117 (13.5)
Apr.	57.4 (13.8)	32.9 (13.2)	24.5 (14.6)	121 (13.0)
May.	58.8 (18.5)	34.0 (17.1)	24.8 (20.7)	129 (13.3)
Jun.	58.0 (5.5)	34.1 (2.0)	23.9 (11.0)	140 (13.1)
Jul.	64.3 (17.6)	37.1 (17.0)	27.2 (18.5)	129 (12.9)
Aug.	62.6 (10)	36.7 (17.0)	25.6 (7.7)	132 (13)
Sep.	65.8 (12.2)	37.64 (11.1)	26.7 (8.5)	39.1 (14.8)
Oct.	60.7 (7.1)	36.8 (9.2)	23.9 (4.0)	135 (12.7)
Nov.	53.3 (−12.2)	33.8 (−5.1)	19.5 (−22.2)	133 (12.8)
Dec.	52.0 (−13.6)	27.3 (−14.3)	17.5 (−23.7)	142.0 (11.6)
Jan. 2009	36.6 (−31.1)	24.2 (−31.1)	12.4 (−42.1)	96.5 (−13.8)
Feb.	34.0 (−19.2)	19.4 (−16.9)	14.6 (−22.0)	87.8 (−4.6)
Mar.	44.8 (−18.2)	27.3 (−14.3)	17.5 (−23.7)	116 (−0.8)
Apr.	47.1 (−18.1)	27.7 (−16.1)	19.5 (−20.9)	117 (−3.3)

Source: Guangdong Statistical Bureau.

Table 3. Indicators of educational level for selected provinces, 2006.

Region	Percentage of college graduates in the population (%)	Average education annual per urban household (RMB)	Average education annual per rural household (RMB)	Average years of education (years)	Gov spending in education (billion RMB)
Beijing	10.8	975	844	10.8	52
Shanghai	9.9	1225	920	9.9	42
Jiangsu	8.7	722	544	8.7	67
Guangdong	4.3	604	303	8.9	89

Source: China Demographic Yearbook, 2008.

---

[30] The percentage change from the same month in 2007 is in parentheses.

Table 4. Indicators of techological capacity of selected provinces, 2006.

Province	R&D personnel per 10,000 population	R&D spending (billion RMB)	Number of invented applied	Percentage of research personnel in the workforce	Number of technology transfer contracts with foreign companies
Beijing	35.9	87.3	751	6.7	1857
Shanghai	9.3	48.6	2488	4.9	2879
Jiangsu	1.7	71.4	1297	5.1	843
Guangdong	0.5	56.1	801	3.1	668
Zhejiang	0.7	47.6	372	4.5	547

Source: China Technology Yearbook, 2007.

Chapter 5

Impact of the Global Economic Crisis on the Pearl River Delta and Yangtze River Delta Regions

YU Hong

The Pearl River Delta (PRD) and Yangtze River Delta (YRD) regions have achieved impressive rates of economic growth to become two "growth engines" for China during the reform decades. This chapter attempts to investigate the impact of the global recession on the foreign trade and economic development of the PRD and YRD regions, and identify their similarities and differences with regard to state anti-crisis agendas. It also discusses the different long-term challenges faced by these two regions.

Over the last decade, the Pearl River Delta (PRD)[1] and the Yangtze River Delta (YRD)[2] regions have been the major engines of foreign trade and emblems of economic development for China. These two regions jointly accounted for around 27.8% of China's Gross Domestic Product (GDP) in 2008. The shares of export in China contributed by the YRD and PRD regions were around 35% and 27%, respectively, in 2008.[3] These two regions are also the leading destinations for foreign capital inflow (see Table 1).

However, as the ratios of export to Gross Regional Product (GRP) in both the YRD and PRD regions were very high, around 63% and 74% in 2008 respectively, the two deltas were naturally confronted with a contraction in their total economic activities as orders from overseas markets and foreign direct investment (FDI) plunged in the financial crisis. Indeed, the global economic crisis has hit China the hardest in what have been ranked as its most open and developed economic regions: the PRD and the YRD. Both regions are suffering greatly from the sharp fall in foreign trade and a drastic slowdown in economic growth. The total value of foreign trade in the YRD region fell sharply to US$150.4 billion in the first quarter of 2009 from US$251.1 billion in the third quarter of 2008, a drop of 66.9%. For the PRD region,[4] the corresponding figure decreased to US$115.4 billion in the first quarter of 2009 from US$192.4 billion in the third quarter of 2008, a decline of 66.7%. Battered by the decline in external

---

[1] The PRD includes the nine municipalities of Guangzhou, Shenzhen, Zhuhai, Foshan, Huizhou, Dongguan, Zhongshan, Jiangmen and Zhaoqing, and covers Guangdong province.

[2] The territorial boundaries of YRD include 16 municipalities of Hangzhou, Ningbo, Jiaxing, Huzhou, Shaoxing, Zhoushan, Taizhou, Nanjing, Wuxi, Changzhou, Suzhou, Nantong, Yangzhou, Zhenjiang, Taizhou and Shanghai within Jiangsu, Zhejiang and Shanghai, two provinces and a centrally administered municipality, respectively.

[3] National Statistics Bureau of China, 2009.

[4] Guangdong's foreign trade has accounted for the majority of the PRD region's foreign trade over the last decade. In 2008, according to statistics, its share reached 95.8%. Therefore, the data of Guangdong were used in the calculation of foreign trade in the PRD region.

Table 1. General development of the Pearl River and Yangtze River Delta regions, 2007.

Indicator	PRD	YRD
Administrative areas	Guangdong	Shanghai, Jiangsu, Zhejiang
Land area (square kilometres)	24,437	99,600
Population (million)	42.8	75.0
Average per capita gross regional product (GRP) (*yuan*)	48,682	44,787
Exports (US$ billion)	369.2	475.9
Foreign capital inflow (US$ billion)	17.1	40.1
Shares in China's total export (%)	30.3	39.0
Shares in total foreign capital inflow to China (%)	22.9	53.5
Shares of high-tech manufacturing in total industrial output (%)	26.5	31.5
Contribution of service sector to GRP (%)	41.1	36.7

Note: The figures on per capita GRP have been population weighted.
Sources:
1. China Statistical Yearbook, 2008.
2. Guangdong Statistical Yearbook, 2008.
3. Shanghai Statistical Yearbook, 2008.

demand and capital inflow, these two regions may cede much of their glory as engines of economic growth to inland regions.

In the first quarter of 2009, economic growth in the PRD and YRD regions had decreased considerably. Indeed, compared to the corresponding figures in the previous year, several municipalities in the PRD region, such as Dongguan, Zhuhai, and Zhaoqing, even recorded negative growth, at −3.5%, −6.9%, and −0.4% respectively. Economic growth was also disappointing in the YRD region. Although some municipalities achieved decent growth, municipalities such as Shanghai, Hangzhou and Ningbo recorded very low GRP growth (Table 2).

In terms of industrial sectors, the average ratio of high-tech industries' output to total industrial output value was 26.5% in the PRD

Table 2.   Economic growth in the Pearl River and Yangtze River Delta regions in the first quarter of 2009.

Municipality	GRP (billion *yuan*)	Growth rate (%)
Pearl River Delta		
Guangzhou	183.7	5.2
Shenzhen	174.0	5.3
Foshan	98.1	7.5
Dongguan	77.0	−3.5
Zhongshan	33.0	3.5
Jiangmen	28.6	4.0
Huizhou	25.9	5.1
Zhuhai	20.4	−6.9
Zhaoqing	14.2	−0.4
Yangtze River Delta		
Shanghai	315.0	3.1
Hangzhou	95.2	3.4
Ningbo	80.0	1.0
Jiaxing	38.1	4.6
Huzhou	22.4	5.3
Shaoxing	45.9	4.3
Zhoushan	10.3	11.8
Taizhou	40.2	2.0
Nanjing	88.2	9.3
Wuxi	105.6	9.7
Changzhou	54.7	10.0
Suzhou	162.6	9.5
Nantong	60.0	13.2
Yangzhou	38.1	13.1
Zhenjiang	37.1	12.6
Taizhou	40.0	12.9

Sources:
1. Shanghai Statistics Bureau, 2009.
2. Jiangsu Statistics Bureau, 2009.
3. Zhejiang Statistics Bureau, 2009.
4. "Wang Yang: Push forward the development strategy of 'double transformation of industries and labour force'", Mingpao News, 29 May 2009, http://news.mingpao.com/cfm/Print. cfm?Publishdate=20090529&File=ca/ca/caa1h.txt, 4 Jun. 2009.

region compared to 31.5% in the YRD region in 2007, indicating that the YRD region had a relatively high value-added industrial structure. In contrast, the PRD region has traditionally been more reliant on low-end export-process sectors. Overall, the economy of the PRD region is widely known as the "global manufacturing factory", especially of low value-added products. The economic problems faced by both the PRD and YRD regions require drastic measures from their governments. However, their different economic structures and regional characteristics mean that local governments need to formulate both similar and different agendas.

The governments of both regions are taking prompt measures to prevent a freefall in the economies. These include increasing government spending on public works and boosting consumer spending to stimulate the local economy. For example, the provincial governments of Guangdong, Jiangsu and Zhejiang have, in 2009, successively announced ambitious stimulus packages of 303 billion,[5] 300 billion,[6] and 300 billion[7] *yuan* investment respectively in sectors like transportation infrastructure, energy, modern industries and environment. Both regions are putting more emphasis on domestic investment and consumption as the economic crisis has pushed for a transition from a development model that is over dependent on trade and inward foreign investment.

While the agendas for both regions bear certain similarities, there were different priorities on anti-crisis policies. In the PRD, the global financial crisis has forced many of the region's low-end manufacturing

---

[5] "Response to global financial crisis: A stimulus package of 303 billion yuan investment on 200 key development projects", http://www.gd.gov.cn/govpub/rdzt/nxcfz/jknxzfjc/200901/t20090119_84133.htm, 1 Mar. 2009.

[6] "Response to the policies of domestic demand expansion announced by the central government: a stimulus package of 300 billion yuan investment is allocated by Jiangsu", http://202.123.110.5/gzdt/2008-11/14/content_1148725.htm, 2 Jun. 2009.

[7] "Zhejiang plans to spend around 300 billion yuan to stimulate domestic demand in 2009", *Sina News*, http://news.sina.com.cn/c/2008-11-13/162816648023.shtml, 2 Jun. 2009.

firms out of the market,[8] and it is now vital that the government plays a decisive role in shaping the economic fortune of the region. Hence, the provincial government of Guangdong is assigning top priority to upgrade the industrial structure.

In contrast, the YRD region focusses more on regional coordination. It is likely to suffer from its innate lack of regional integration and coordination since it comes under three different administrative jurisdictions. This may put severe constraints on the effectiveness of the collective response to the crisis as the lack of industrial cooperation within this region may result in duplicated development and cut-throat style competition. It also limits the development of an integrated domestic market, which is badly needed in the aftermath of a sharp fall in external demands.

DIFFERING PATHS TO INDUSTRIAL DEVELOPMENT

During the reform period, particularly since 1992, the PRD and YRD regions have been the major players in foreign trade and emblems of economic development for China. Contributions made by these two regions jointly accounted for 27.8% of GDP in China in 2008. According to the custom statistics, the shares of exports in China contributed by the YRD and PRD regions were around 35% and 27%, respectively, in 2008. Thanks to its rapid growth of foreign trade and capital inflow, both regions have achieved a high annual growth rate of around 15% over the past 30 years.[9]

Both regions have also been the most important centres for export-oriented manufacturing industries in China over the last decade. The large export-process production bases in Shenzhen and Dongguan serve as flagships in the PRD region: the shares of exports from the PRD region contributed by these two municipalities were

---

[8] "Testing times for China's economy", *BBC News*, http://news.bbc.co.uk/2/hi/programmes/from_our_own_correspondent/7937773.stm, 4 Jun. 2009.
[9] China Statistical Yearbook, 2008.

44.4% and 16.2%, respectively, in 2008. For the YRD, Shanghai and Suzhou, where large numbers of export-oriented and high value-added factories conglomerate, are leading the region's industrial development. In 2008, the shares of exports from the YRD region contributed by these two municipalities were 33.8% and 26.3%, respectively.[10]

The PRD and YRD regions spearheaded economic opening up and reform on a scale unprecedented in China. Since the initial establishment of Shenzhen as a Special Economic Zone in 1980 and the development of Pudong New District in 1992, Shenzhen and Pudong have based their development on trade and foreign capital after low-end export-oriented industries began to shift from the more industrialised economies of Asia into regions with abundant supplies of cheap labour, land and other factors of production. With acute business acumen, foreign businessmen were able to shift their production bases into the PRD and YRD regions to take advantage of low production costs and superior coastal location.

Foreign trade in the two regions has developed rapidly since 1990. For the YRD region, total value of foreign trade in Shanghai, Jiangsu and Zhejiang was US$322.1, US$392.2 and US$211.1 billion in 2008, with annual growth of 23.3%, 28.8% and 27.4% between 1990 and 2008 respectively. In the PRD region, trade in Guangdong achieved annual growth of about 16.8%, reaching US$683.2 billion in 2008 from US$41.8 billion in 1990 (Figure 1).

Figure 2 shows that in the YRD, foreign capital inflow to Shanghai, Jiangsu and Zhejiang has increased remarkably over the last decade. For Shanghai, the total value of foreign capital reached US$10.0 billion in 2008 from US$1.2 billion in 1992, with annual growth of around 14.2%. The foreign investment inflow to Jiangsu and Zhejiang jumped to US$25.1 billion and US$10 billion respectively, in 2008, a big leap from the corresponding figures in 1992 of only US$1.4 and US$0.1 billion respectively. For the PRD region, the value of foreign capital inflow also hit US$19.1 billion in 2008 from US$4.8 billion in 1992.

---

[10] Guangdong Statistics Bureau, 2009 and Shanghai Statistics Bureau, 2009.

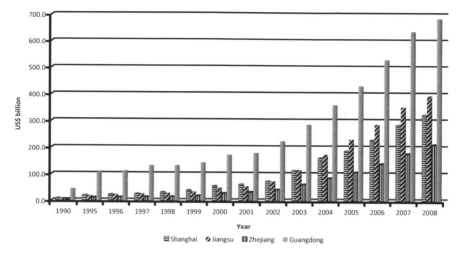

Note: The YRD region includes Shanghai, Jiangsu and Zhejiang; the PRD region covers Guangdong.

Sources:

1. Guangdong Statistical Yearbook, 2008.
2. Public Report of National Economic and Social Development Statistics of Guangdong, 2008.
3. Shanghai Statistical Yearbook, 2008.
4. Public Report of National Economic and Social Development Statistics of Shanghai, 2008.
5. Jiangsu Statistical Yearbook, 2008.
6. Public Report of National Economic and Social Development Statistics of Jiangsu, 2008.
7. Zhejiang Statistical Yearbook, 2008.
8. Public Report of National Economic and Social Development Statistics of Zhejiang, 2008.

Fig. 1.　Foreign trade development in the Yangtze River and Pearl River Deltas.

Thanks to increases in trade and foreign capital investment, both regions have achieved rapid industrialisation and growth since 1992. In the YRD region, Shanghai, Jiangsu and Zhejiang's industrial output had grown to 578.4 billion, 1475.9 billion and 1035.9 billion *yuan* in 2008 from 63.6 billion, 101.7 billion and 58.1 billion *yuan* respectively in 1992. For the PRD region, Guangdong's industrial output increased to 1.73 trillion *yuan* in 2008 from 89.9 billion *yuan* in 1992 (Figure 3). Compared to the 2001 figures of 44.2% and 45.1%, the shares of industrial output in GRP in the YRD and PRD regions rose to their peaks in 2006 of 48.1% and 51.3%

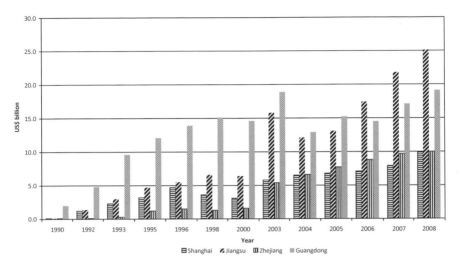

Note: The YRD region includes Shanghai, Jiangsu and Zhejiang; the PRD region covers Guangdong.

Sources:

1. Guangdong Statistical Yearbook, 1991–2008.
2. Public Report of National Economic and Social Development Statistics of Guangdong, 2008.
3. Shanghai Statistical Yearbook, 1991–2008.
4. Public Report of National Economic and Social Development Statistics of Shanghai, 2008.
5. Jiangsu Statistical Yearbook, 1991–2008.
6. Public Report of National Economic and Social Development Statistics of Jiangsu, 2008.
7. Zhejiang Statistical Yearbook, 1991–2008.
8. Public Report of National Economic and Social Development Statistics of Zhejiang, 2008.

Fig. 2.　Foreign capital inflow in the Pearl River and Yangtze River Deltas.

before declining slightly to a respective 46.5% and 49.1% in 2008 (Figure 4).

Both regions have also achieved rapid economic growth since 1992. In the YRD region, Shanghai, Jiangsu and Zhejiang's GRP in 1991 was a respective 111 billion, 214 billion and 138 billion *yuan*. In 2008, it had grown to 1,370 billion, 3,000 billion and 2,149 billion *yuan* respectively. For the PRD region, Guangdong's GRP increased to 3,570 billion *yuan* in 2008 from 245 billion *yuan* in 1992, with annual growth of about 18.2% (Figure 5).

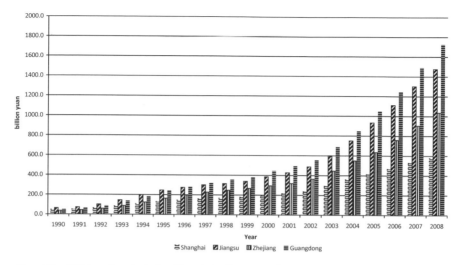

Note: The YRD region includes Shanghai, Jiangsu and Zhejiang; the PRD region covers Guangdong.

Sources:

1. Guangdong Statistical Yearbook, 2007.
2. Public Report of National Economic and Social Development Statistics of Guangdong, 2008.
3. Shanghai Statistical Yearbook, 2007.
4. Public Report of National Economic and Social Development Statistics of Shanghai, 2008.
5. Jiangsu Statistical Yearbook, 2008.
6. Public Report of National Economic and Social Development Statistics of Jiangsu, 2008.
7. Zhejiang Statistical Yearbook, 2007.
8. Public Report of National Economic and Social Development Statistics of Zhejiang, 2008.

Fig. 3.   Total value-added industrial output in the Pearl River and Yangtze River Deltas.

Although the YRD region is on the path of export-oriented development with heavy reliance on foreign capital, it is also techno-logically more advanced. The share of low-end manufacturing products in total exports in the YRD region was only 46.6% in 2007, compared to 66.6% in the PRD region (Table 3). The PRD region has experienced a different pattern of industrial development from the YRD region over the last decade. In PRD, industries such as electric machinery and equipment are dominated by low-end processing and assembling activities, rather than high-end advanced manufacturing, technological research and new product designing. The economy of

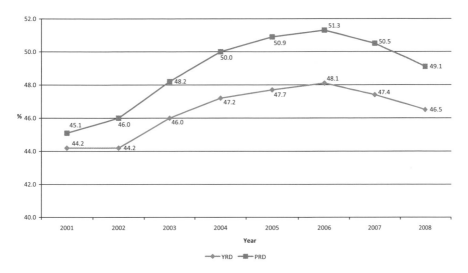

Note: Compilation based on the data of industrial output and GRP in the various regions.

Fig. 4. Share of industrial output in GRP in the Pearl River and Yangtze River Deltas.

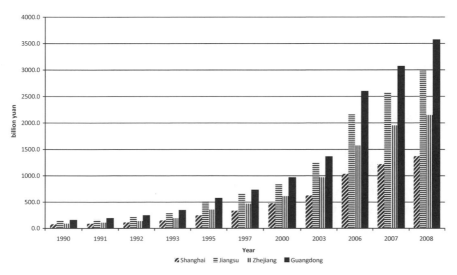

Note: The YRD region includes Shanghai, Jiangsu and Zhejiang; the PRD region covers Guangdong.

Source: As in Fig. 2.

Fig. 5. Total GRP in the Pearl River and Yangtze River Deltas.

Table 3.   Share of low-end manufacturing products in exports from the Pearl River and Yangtze River Delta regions (US$ billion).

Name	YRD				PRD			
	2004	2005	2006	2007	2004	2005	2006	2007
Total value of exports	306.7	412.1	527.7	660.3	191.5	238.1	301.9	369.2
Low-end manufacturing products	142.9	198.8	255.5	307.8	145.5	174.9	208.3	246.1
Share of low-end products in exports (%)	46.5	48.2	48.4	46.6	75.9	73.4	68.9	66.6

Sources:
1. Guangdong Statistical Yearbook, 2008.
2. Shanghai Statistical Yearbook, 2008.
3. Jiangsu Statistical Yearbook, 2008.
4. Zhejiang Statistical Yearbook, 2008.

the PRD region is widely known as the "global manufacturing factory". This relative weakness is exemplified by the fact that, in 2007, the average ratio of high-tech industries to total industrial output value was 26.5% in the PRD region compared to 31.5% in the YRD region.

IMPACT OF THE GLOBAL ECONOMIC CRISIS

The global economic crisis, triggered by the American sub-prime mortgage crisis in April 2007, has hit the export-oriented PRD and YRD regions hard. Both regions witnessed a rapid decline in foreign trade and investment, rising unemployment[11] and a slowdown in economic growth.

Figure 6 shows that the total value of foreign trade in the YRD region fell sharply to US$150.4 billion in the first quarter of 2009 from US$203.4 billion in the first quarter of 2008. Likewise, the

---

[11] "China's worst nightmare: unemployment", *Times*, http://www.time.com/time/world/article/0,8599,1855400,00.html, 7 Jun. 2009.

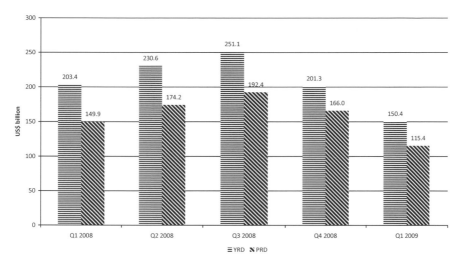

Sources:

1. Shanghai Statistics Bureau, 2009.
2. Jiangsu Statistics Bureau, 2009.
3. Zhejiang Statistics Bureau, 2009.
4. Guangdong Statistics Bureau, 2009.

Fig. 6.   Total value of foreign trade in the Pearl River and Yangtze River Deltas.

PRD region registered a fall to US$115.4 billion in the first quarter of 2009 from US$149.9 billion in the first quarter of 2008.

Due to their overdependence on foreign trade and investment, these two regions are the hardest hit in this global economic slow-down. The global economic crisis has heightened the risk that both the PRD and YRD regions may lose out to China's inland regions in terms of pace of development and transfer of capital and technology. For PRD and YRD, existing industrial structure is a double-edged sword. Whilst the export-oriented and low-end manufacturing industries have contributed greatly to the two regions' fast economic growth in the past, they are also responsible for the regions' downfall in this crisis.

The problem of an over-reliance on trade and foreign capital is most seriously felt in the PRD region.[12] A recent survey indicates that many Hong Kong-based factories in the PRD have been considering shifting their production facilities to inland regions since the onset of the crisis; 90% recognise that upgrading their industries is the ultimate solution to their predicament.[13] While similar challenges also apply to the YRD region, the risk of such capital outflow from the region is lower, thanks to its better positioning in the value chain.

GOVERNMENT AGENDAS TO FIGHT THE CRISIS IN THE TWO DELTAS

Similarities in Anti-crisis Policies

The economic problems faced by both regions require drastic measures by their governments and many common elements exist in the two regions' policy responses to fight the crisis. First, both regions have placed more emphasis on boosting domestic spending and investment, thus departing from a development model that depends too much on inward foreign investment and trade.

The global crisis has highlighted the importance of rebalancing economic growth by focussing on domestic demand in the long run. It may open new avenues to a more self-reliant and sustainable developmental pattern for these two deltas. Although their trade and in particular export-oriented industrial sectors have been hit hard by the global economic recession, the economic growth of the PRD and YRD regions is likely to continue in 2009 under the huge investment stimulus plans issued by the central and local governments.

Second, to capitalise on the dip in prices, the PRD and YRD regions have announced key policies to upgrade their backward industrial structures by focussing on the development of more advanced manufacturing industries.

---

[12] "Guangdong seeks to upgrade its way out of slump", *China Daily*, online edition: http://www.chinadaily.com.cn/bw/2009–02/16/content_7478529.htm, 3 Jun. 2009.

[13] "Hong Kong businessmen at PRD: Transformation as the key solution for crisis", *Mingpao*, 21 Apr. 2009.

In the PRD region, the Reform and Development Plan 2008–2020 (henceforth the Plan), was unveiled in January 2009, outlining key policies to help cope with the global economic crisis and resolve problems of the existing industrial and economic structure. Various preferential policies such as tax cuts and funds to support technological advances are expected to be provided for the upgrading of the region's manufacturing industries.

These policies targeted key sectors of modern equipment manufacturing, automobile, ship building, electronic information and new materials. Guangzhou and Shenzhen are expected to emerge as two leading national high-tech industry development areas in China. As outlined by the Plan, the local governments will bolster the construction of the Guangzhou Science City (northern region), Guangzhou International Biological Island and Shenzhen High-tech Industrial Area to speed up economic restructuring and industrial upgrading in the PRD region.

For the YRD region, government policies are specifically directed towards the developing of advanced manufacturing industries such as electronic information, equipment manufacturing, automobile and new energy industries in Shanghai,[14] and electronic information, equipment manufacturing, energy-conservation equipment, medicines and telecommunication industries in Jiangsu.[15] The traditional industries such as textile and garment industries in Zhejiang will also be reformed and updated. The provincial government has given priorities to the development of high-technology and modern equipment manufacturing.[16] These sectors need to improve on their product quality and strengthen their overall competitiveness.

---

[14] "Shanghai plans to give development priority to the 20 key industries", *STNN News*, http://www.stnn.cc/chinafin/200807/t20080703_806584.html, 4 Jun. 2009.

[15] "Jiangsu chooses 100 key industrial projects to push forward industrial upgrading", http://www.gsiic.com.cn/Article/200905/20090518091623_85232.html, 3 Jun. 2009.

[16] "Changing danger into an opportunity: the economic restructuring in Zhejiang", *Xinhua News Agency*, http://www.zj.xinhua.org/special/2009–05/05/content_16434932.htm, 4 Jun. 2009.

The PRD and YRD regions are promoting the development of high value-added industries, as the crisis has effectively exposed the vulnerability of labour-intensive and low value-added manufacturing activities. Both regions hope to steadily become advanced manufacturing bases. Meanwhile, low value-added economic activities will be gradually transferred to inland regions.

Differences in Anti-crisis Policies

While the agendas for both regions bear certain similarities, some differences in anti-crisis policies are also evident. The PRD region assigns top priority to salvaging losses caused by the economic crisis and implementing industrial upgrading. The Party Secretary of Guangdong, Wang Yang, has expounded the idea of "double restructuring of industries and labour force" (known also as the so-called "emptying the cage and changing the bird" policy), which lays out the need to upgrade the value-added and technological level of PRD's industries while transferring the low value-added and labour-intensive industrial sectors outside the PRD region. The idea was later endorsed by President Hu Jintao during the People's Congress yearly session in early March 2009.[17]

The Guangdong government has identified the changing industrial structure as the leitmotif of crisis management. The ability to move up the production value chain and to ride on the wave of the next phase of economic development in China has been singled out for this purpose.

The YRD region, on the other hand, focusses more on regional integration and coordination.[18] This is quite understandable since the

---

[17] "Hu Jintao discusses national matters with members of the NPC and CPPCC Sections", http://hebnews.cn/zt/2009qglh/09lhjjlh/2009/0313/bdb70d961-ff40dff011ffce2edd22719.html, 19 Apr. 2009.

[18] "Strengthening regional economic coordination and cooperation within the Yangtze River Delta", The Chinese Academy of Social Science, http://myy.cass.cn/file/2004020915981.html, 5 Jun. 2009.

PRD region is under the single administration of a province, while the YRD region falls under the administration of two provinces and one centrally administrated municipality. In March 2009, during the Ninth Economic Coordination Meeting within the YRD, it was agreed among local leaders that the YRD region needs concerted efforts to improve its economic competitiveness and resistance to the crisis. Since the lack of coordination and integration directly limits the much needed development of the regional market, the panel of local leaders has expressed the same urgency for measures to improve internal links, accelerate cooperation in fields such as environmental protection and increase healthcare and financial integration.[19]

DIFFERENT CHALLENGES AHEAD FOR THE TWO DELTAS

Regional Cooperation within the YRD Region

Although both the PRD and YRD regions need to work on industrial upgrading and regional cooperation, the governments in both regions are facing different long-term challenges in coping with the global economic slowdown and sustaining regional competitiveness. For the YRD, without the support of other neighbouring regions, its development goal of becoming a globally competitive region is doomed to fail.

Cooperation within this region (Shanghai, Zhejiang and Jiangsu) would provide a big domestic market for goods produced in the YRD region. It could also attract more skilled labour from the periphery to support the development of advanced manufacturing sectors in this region. However, fulfillment of the potential of this region through coordinated development of an integrated domestic market is a challenging task for the local government.

---

[19] "Stimulating economic growth and ensuring people's living standard: regional cooperation within the YRD region enters a new era", *Xinhua News Agency*, the http://news.xinhuanet.com/newscenter/2009-03/30/content_11098866.htm, 2 Jun. 2009.

Zhang and Wu's study[20] offers detailed research on the regional conflict and competition within the YRD during the reform period since 1978. This research demonstrates that there was intense competition among Shanghai, Jiangsu and Zhejiang in areas such as foreign investment and construction of infrastructure due to administrative divisions and diverging economic interests. It is evident in the construction of Shanghai's Yangshan Deep Port and the transfer of Hongqiao International Airport. Moreover, within the YRD region, various local governments have implemented different development policies to achieve local economic growth and established administrative barriers which hamper inter-regional cooperation.

The YRD region suffers from its innate lack of regional integration and coordination since it comes under three different administrations. The lack of coordination and integration may result in duplicated development and "cut-throat" style competition in areas such as modern equipment manufacturing.

In the YRD region, the local governments may need to adopt certain key measures to promote regional coordination and economic cooperation, such as a mechanism for coordination and regular meetings to link Shanghai, Jiangsu and Zhejiang in discussions on industrial cooperation, regional transportation construction, writing common development plans and environmental protection.

Since the nine municipalities within the PRD region are located within Guangdong, the provincial government is able to effectively push forward regional cooperation on industrial modernisation unlike leaders of the YRD region. The PRD's collective anti-crisis response of the "double transformation" strategy to speed up local industrial upgrading is thus bearing fruit.

---

[20] Zhang Jingxiang and Wu Fulong, "China's Changing Economic Governance: Administrative Annexation and the Reorganization of Local Governments in the Yangtze River Delta", *Regional Studies 40*, no. 1 (2006): 3–21. For more details on regional conflict and competition within the YRD region, please also refer to Zhang Tingwei, "From Intercity Competition to Collaborative Planning: The Case of the Yangtze River Delta Region of China", *Urban Affairs Review 42*, no. 1 (2006), pp. 26–56.

Industrial Upgrading in the PRD Region

The goal of industrial restructuring in the PRD region set by the local government is indeed ambitious and very difficult to achieve. Moreover, the existing structure may create serious obstacles for the transformation. The shortage of both skilled human capital and government research and development (R&D) expenditure in the PRD region is another main roadblock for the development of advanced manufacturing and other high-technology industries. In the training of skilled personnel, the PRD region has been lagging behind that of the YRD region over the last decade. The share of professional personnel in total labour force was 6.7% in the PRD region compared to 9.3% in the YRD region in 2007 (Figure 7).

The YRD region has shown stronger capability for industrial modernisation and economic restructuring than the PRD region.

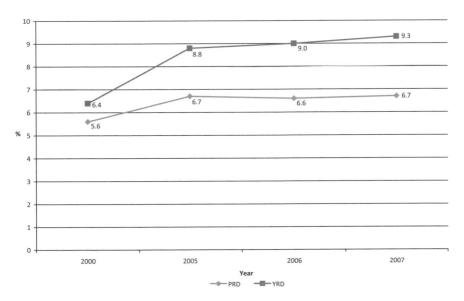

Note: Compilation based on the data of professional personnel and total labour force in the various regions.

Fig. 7. Share of professional personnel in total numbers of labour force in the Pearl River and Yangtze River Deltas.

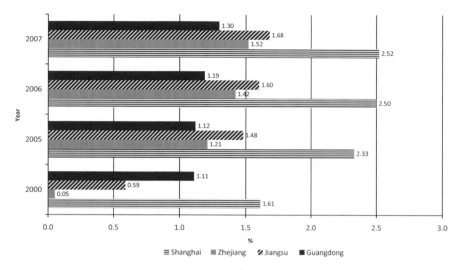

Sources:

1. Guangdong Statistical Yearbook, 2002–2008.
2. Jiangsu Statistical Yearbook, 2002–2008.
3. Zhejiang Statistical Yearbook, 2002–2008.
4. Shanghai Statistical Yearbook, 2002–2008.

Fig. 8.   Ratio of R&D expenditure to GRP in the Pearl River and Yangtze River Deltas.

More was spent on R&D, which is essential for industrial upgrading and the development of an innovation-based economy. In 2007, government expenditure on R&D in Guangdong amounted to 1.3% of its GRP, considerably lower than those for Shanghai (2.5%), Jiangsu (1.7%), and Zhejiang (1.5%) in the YRD region (Figure 8). Such gaps in government's R&D spending will inevitably affect the development of high-tech industries in the PRD region, and further widen the development gap in high-end technological industries between the two deltas.

It is unclear if the local government in the PRD region is making efforts to develop human capital and increase R&D expenditure. There is also a lack of specific measures for upgrading the industrial structure and developing high-tech enterprises in this region. Certain key measures such as tax incentives, capital subsidies and manpower training should be adopted to promote industrial upgrading.

In the PRD region, state support of industrial upgrading and R&D activities are not sufficient without the necessary tax incentive schemes. Tax incentives have become accepted worldwide as the tool for industrial upgrading and an effective means to encouraging investment in advanced manufacturing, high-technology industries and R&D activities.

To make the transition from low-end processing to high-end sectors, industrial firms in the PRD region will need to acquire advanced technology, which requires sufficient capital investment particularly in the early stages. State-oriented capital subsidies are thus crucial for these firms to meet the capital investment requirement for importing technology.

The local governments in the PRD region may also need to set up publicly funded manpower training and research in training centres and research institutes to ensure a plentiful supply of trained and skilled labour. A user-friendly and effective infrastructure for developing human resources is thus necessary.

The Singapore model of industrial upgrading in the 1970s and 1980s can provide very useful lessons for the PRD region. For example, this region can learn from Singapore in the fields of tax incentives (e.g. the investment tax credit scheme introduced in 1979),[21] state capital subsidies and creation of training schemes to support workers in upgrading skills (e.g. Singapore Workforce Skills Qualifications). Pro-industrial upgrading measures such as these are certainly worthy of consideration.

In conclusion, the global economic crisis has hit China the hardest in its export-oriented eastern regions of the PRD and YRD.

---

[21] To read more about the industrial upgrading model of Singapore during the 1970s and 1980s, please refer to the following: (1) Yue, Chia Siow, "The Character and Progress of Industrialization", in *Management of Success: The Moulding of Modern Singapore*, eds. Sandhu, Kernial Singh and Paul Wheatley (Singapore: Institute of Southeast Asian Studies, 1989), pp. 250–279. (2) Khondker, Habibul Haque, "Science and Technology Policies for Development: The Case of Singapore", in *Handbook of Development Policy Studies*, eds. Mudacumura, Gedeon, M. and M Sharnsul. Haque (Florence: CRC Press, 2004), pp. 331–344.

Due to their overdependence on trade and foreign capital inflow, both regions are suffering greatly from the sharp fall in foreign trade, leading to a drastic slowdown in economic growth.

Many common elements exist in the two regions' anti-crisis agendas, in areas such as boosting domestic investment. However, the two regions have different priorities for their anti-crisis policies. The PRD region has established itself as a low-end, labour-intensive manufacturing base; thus, the provincial government of Guangdong has assigned top priority to upgrading the industrial structure in this region. However, the YRD region is likely to suffer from its innate lack of regional coordination and its focus is thus on regional cooperation. In order to help these two regions to cope with different long-term challenges faced by them, the local governments in the PRD and YRD regions may need to adopt various key measures to push forward industrial upgrading and to promote regional cooperation respectively.

APPENDIX 1

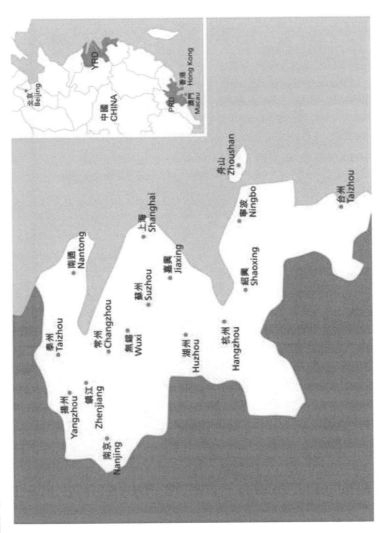

Source: http://www.reedexpo.com.cn/en/Upload/WebEditor/2007_02/25141203522.jpg, 15 May 2009.

Location and jurisdictions of the Yangtze River Delta.

APPENDIX 2

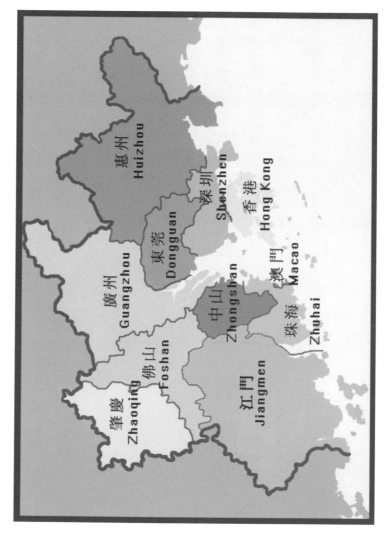

Source: http://www.cityu.edu.hk/lib/collect/prdyrd/about_us/prdmap.jpg

Location and jurisdictions of the Pearl River Delta.

Chapter 6

Taiwan's Economy in the Financial Crisis and Its Outlook

ZHAO Hong

As the US-led financial crisis spread globally, Taiwan found itself in depression as well. To quickly revive the economy and improve on its long-term prospects, the Ma Ying-jeou administration has introduced a series of policies and measures to stabilise its economy. Ma's policies mainly cover two aspects: implement stimulus programmes and enhance economic ties with mainland China. Whether Taiwan's economy can recover soon and emerge stronger in the coming years largely depends on the Ma administration's domestic expansion policies and the revivification of the world economy in the short run; in the long run, the question is whether it can adjust its domestic industrial structures properly and transfer its economy that is heavily dependent on Western markets to one which is dynamic, integrated and driven by domestic and regional demands.

As the US-led financial crisis spread globally, Taiwan found itself in depression as well. In December 2008, the Central Bank of Taiwan

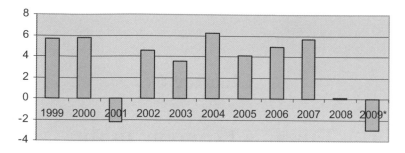

Source: Directorate-General of Budget, Accounting and Statistics, Executive Yuan, Taiwan; figures for 2009 are forecast.

Fig. 1.   Taiwan's GDP growth.

acknowledged that the economy had slipped into a recession. As shown in Figure 1, Taiwan's economic growth moderated significantly to just 0.12% in 2008, down from 5.9% in 2007. The Cabinet-level Directorate General of Budget, Accounting and Statistics (DGBAS) forecasted in early 2009 that Taiwan's gross domestic product (GDP) would shrink by 2.97% in 2009.

The pessimistic view was based on the sharp deterioration since the third quarter of 2008. As depicted in Figure 2, the last quarter of 2008 dipping deeply into negative growth of 8.36% has been Taiwan's worst performance since 2001's contraction of 2.2% when the global information technology bubble deflated.[1] The recent negative growth indicated a downward spiral and even tougher times ahead.

Indeed, Taiwan's economy held firm in the first half of 2008, but took an abrupt turn after September when the global financial crisis intensified with the collapse of the Lehman Brothers. Industrial production has since slowed, plunging by 32% in December 2008 (year-on-year). Manufacturers cut production of electronic parts and components, which account for nearly 10% of

---

[1] Asian Development Bank Outlook 2009, p. 180, http://www.adb.org/Documents/Book/ADB/2009/default.asp.

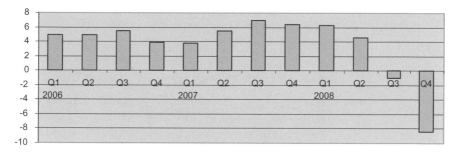

Source: Monthly Bulletin of Statistics, Taiwan.

Fig. 2. Taiwan's quarterly GDP growth (year-on-year % change).

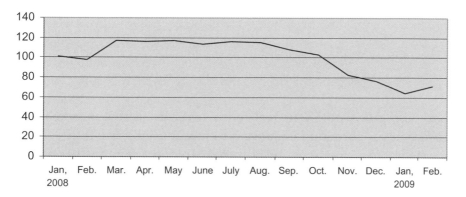

Source: Monthly Bulletin of Statistics, Taiwan.

Fig. 3. Indexes of manufacturing production (index 2006 = 100).

GDP, as global demand for these items shrivelled. Indexes of manufacturing production declined by 38% from January 2008 to January 2009 (Figure 3).

The labour market also saw rapid deterioration and rising unemployment. Unemployment rose to a six-year high of 5% in December 2008, hitting a record of 549,000; the upward trend continued in January to reach 5.3%, a figure which was higher than those of most East Asian economies but lower than those in some industrial countries such as the US, Germany and Canada (Figure 4). "Average wages

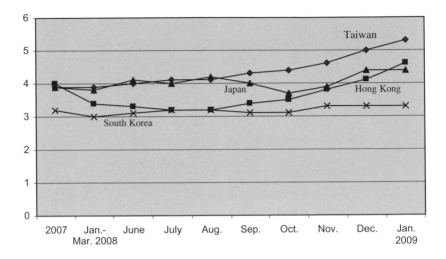

Source: Directorate-General of Budget, Executive Yuan, Taiwan.

Fig. 4.   Unemployment rates of selected economies.

have also fallen by 5% in real terms over the past year, and many companies are ordering employees to take unpaid leave".[2]

Taiwan's economy in 2009 is likely to deteriorate further before getting better and is projected to shrink by 2.97% with turbulent financial markets and a synchronised global economic downturn. Exports will be reined in by waning global demand while domestic demand looks unlikely to pick up soon. Unemployment rate will continue to rise as hiring demand remains low.

MAIN ATTRIBUTES OF THE ECONOMIC RECESSION

Among the drags on Taiwan's GDP are exports and domestic private demands (investment and consumption) which accounted for 74% and 62% of the expenditure on GDP respectively in 2008 (Table 1).

---

[2] "Taiwan's economy: mirror, mirror on the wall", *The Economist*, 12 Feb. 2009, http://www.economist.com/world/asia/PacificFriendly.cfm?story_id=13109874.

Table 1. Structure of expenditure on GDP (%).

Year	Private consumption expenditure	Government consumption expenditure	Gross fixed capital formation	Increase in stocks	Exports of goods and services	Imports of goods and services
2001	62.2	14.2	19.4	−1.0	50.3	45.1
2002	61.1	13.9	18.6	−0.6	52.9	45.8
2003	60.4	13.9	18.6	−0.2	57.0	49.7
2004	60.7	13.2	21.9	0.8	63.1	59.7
2005	61.3	13.1	21.3	0.1	64.2	60.0
2006	60.2	12.6	21.2	0.3	69.7	64.0
2007	58.9	12.1	21.1	0.4	73.5	66.0
2008	61.6	12.6	20.6	0.6	74.4	69.8

Source: Directorate-General of Budget, Accounting and Statistics, "Monthly Bulletin of Statistics", May 2009.

External demand for Taiwan's export worsened over the course of 2008 with the deepening of the global economic downturn. Domestic demand also lost much of its momentum with weaker consumer and investor confidence.

With developed economies sliding into recession and the result-ant weaker demand for products, Taiwan's export of goods and services slackened during 2008. Total export of good in 2008 grew by 3.6 in real terms, a notable drop from the 10.1% increase in 2007 (Figure 5). Negative growth kicked in from October 2008, and regis-tered a year-on-year decrease of 36.6% in the first three months of 2009. DGBAS chief forecasted that Taiwan's export would plunge by 20.1% and imports would plummet by 26.2% in 2009 with a foreign trade surplus of US$26.3 billion.[3]

Taiwan's economy is heavily dependent on the export of goods and services. This reflects the expansion of manufacturing production chains with neighbouring economies, particularly mainland China,

---

[3] "Taiwan GDP to contract 2.97%", *The China Post*, 19 Feb. 2009, http://www.chinapost.com.tw/taiwan/t-business/2009/02/19/196692/Taiwan's-GDP.htm.

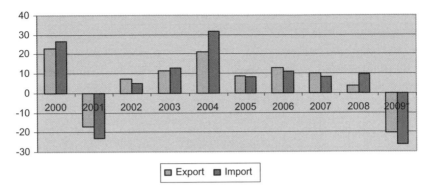

Source: Monthly Bulletin of Statistics, Taiwan; figures for 2009 are forecast.

Fig. 5.   Export and import growth rate.

where scores of electronics factories assemble Taiwan-made components for onward export to the US and other foreign markets. Due to
the global crisis, growth in exports to mainland China in 2008 slowed
to 7.2% from 20.5% in 2007, while exports to the US fell in absolute
terms by 4%.[4]

It seems that the situation has not been improving. According to
the Ministry of Economic Affairs, export orders sank to US$17.7 bil-
lion in January, a drop of 41.7% from the same month of last year, with
orders from mainland China (including Hong Kong) down by 54.7%,
US 36.6%, Japan 35.1%, and Europe 30.7%.[5] As a result, export to
mainland China (including Hong Kong) in the first two months fell
44.3% from a year earlier, while export to US fell 25.7%. Sales to mainland China (over one-quarter of the total), which consist largely of
electronic components, have been hit by massive Chinese destocking.
The island's electronics industry is enduring its worst-ever slump;
Taiwan Semiconductor Manufacturing Company, the world's biggest
contract chipmaker, is running at around 35% of capacity.[6]

---

[4] Monthly Bulletin of Statistics, Taiwan, March 2009.
[5] Directorate-General of Budget, Accounting and Statistics, Executive Yuan, Taiwan,
http://www.moea.gov.tw/~ecobook/eco/1980eco.pdf.
[6] "Taiwan's economy: mirror, mirror on the wall", *The Economist*, 12 February 2009,
http://www.economist.com/world/asia/PacificFriendly.cfm?story_id=13109874.

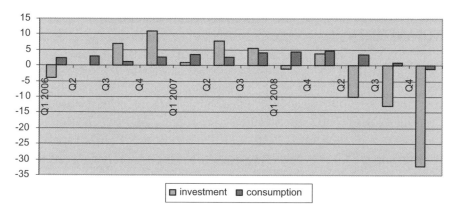

Source: Monthly Bulletin of Statistics, Taiwan.

Fig. 6. Private investment and consumption growth.

Evaporating overseas demand was compounded by poor domestic private consumption which accounts for over 62% of Taiwan's GDP. Figure 6 shows that private consumption did relatively well in the first and second quarters of 2008 before spiralling downwards as a result of gloomy job prospects and the negative wealth effect of a downward correction in local asset markets. Private consumption expenditure grew by only 2% for 2008 as a whole.[7] It posted a contraction of 1.7 in the last quarter of 2008.

Due to the slowdown of overseas and domestic demand, and the cooling down of the local property market, private investment in production and construction activities shrank by 32.2% in the last quarter of 2008 (Figure 6), and plummeted by 41.2% in the first quarter of 2009. Overall private investment registered a decline of 13.5% for the year of 2008, and is predicted to decline by 28.1% in 2009.[8] Fixed capital formation in machinery, equipment and computer software also posed a decline of 10.7%.

---

[7] Monthly Bulletin of Statistics, Taiwan, March 2009.
[8] Directorate-General of Budget, Accounting and Statistics, Executive Yuan, Taiwan, http://www.moea.gov.tw/~ecobook/eco/1980eco.pdf.

GOVERNMENT'S COUNTER-RECESSION MEASURES

Although the global recession only began to put a squeeze on Taiwan's economy early last fall, the debate over the best way to revive the island's economy could be traced back to the campaigning months of the 2008 presidential election in March. At that time, Democratic Progressive Party (DPP) candidate Frank Hsieh and Kuomintang (KMT) Ma Ying-jeou proposed competing stimulus strategies to revive the flailing economy after years of relatively slow growth under former President Chen Shui-bian.

After assuming office, the Ma administration immediately introduced a series of policies and measures to stabilise the financial market, support enterprises and create jobs. Ma's policies mainly cover two aspects: one is to implement stimulus programmes to increase domestic consumption and demand, and the other is to enhance economic ties with mainland China to enlarge the export market.

Implementing Stimulus Programmes

Since September 2008, loose monetary policies have been implemented to complement the fiscal stimulus programme to prop up the economy. From September to February 2009, the Central Bank lowered policy rate by a total of 238 basis points to 1.25%.[9] For consumers, this is good news as it reduces interest rates on loans for big-ticket items such as housing and automobiles. Broad money supply (M2) grew by a sluggish 2.67 on average in 2008 before picking up from the fourth quarter (Figure 7).

On 18 January 2009, the Taiwan government issued consumer vouchers totalling NT$83 billion (US$2.52 billion). According to the Ministry of the Interior, around 21 million people had collected their vouchers from 14,202 distribution stations across Taiwan proper and offshore islands. As the coupons must be used before 30 September,

---

[9] "The Road to Revitalization", *Taiwan Review*, 3 Jan. 2009, available at http://taiwanreview.nat.gov.tw/fp.asp?xItem=48013&CtNode=119.

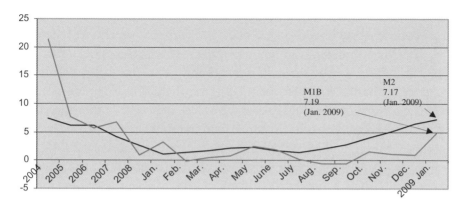

Source: Monthly Bulletin of Statistics, Taiwan.
Note: M1B = cash + cheque deposits + demand deposits; M2 = M1 + time deposits.

Fig. 7. Money supply growth rate.

this represented a potential NT$76.2 billion boost for Taiwan's economy. Investment in public infrastructure of NT$500 billion (US$15.6 billion) has also been planned over the next few years, with about 30% (0.1% of GDP) allocated for this year.[10] The infrastructure construction not only leads to upgrades in rapid transit systems, bridges, sewerage systems and railways, but also jobs to commissioned companies thus stimulating private investment.

On 12 January, the Legislative Yuan passed amendments to Gift and Inheritance Tax Act to boost domestic investment. The amendments reduce gift and inheritance tax rates from as much as 50% to a flat rate of 10% to encourage local investors to retain funds in or return them to Taiwan.[11] In late December 2008, the Ma administration approved the "New Zheng He Plan" (expanding global market programme), which will tap an NT$8.53 billion (US$258.5 million)

---

[10] "Weathering the Financial Storm", *Taiwan Review*, 3 Jan. 2009, http://taiwanreview.nat.gov.tw/fp.asp?xItem=48013&CtNode=119.
[11] "The Road to Revitalization", *Taiwan Review*, 3 Jan. 2009, http://taiwanreview.nat.gov.tw/fp.asp?xItem=48013&CtNode=119.

fund to assist local companies in broadening their exports to emerging economies such as Brazil, Russia and those in the Middle East.[12]

The Ma administration has also implemented three policies to stabilise and enhance the financial services industry. One is "government support for banks". In October 2008, the Executive Yuan announced that the government would guarantee savers' deposits. Under the effect of this measure, deposits in small and medium-sized private banks increased by some NT$171.2 billion by the end of February 2009. The second is "bank support for business". In October 2008, the government established a special task force to finance business operations. Business enterprises in operation may apply for a six-month extension of industrial and commercial loans from commercial banks for loans expiring before the end of 2009. The third is "business support for workers". Launched in January 2009, this project involves integrating local and central government resources and collaborating with private industrial associations to provide proactive care for local small- and medium-sized enterprises. The scope of services offered under the project includes assistance to financial, technological, marketing and labour problems, and help in solving operational difficulties.

To reduce unemployment, in the second half of 2008, the Council of Labour Affairs (CLA) launched a plan to create 117,000 short-term jobs. The programme is scheduled to run until August this year with government spending of NT$9.62 billion (US$292 million) to create job opportunities and train workers. As part of the CLA plan, the Immediate Placement Project will allow any legally established company to receive a subsidy when hiring Taiwanese workers who have been unemployed for more than 90 days. Moreover, starting on 15 December 2008, the CLA began to provide loans of as much as NT$100,000 (US$3,030) to each worker that requests for such assistance.[13]

---

[12] This plan was named after Zheng He, the legendary Ming dynasty (1368–1644) mariner who sailed from China as far as Saudi Arabia and the east coast of Africa, trading with locals and introducing Chinese products in those regions.
[13] "The Road to Revitalization", *Taiwan Review*, 3 Jan. 2009, http://taiwanreview.nat.gov.tw/fp.asp?xItem=48013&CtNode=119.

To assist low-income households hardest hit by the recession, in August 2008, the Ministry of the Interior launched the Instant Care Programme to offer cash subsidies to households whose household income is close to poverty line but are ineligible for government assistance. Under the programme, 290,000 people from 96,000 households in Taiwan are eligible to receive NT$10,000 to NT$30,000 (US$303–US$909) per family per month in emergency cash subsidies. They are encouraged to use these cash transfers to buy energy-saving products such as solar water heating systems and low-emission vehicles. Furthermore, the government has allocated NT$13.5 billion (US$409 million) to provide support to 450,000 individual workers whose income level is close to poverty line.

Improving Cross-Strait Relations

To quickly revive the economy and to improve its long-term prospect, Ma Ying-jeou moved quickly to focus on economic issues, declaring that "Taiwan should get its priority right. Lofty political agenda should give way to the urgent issue of economic rejuvenation, social protection and aging population".[14] Indeed, cross-Strait relationship has taken a dramatic turn since Ma took office in May 2008. In less than a year, Taiwan's Straits Exchange Foundation (SEF) and the mainland's Association for Relations Across the Taiwan Strait (ARATS) have held three rounds of talk on 13 June, 14 November 2008 and 26 April 2009 respectively.

In early 2008, the Ma administration proposed signing an Economic Cooperation Framework Agreement (ECFA) with the mainland. According to Ma's proposal, the ECFA will allow free flow of merchandise, services and capital between Taiwan and the mainland. Issues to be addressed include tariffs, nontariff measures, investment protection, intellectual property rights and a mechanism for dispute mediation. Under such a framework, the two sides

---

[14] Yun-han Chu. "Rapprochement in the Taiwan Strait: The Opportunities and Challenges for Taipei and Beijing", presented at the East Asian Institute, National University of Singapore, 7 May 2009.

will also coordinate industrial policies: making joint efforts to incubate world-class industrial giants and brand names; establishing joint ventures in solar energy, automobile, Chinese medicine, aerospace, next-generation telecommunication and materials; jointly developing industrial and technical standards; and forming strategic alliance between state-owned corporations in energy, steel and telecommunication.

Alongside the talks and ECFA proposal are concrete steps to normalise and to improve economic relations. By late 2008, the "three links" have been largely achieved with the signing of four agreements, including those on air transport, direct sea transport, postal cooperation and food safety. Moreover, restrictions on two-way investment are expected to be gradually lifted, after the two sides reached a consensus on 26 April 2009 to jointly promote mainland Chinese investment in Taiwan.

In the recent talk between Taiwan's SEF and the mainland's ARATS, there was also effort to establish institutionalised cooperation platforms, such as the signing of the "Agreement on Joint Cross-Strait Crime-fighting and Mutual Judicial Assistance". In the area of cross-Strait financial cooperation, besides the signing of "Cross-Strait Financial Cooperation Agreement", the two sides also include financial supervision and management mechanism (in the banking, securities and futures sectors) and currency management for follow-up negotiations.

It is expected that economic relations across the Taiwan Strait will continue to improve. The two sides already agreed on issues for negotiation during the fourth talk between SEF and ARATS in 2009, including "cross-Strait fishery labour cooperation", "cross-Strait quarantine and inspection of agricultural products", "cross-Strait cooperation on standard inspection, measurement and certification", and "avoidance of double taxation". The Ma administration believes that such an adjustment of cross-Strait economic and trade policies will not only help Taiwan overcome its current crisis, but also create long-term positive effects on Taiwan's future economic development.

Taiwan's Economy to Benefit from Improving Cross-Strait Relations

The Ma administration's measures to boost economic relations with mainland China have in the first place largely helped businesses cut costs at a time when both Taiwan and the mainland are experiencing the pinch of the global recession. For instance, in the past, without direct shipping, vessels sailing to mainland Chinese ports must detour via Japan's Ishigaki Island before sailing on to their mainland destination, wasting both time and fuel. This has not only reduced the competitiveness of Taiwanese enterprises, but also caused Taiwan's ports to gradually slip down world rankings of international container ports (for instance, Kaohsiung Port's container through-put fell from fourth highest in the world in 2003 to 12th at present), thus badly affecting the important role Taiwan can play in Asian sea transport.

After reaching agreement on direct sea transport on 4 November 2008, vessels no longer need to sail via Ishigaki, thus saving on average 16–27 hours per voyage, and reducing shipping costs by 15–30%. According to the Ministry of Economic Affairs, Taiwan's businesses will thus save at least NT$4.53 billion (US$137 million) each year in transportation costs. The Council of Agriculture under the Executive Yuan has also said that the shorter shipping time will decrease the transportation damage rate for agricultural products from 15% to 5%, thus boosting profits.[15]

A study has also found that a 10,000-ton container ship can save approximately NT$600,000 per voyage, and a regular container line can save from NT$620 million to NT$1.3 billion per year (depending on the port of detour). A bulk carrier operating under a nonscheduled service can save one to two days per voyage, reducing ore and coal shipment costs by roughly 18.7%, and reducing the shipment cost of other trade goods and materials by roughly 33.4%, with

---

[15] "The Road to Revitalization", *Taiwan Review*, 3 Jan. 2009, http://taiwanreview.nat.gov.tw/fp.asp?xItem=48013&CtNode=119.

annual cost savings estimated at up to NT$1 billion.[16] Finding such ways to enhance efficiency and reduce cost are crucial at a time when some businesses in Taiwan are fighting for survival and laying off employees, which could exacerbate an already gloomy macroeconomic outlook and increase social instability.

The Ma administration believes that Taiwan's economy will benefit from improving cross-Strait relations or the signing of a regional trade arrangement (ECFA) with the mainland. The mainland is not only an important manufacturing platform and the biggest export market for Taiwan, but also an important source of tourists, investment and consumer demand. The huge domestic market of the mainland is expected to be the most important driving force for the recovery and development of neighbouring economies including Taiwan. As shown in Table 2, cross-Strait trade amounted to over US$100 billion in 2008, where Taiwan enjoyed a trade surplus of US$43 billion. With the signing of an ECFA which leads to zero tariff, Taiwan's more developed service industries and agriculture could gain better access to the mainland's markets.

There has also been a large amount of Taiwanese capital investment in the mainland. According to Taiwan's Investment Commission, the accumulated amount of indirect investment by Taiwanese businesses to the mainland between 1988 and January 2009 reached US$75.9 billion. Unofficial estimates of Taiwanese investment in mainland China, on the other hand, range from US$200 billion to US$400 billion. Currently, there is no direct investment in the other direction, since Taiwan does not allow investments from the mainland.

During the recent round of cross-Strait talks in Nanjing in April 2009, the two sides worked to reduce such disparity and reached a consensus on jointly promoting mainland investment in Taiwan based on the principles of "complementary strengths, mutual benefit and a win–win situation". The Ministry of Economic Affairs announced

---

[16] "The Results of the Second Chiang-Chen Talks", Mainland Affairs Council, Taiwan, November 2008.

Table 2. Taiwan's trade with mainland China.

Year	Total trade			Export from Taiwan to the mainland			Import from the mainland to Taiwan			Surplus
	Amount (US$ bil)	Change (%)	% in total	Amount (US$ bil)	Change (%)	% in total	Amount (US$ bil)	Change (%)	% in total	Amount (US$ bil)
2001	31.5	−6.7	13.4	25.6	−6.7	20.3	5.9	−5.2	5.5	19.7
2002	39.5	25.3	15.9	31.5	23.1	23.3	7.9	35.0	7.0	23.6
2003	49.3	24.8	17.7	38.3	21.5	25.4	11.0	38.3	8.6	27.3
2004	65.7	33.3	18.7	48.9	27.8	26.8	16.8	52.4	10.0	32.1
2005	76.4	16.2	20.0	56.2	15.0	28.4	20.1	19.7	11.0	36.2
2006	88.1	15.4	20.7	63.3	12.5	28.3	24.8	23.3	12.2	38.6
2007	102.3	16.1	21.9	74.3	17.3	30.1	28.0	13.1	12.8	46.3
2008	105.4	3.1	21.2	74.0	−0.4	28.9	31.4	12.1	13.0	42.6

Source: Board of Foreign Trade, Ministry of Economic Affair, Taiwan, http://www.cweb.trade.gov.tw.

on 12 May that Taiwan will open to Chinese investments in Taiwan's 99 industries and business lines in the manufacturing and service sectors as well as the infrastructure sector.[17]

There is little doubt that Taiwan stands to benefit significantly from mainland investments. The island enjoys comparative advantages over the mainland in areas such as research and development, consumer-oriented brand development and management. Such "high-margin contributions depend on Taiwan's strong intellectual property rights protection and regulatory regimes, not just low labour costs. They are likely to stay in Taiwan long after Chinese investment is permitted".[18] In fact, investment from the mainland will help buffer Taiwan's economy from falling demand for its products in the West and bring the island closer to China's emerging domestic market demand.

Taiwan will also benefit from the rapidly increasing number of tourists from the mainland. According to the Taiwan Immigration Agency, the number of mainland tourists to Taiwan hit 288,599 by the end of 2008 and reached 30,518 in January 2009, an increase of 130% over January 2008. Unofficial sources estimate that daily arrivals of mainland tourists have gone up from less than 300 to around 5,000.[19] This has markedly invigorated Taiwan's domestic tourism-related industries, such as restaurants, hotels and catering, retail and real estate. It is estimated that more than 5.5 billion RMB of tourism income can be generated annually.

Moreover, improving cross-Strait relations will help reduce risks of cross-Strait hostility, which in turn increases Taiwan's economic outlook. In the last decade, despite Taiwan's close proximity to the world's largest emerging economy, as well as a robust regulatory and legal environment, international investors have not viewed the island as an attractive investment destination due to the potential risk of cross-Strait conflict. With improved economic relations with the

---

[17] "Taiwan ready for Chinese investment", *The China Post*, 13 May 2009.

[18] Daniel H. "Investing in Cross-Strait Relations", *Wall Street Journal Asia*, 4 May 2009.

[19] Yun-han Chu. "Rapprochement in the Taiwan Strait: The Opportunities and Challenges for Taipei and Beijing", presented at East Asian Institute, National University of Singapore, 7 May 2009.

mainland, Taiwan could look forward to enhancing the island's competitiveness in attracting more FDI from multinationals and to take part in the emerging East Asia economic community.

CAN TAIWAN'S ECONOMY RECOVER SOON?

Taiwan's exports continued to decline 36.6% (year-on-year) for the first quarter of 2009, reducing hopes of any early recovery for the export-oriented island economy. Major industrial economies have slipped into recession, with the International Monetary Fund (IMF) projecting GDP in advanced countries to fall 0.3% in 2009. G3 economies (the US, eurozone, and Japan) have contracted in recent quarters with domestic demand cooling fast. While the measures authorities have taken so far around the globe should help reduce the severity and duration of the crisis, the damage to the global economy and credit conditions is significant. In its latest economic outlook on Asia, the IMF forecasts that the region excluding China and India would grow by only 1.6% in 2010, largely because it expects the American economy to be flat.[20] The inability of the US to achieve wide-scale modifications in the growing number of distressed and negative equity mortgages has well delayed its economic recovery. The sluggish world economy is expected to increase Taiwan's downside risks in 2009 and reduce its economic growth momentum. The slump in global demand for machinery and electronics products (about half of all merchandise exports), and the knock-on effects to consumption and investment, will hinder Taiwan's economy to recover.

Domestically, the DGBAS estimated that the private investment in Taiwan would shrink by 28.1% in 2009, the annual consumer price index (CPI) would decline by 0.82% and per capita GNP would shrink to US$15,957.[21] Private investment strongly correlates with

---

[20] "Crouching tigers, stirring dragons", *The Economist*, 14 May 2009, http://www.economist.com/world/asia/PacificFriendly.cfm?story_id=13649520.
[21] "Taiwan GDP to contract 2.97%", *The China Post*, 19 Feb. 2009, available at http://www.chinapost.com.tw/taiwan/t-business/2009/02/19/196692/Taiwan's-GDP.htm.

the performance of merchandise exports, so it is unlikely to pick up significantly until manufactured exports rise. In short, Taiwan's economic recovery is hindered by weak international demand which has caused soft domestic investment intentions. Hence, for Taiwan's economy to recover or even emerge stronger, the government needs to implement stimulus packages efficiently in the short term as well as readjust its industrial structures properly and change its export-driven development model in the long term.

Table 3 shows that among these four NIEs (newly industrialised economies), namely, Taiwan, South Korea, Singapore and Hong Kong, Taiwan's fixed capital formation growth rate and its percentage in GDP are the lowest. Figures also show that from 1999 to 2008, the percentage of private investments in GDP was 14.9%, accounting for over 65% of the total fixed capital formation, while the percentage of government and public investments in GDP was 6%, accounting for less than 35% of the total capital formation.[22] This implies that there

Table 3.   Capital formation of Asian NIEs (%).

Year	Taiwan		South Korea		Singapore		Hong Kong	
	Growth	Percent	Growth	Percent	Growth	Percent	Growth	Percent
1999	2.9	23.1	8.3	29.7	−8.4	34.2	−16.7	25.7
2000	9	23.9	12.2	31.1	2.3	30.6	7.9	26.4
2001	−19.9	19.4	−0.2	29.5	−5.9	30	2.6	25.6
2002	1.1	18.6	6.6	29.1	−12.3	25.5	−4.7	22.4
2003	1.7	18.6	4	29.9	−3.6	24.1	0.9	21.2
2004	19.5	21.9	2.1	29.5	9.5	23.2	2.5	21.3
2005	1.2	21.3	2.4	29.3	−0.1	21.3	4.1	20.9
2006	0.9	21.2	3.6	29	13.3	22.1	7.1	21.9
2007	1.9	21.1	4	28.8	19.2	24	3.4	20.1
2008	−10.8	20.6	−1.9	—	13.7	28.5	−0.3	19.5
1999–2008	0.7	21	4.1	29.5	2.8	26.3	0.7	22.5

Source: Ministry of Economic Affairs, Taiwan, http://www.moea.gov.tw/~ecobook/eco19802-eco.pdf.

---

[22] Ministry of Economic Affairs, Taiwan, http://www.moea.gov.tw/~ecobook/eco19802eco.pdf.

is much room for the government to invest further in infrastructure and the public sector for several years. However, it is also necessary to encourage more consumption to fill the gap after the infrastructure projects are completed.

Private investments are mainly on electronics industries and remained low in the past years. This fact implies that Taiwan's economy was no longer mainly driven by capital-intensive sectors. It has been developing noncapital-intensive sectors, such as knowledge-based or brain renovation-based industries. It also indicates that private investment intentions are turning weak and reluctant because of poor demand in manufactured exports abroad. Taiwan needs to find new investment opportunities and alternatives to induce and stimulate its industrial structural development.

Taiwan has a population of 2.3 million and its domestic market has much potential. The government might enlarge domestic demand by further developing its service sectors and improving its public facilities and its education and health care quality. In fact, Taiwan's public construction compared to the level of per capita income level shows that there is a great deal of room for improvement; the bridges that collapsed in the rain, pot-holes in the roads and untreated sewage highlight the inadequate public constructions rated by international public construction standards. Government investments in these areas can compensate for and stimulate sluggish private investments, and make these infrastructures beneficial to Taiwan's economic development in the long run.

Regional markets in Asia also present great opportunities, especially some emerging economies (including some ASEAN countries). The Asian Development Bank predicted that, in spite of the current global financial crisis, India's GDP growth rate will remain at 5% in 2009 and 6.5% in 2010; China's GDP will remain at 7% and 8%; Vietnam's GDP will remain at 4.5% and 6.5%; Cambodia's GDP will remain at 2.5% and 4% while Lao's GDP will be at 5.5% and 5.7%.[23] These dynamic economies will help pick up the demand slack as they have

---

[23] Asian Development Bank Outlook 2009, http://www.adb.org/Documents/Book/ADB/2009/default.asp.

become increasingly important trade partners to Taiwan since 2000. According to statistics from Taiwan's Ministry of Finance, from 2002 to 2008, export shares of China (including Hong Kong) and the ASEAN-6 countries (Indonesia, Malaysia, the Philippines, Singapore, Thailand, and Vietnam) in Taiwan's total exports increased from 10.1% and 9.8% to 39% and 15% respectively, while that of the US and Europe had narrowed from 18.6% and 15.1% to 12% and 11.7% respectively.

Regional economic integration in East Asia is a development trend. Yet for some political reasons, over the last decade, Taiwan is feeling increasingly marginalised and excluded from East Asia's move towards regional integration. The consequent concern is that, being excluded from the expected free trade area in East Asia, Taiwan's businesses will be at a serious disadvantage due to higher import tariffs as well as other trade and business barriers. This is especially true for Taiwan's small- and medium-sized enterprises which account for over 90% of its economic activities. According to a recent report from Taiwan, 110,000 workers may lose their jobs as a result of the ASEAN–China FTA coming into effect in 2010, since Taiwan's exports of petrochemical, electronics, textiles and machine tools to the mainland will be subject to the 6.5% import duty.[24] In contrast, if Taiwan were to join the ASEAN+3 FTA, its GDP will increase by 3.3%–3.4%.

In reality, Taiwan can initiate some specific cooperative projects as a means to participate in the regional integration process. For instance, ASEAN views the food security issue very seriously as its members are struggling to make efficient use of land and natural resources to develop their agriculture. Taiwan is well known for its ability to develop agriculture and is very strong in orchid growing and fish farming. The Taiwan government can utilise this ability to co-develop agriculture with other governments, and strengthen its international competitiveness in agriculture and other related industries. By integrating domestic resources (economic resources, relevant industries, and scientific research and development) and leveraging on

---

[24] "Taiwan should sign CECA with China as soon as possible", *Central News Agency*, 23 Feb. 2009.

Table 4. Trade dependence of major East Asian economies (%).

Year	Taiwan	South Korea	Japan	Singapore	Hong Kong
1999	78.6	65.2	15.6	—	214.9
2000	91.9	59.2	17.2	—	243.6
2001	80.3	65.0	17.0	251.0	233.2
2002	83.5	60.5	17.8	273.5	247.7
2003	91.2	57.5	18.7	317.9	287.0
2004	106.1	61.3	20.6	340.9	319.4
2005	107.0	70.2	22.9	354.7	330.0
2006	116.5	69.0	26.4	364.0	341.9
2007	121.1	71.5	28.5	335.5	343.7
2008	126.6	75.1	29.7	360.5	349.6
1999–2008	111.3	65.5	21.4	324.8	291.1

Note: Trade dependence = total trade value ÷ GDP.
Source: Ministry of Economic Affairs, Taiwan, http://www.moea.gov.tw/~ecobook/eco19802-eco.pdf.

its advantages, Taiwan can speed up its integration with this dynamic region and thus largely reduce its reliance on the dollar economy.

Table 4 shows that in the past decades, Taiwan's economy was mainly export-oriented and its trade dependence in 2008 was 126.6%, higher than that of Japan (29.7%) and South Korea (75.1%), but lower than that of Singapore (360.5%) and Hong Kong (349.6%). Moreover, in Taiwan's total exports, 40% goes to mainland China and is mostly on electronic parts, equipment and raw materials. This part of trade was mainly created by Taiwanese investors in the mainland who bought equipment and spare parts from Taiwan. However, evidence shows that these investment-created trade effects have been diminishing these years due to Taiwan's industrial structural problems which are showing after the financial crisis.

In fact, these years saw domestic- or foreign-invested industries in China transforming rapidly to midstream or downstream operations, thus reducing the Taiwanese mainland investment-created trade effects. This was evidenced by the findings of the Taiwan Institute of Economic Research. For example, in September 2008, China's exports to the US increased by 15.4%, yet Taiwan's exports to mainland decreased by 16.3%; in October, November and December, China's exports to the US increased by 12.4%, down by 6.13% and up by 4.1%, respectively, yet Taiwan's exports to mainland seriously decreased by 19.9%, 38.5% and 54.0%, respectively.[25] These changing figures show that when China's exports to the US decreased, Taiwan's exports to mainland China decreased even further. This phenomenon indicates that Taiwan needs to adjust its own industrial structures and move into higher end-products so as to match the structural development in the mainland and thus maintain its investment-created trade effects.

Recently, the Taiwan government is planning to promote several industries as the island's future or "star" industries. The first one is biotechnology industry. Taiwan recently announced a plan to establish an NT$60 billion (US$1.78 billion) venture capital fund to transform the biotechnology sector into the island's next star industry.[26] This project is expected to span 10 years. Biotech is said to have global demand and is almost "recession-proof" as stock prices of related forms reportedly suffered the smallest Wall Street losses on average. Domestically, by 2026, 20% of the Taiwanese population will be over 65 years old, necessitating more development in the medical and health care industry.

Others include green energy, of which the twin pillars will be solar energy and light-emitting diode industries. The current value of production is about US$4.7 billion. The figure is expected to increase to US$14 billion by 2012 and over US$20 billion by 2015.[27] Taiwan's cultural and creative industry have also been targeted as another future star industry. Through deregulation and enlarging the domestic market, more resources could be dedicated to this industry. By electing to promote these prospective sectors, the government is demonstrating

---

[25] Taiwan Institute of Economic Research, "Taiwan's Industrial Structures After Financial Crisis", http://www.tier.org.tw/comment/tiermon200903.asp.

[26] "The nation's next star industry", *Taiwan Journal*, 4 Mar. 2009, http://taiwan-journal.nat.gov.tw/ct.asp?xItem=49502&CtNode=118.

[27] "An economic power's blueprint for future success", *Taiwan Journal*, 2 Apr. 2009, http://taiwanjournal.nat.gov.tw/ct.asp?xItem=49502&CtNode=118.

its commitment to the process of diversification, which is seen as the key to Taiwan's future economic development.

In sum, in the short run, whether Taiwan's economy can recover in 2009 and emerge stronger in the coming years largely relies on Ma administration's expansion policies and the revivification of the world economy. In the long run, it also depends on whether it can develop its domestic industrial structures fully and transform itself into a dynamic integrated economy driven by domestic and regional demands rather than depending excessively on electronics and information technology exports to the US and the European markets.

Chapter 7

Hong Kong's Economy on the Road to Recovery?

ZHANG Yang

Hong Kong's economic growth moderated significantly to 2.4% in 2008. In the first quarter of 2009, it registered a negative growth of 7.8%, the worst performance since 1998. Underlying this economic downturn are slackening exports, weaker domestic demand and withering investment. The Hong Kong government has responded swiftly to this "once-in-a-century financial turmoil" by putting forward measures to stabilise the financial market, support enterprises and create employment, including a proposed budget deficit of about HK$40 billion. Cushioned by a growing hinterland in mainland China, Hong Kong's economy in 2009 is projected to shrink modestly by 5.5–6.5% according to the updated forecast.

The global economic slowdown has left an indelible mark on economies worldwide. Hong Kong is no exception. Its economic growth moderated significantly to 2.4% in 2008, down from 6.4% in 2007. This deceleration of growth indicated a below-trend

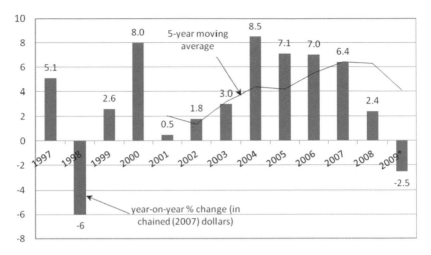

Source: Hong Kong Census and Statistics Department; *: Projected by the government in February; forecast revised to 5.5–6.5% in May.

Fig. 1.   Hong Kong's economic growth.

performance and a derail from the upturn since 2002 (Figure 1). The 2.4% annual GDP growth rate, however, was not representative of the annualised quarterly rate of 1.5% in the third quarter and a contraction of 2.6% in the fourth, mainly due to the outbreak and ramification of the global financial crisis. These numbers show a marked slowdown from the strong 7.3% growth in the first quarter and 4.1% in the second.

In retrospect, Hong Kong's economy was hit hard by the catastrophic ripples of the Asian financial crisis in 1998, the global economic downturn in 2001 and the outbreak of Severe Acute Respiratory Syndrome (SARS) in 2003. As depicted in Figure 2, the last quarter of 2008 dipping deep into the negative growth of 2.6% has been Hong Kong's worst performance since 1999, echoing sharp declines reported recently by China, Taiwan, Japan and Singapore (Figure 3), and indicating a downward spiral and even tougher times ahead.

Indeed Hong Kong's economy still held firm in the first half of 2008, but took an abrupt turn after September when the global financial crisis intensified with the collapse of the Lehman

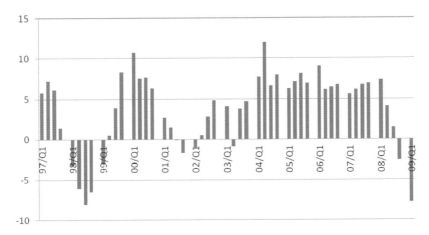

Source: Hong Kong Census and Statistics Department.

Note: 08/Q4 and 09/Q1 figures subject to revision.

Fig. 2. Quarterly GDP growth (year-on-year % change, in chained (2007) dollars).

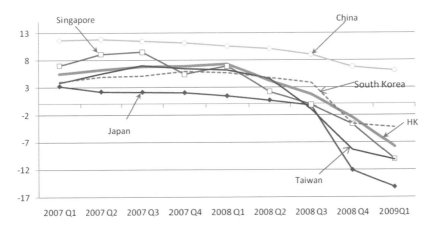

Source: EIU Country Data.

Fig. 3. Economic performance of selected Asian economies.

Brothers. The labour market has since seen rapid deterioration with unemployment rate on the rise. On close examination, unemployment rate climbed up distinctly towards the end of 2008, reversing the declining trend prevalent for more than five years which led to a 10-year low of 3.2% in mid-2008. For the three-month period ending February 2009, unemployment rate registered 5%, compared to 3.3% a year earlier. Meanwhile, inflation pressure receded considerably where Consumer Price Index fell notably from its peak in July 2008 (Figures 4 and 5).

The residential property market had also lost its growth momentum in the previous year and began faltering in the second half

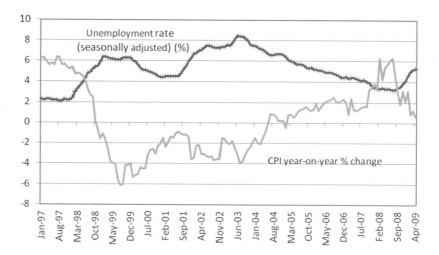

Source: Hong Kong Census and Statistics Department.

Fig. 4. Hong Kong's unemployment and inflation.

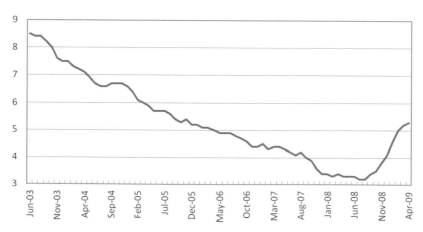

Source: Hong Kong Census and Statistics Department.

Fig. 5. Unemployment rate since 2003 (seasonally adjusted, %).

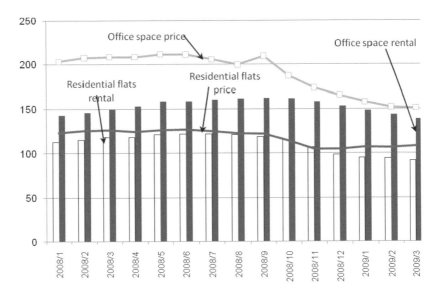

Source: Rating and Valuation Department, http://www.rvd.gov.hk.

Fig. 6. Property prices and rentals index (1999 = 100).

of 2008. By December 2008, flat prices, rentals and the number of transactions in residential properties fell notably by 18%, 19% and 22% respectively, from their peaks in early 2007. Another indicator of the local asset market, Hong Kong's stock market continued its downward adjustment that started in late 2007, but registering a sharper decline after September 2008. The Hang Seng index closed the year at 14,387, plunging 48% from a year before, unseen since 1974, and wiping out more than HK$6 trillion of wealth.[1] Due to doom market sentiments, market capitalisation shrank and fund-raising activities also receded (Figures 6 and 7).

MAIN ATTRIBUTES OF THE ECONOMIC SLOWDOWN

With Hong Kong's economy adversely hit as reflected by key macro-economic indicators, it is worth our while to analyse the underlying

---

[1] "HK Stock Market Capitalization Halved in 2008", *Xinhua net*, 3 Mar. 2009, http://english.cri.cn/6826/2009/03/03/1722s459965.htm.

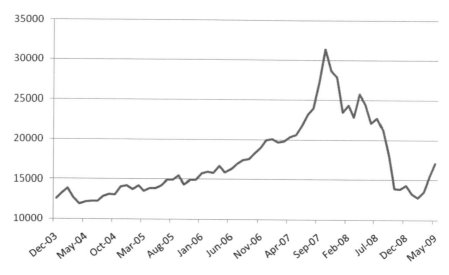

Source: Yahoo Finance.

Fig. 7.   Hang Seng index (close price adjusted for dividents and splits).

attributes to this economic slowdown amid this "once-in-a-century financial turmoil". Owing to a deepening global economic downturn, the external demand for Hong Kong exports worsened over the course of 2008. More importantly, domestic demand lost much of its momentum with weaker consumer and investor sentiments amid tighter credit market. As shown in Figure 8, of the −2.6% GDP contraction in the last quarter of 2008, net export contributed 4%, government spending 0.1% while investment −4.4% and private consumption −2.4%.

Specifically, Hong Kong's exports slackened during 2008 with the advanced economies sliding into recession and the resultant weaker demand for products from emerging economies. Total export of goods in 2008 grew by 2% in real terms, a notable drop from the 7% increase in 2007, and registered a year-on-year decrease of 4.9% in the fourth quarter. Hong Kong's main export markets are the mainland and the US, accounting for 49% and 13%, respectively, in 2008. Exports to the former increased by 4.7% while sales to the latter fell

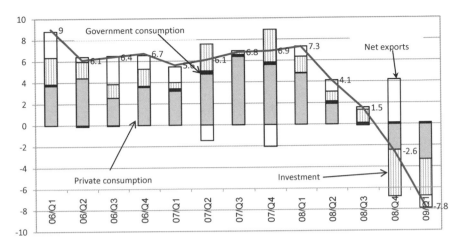

Source: Hong Kong Census and Statistics Department.

Fig. 8. Contributions to quarterly GDP growth (percentage point).

by 2.4%. What is more, total exports dropped by 21.8% year-on-year in January 2009[2] (Figure 9).

Resembling the decelerating trend in trade of tangible goods, exports of services rose by 5.6% over the year 2008, much slower than the 14.1% in 2007. In the last quarter of 2008, exports of services declined by 0.2%. This was particularly significant given the predominance of the service sector in Hong Kong's economy with its contribution to GDP rising from 70% in 1980 to 92.3% in 2007, as shown in Figure 10. Indeed, the service sector accounted for 87% of total employment in the first three quarters of 2008.

Weakness stemming from evaporating demand overseas was compounded by poor domestic demand, the key pillar of growth for the previous few quarters. Domestic demand held up relatively well in the

---

[2] "HK export value shrinks 21.8% in Jan", *Hong Kong Trade Development Council*, 27 Feb. 2009, http://hongkong.hktdc.com/content.aspx?data=hk_content_en& contentid=1073271&src=HK_BuNeTr&w_sid=194&w_pid=644&w_nid=10027& w_cid=1073271&w_idt=1900-01-01&w_oid=343&w_jid=.

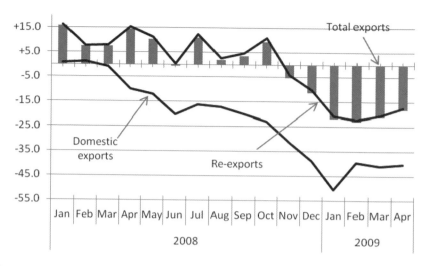

Source: Hong Kong Census and Statistics Department.

Fig. 9.   Exports of goods (year-on-year % change).

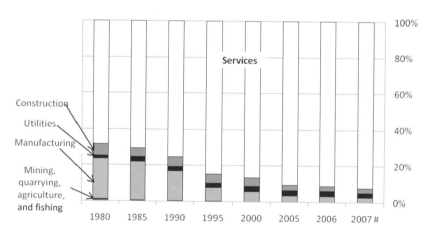

Source: Hong Kong Census and Statistics Department; # Figures subject to revision.

Fig. 10.   Composition of Hong Kong GDP by sectors.

first quarter of 2008 after which the deceleration in private consumption became evident due to gloomy job prospects and negative wealth effect from a downward correction in local asset markets. Private consumption grew by 1.8% in real terms for 2008 as a whole, down from a robust 8.5% rise in 2007. Worse, it posted a contraction of 3.2% in the last quarter of 2008. Partly due to the cooling down of the local property market from the second half of 2008, investment in building and construction activities shrank by 3.6% in the last quarter. Fixed capital formation in machinery, equipment and computer software posted an even bigger decline of 18.7%. Overall investment remained sluggish and registered a marginal decline of 0.3% for the year.

GOVERNMENT'S COUNTER-CYCLICAL MEASURES

In the wake of the worst financial turmoil in decades, the Hong Kong Special Administrative Region (SAR) Government has responded swiftly by putting forward a series of measures since late 2008 to stabilise the financial market, support enterprises and create employment. Indeed the Task Force on Economic Challenges was established in October 2008 to assess the impact of the ongoing crisis on the economy and propose ways and means to address the challenges.

Soon after the outbreak of the financial crisis, two pre-emptive measures were announced in October 2008 by the Financial Secretary. One is to use the Exchange Fund to guarantee repayment of all deposits held with authorised institutions in Hong Kong. The other is the establishment of a Contingent Bank Capital Facility to provide additional capital to locally incorporated banks when necessary. These measures helped to stabilise Hong Kong's financial system and will remain in force until the end of 2010.

Amidst the global credit crunch, small- and medium-sized enterprises (SMEs) inevitably face very tight credit conditions and are crippled by cash flow problems. In response to this, a Special Loan Guarantee Scheme was first introduced in November and then substantially expanded in the Chief Executive's announcement on 8 December 2008. The government's commitment was increased to HK$100 billion with the provision of up to 70% guarantee to participating lending institutions granting loans to Hong Kong companies.

This scheme applied to all firms except listed companies and loans obtained can be used as operating funds, commercial overdrafts or letters of credit.

In the same announcement, the government pledged to provide more than 60,000 employment opportunities in 2009 through expediting projects, recruiting civil servants and creating temporary and other posts. Along with these efforts, the Hong Kong Monetary Authority also rendered liquidity assistance to licensed banks, lowered base interest rates on money borrowed through discount windows and injected Hong Kong dollars into the banking system.

More recently, in the 2009/2010 Budget released by the Financial Secretary John Tsang on 25 February 2009, the government proposed an expenditure of over HK$300 billion for the year and set a budget deficit of about HK$40 billion. Counter-cyclical measures were announced particularly to reduce business costs, secure and preserve jobs and boost consumption. Details are documented in Table 1. In the same Budget, the government pushed forward an array of initiatives to further expand cross-boundary transportation capacity including the construction of the 29 km Hong Kong-Zhuhai-Macau Bridge to commence by 2010 and to be completed in 2016, and the

Table 1.   Key measures announced by the budget.

To reduce business costs	20% rental reduction for government properties and short-term tenancies for three months.
To create jobs	To earmark HK$1.6 billion to create 62,000 jobs over three years: • HK$36,000/HK$24,000 annual internship subsidy to employers who hire university graduates for jobs in the mainland/Hong Kong. • Creating some 14,000 jobs in the next two years by subsidies for building maintenance and cultural events.
To boost consumption	• An one-off rebate of 50% of salary tax paid up to a maximum of HK$6,000. • Exemption of property rates for two quarters for 2009/10, capped at HK$1,500. • Freezing government fees and charges until March 2010.

Source: THE 2009–10 BUDGET, by Hong Kong Financial Secretary.

Guangzhou-Shenzhen-Hong Kong Express Rail Link to start in 2009. These infrastructure projects will boost investment in the short run and foster closer economic integration with the mainland in the long run.

Perceived by many as a conservative fiscal package, the proposed deficit accounts for about 2.4% of Hong Kong's GDP. The concession on property rates and tax rebates have been greatly reduced from 2008 when the economy was growing robustly. Specifically, the bonus of social security allowances for the elderly and disabled and subsidies on electricity bills were no longer offered in 2009. Moreover, tax rebates will only be credited to the following year's bill and therefore have limited immediate impact on consumer sentiments.

On a regional scale, the Budget is considered rather modest by many (Table 2), especially so given Hong Kong's ample fiscal

Table 2. Projected government budget deficit for 2009 in selected Asian economies.

Economies	Local currency	US$	Share of GDP %
Hong Kong	HK$40 billion	5.2 million	2.4
Singapore	S$8.7 billion[3]	6 billion	3.5
China	RMB950 billion[4]	130 billion	3
Taiwan	NT$134.6 billion[5]	4 billion	1.3
South Korea	KRW51,600 billion[6]	34.4 billion	5.4
Malaysia	N/A	N/A	7.6
Japan	YEN13.1 trillion[7]	145.6 billion	2.6

Source: Compiled by the author from different sources.

---

[3] "Budget 2009 Speech", http://www.singaporebudget.gov.sg/resilience.html.
[4] "China's RMB 950 bn deficit budget within safe limits", http://www.chinaknowledge.com/Newswires/News_Detail.aspx?type=1&NewsID=22145.
[5] "Deficit seen rising as Taiwan passes 2009 budget", *Reuters via COMTEX*, 16 Jan. 2009, http://www.zibb.com/article/4725618/Deficit+seen+rising+as+Taiwan+passes+2009+budget.
[6] "Supplementary Budget for Job Creation", http://english.mofe.go.kr/news/pressrelease_view.php?sect=news_press&pmode=&cat=&sn=6363&page=1&SK=ALL&SW=.
[7] "Japan's Budget Hits Record as Aso Seeks for Recovery", (*Bloomberg*), 20 Dec. http://www.bloomberg.com/apps/news?pid=20601087&sid=aJTp3Jx8cyBk&refer=home.

resources with fiscal reserves projected to reach HK$488 billion by 31 March 2009, equivalent to 27.2% of GDP or 18 months of government expenditure. To maintain fiscal prudence, the government reactively fine-tuned revenue and expenditure rather than proactively roll out aggressive stimulus measures and commit to a larger deficit; the budget would probably offer little quick and immediate relief measures to offset the external environment and lift its sagging economy.

OUTLOOK FOR 2009 AND RECENT DEVELOPMENT

In February 2009, the SAR government projected its economy to shrink by 2–3% in 2009, the first annual decline since 1998. This projection is made against the backdrop of turbulent financial markets which have resulted in a synchronised global downturn with advanced economies mostly mired in recession and the emerging economies in a sharp slowdown. Hong Kong's economy is expected to face more pain as job losses mount, exports slump and property prices tumble; economic performance is likely to further deteriorate before getting better. Prospects of a turnaround, however, depend on how the financial crisis plays out globally and when the financial market resumes its function. This in turn hinges on the effectiveness of huge fiscal stimulus measures and aggressive monetary easing policies implemented across the world.

The projection of 2–3% contraction is based on the following factors. First of all, the credit crunch and the global economic downturn have already dampened significantly Hong Kong's external trade. The recent appreciation of US dollar, to which Hong Kong dollar is closely pegged, has weakened to some extent the price competitiveness of Hong Kong's exports. Exports in goods will be reined in further by waning global demand.

Second, the prospects for exports of services are likewise not promising. Inbound tourism growth will be negatively affected by dropping incomes. Exports of financial, business and other services will remain sluggish as financial market sees no solid sign of rebound and commercial activities are dampened greatly by the financial tsunami. Market sentiments are likely to stay fragile in the face of an intensifying financial crisis where huge losses are reported recently by major financial institutions in the US and Europe.

Third, domestic demand may be the sole engine for growth, which too is set to gear down. Local consumer spending is likely to wither further with falling household wealth, rising unemployment and heightened uncertainties. Investment likewise will stall with no clear signs so far of a global economic recovery.

On other aspects of the economy, inflationary pressure will continue to ease, given the retreat of international commodity prices and continuous adjustments in the local property market. The headline Composite CPI will remain depressed amid slackening business conditions. Labour market conditions are about to worsen further, as reflected by the recent cut-back in private sector vacancies. The jobless rate will rise given weaker hiring demand in the financial sector, the main driver of Hong Kong's employment growth. Hence, it is the government's top priority to preserve employment and prevent job loss, which has been deliberately addressed in the Budget.

Indeed, latest available figures indicate that economic recession in Hong Kong has deepened since the beginning of 2009. Following the contraction of 2.6% in the final quarter of 2008, GDP registered an even sharper year-on-year decline of 7.8% in the first quarter of 2009, the worst quarterly performance in a decade.

On the trade front, exports of goods saw a dramatic plunge with total merchandise exports for the first three months of 2009 dropping from a year earlier by 21.8%, 23%, and 21.1%, respectively. Exports of services likewise had deteriorated in the first quarter by 8.2%, compared to a marginal growth of 0.4% in the last quarter of 2008. This drop can be mainly attributed to sluggish financial services activities, dwindling freight transport services and other trade-related services. As evidenced by Figure 9, net exports were the only pillar of moderate economic contraction in the fourth quarter of 2008. When this became negative in the first quarter of 2009, the economy unavoidably registered a much more severe decline.

In domestic demand, private consumption expenditure fell further by 5.5% in real term year-on-year in the first quarter of 2009, following the decline of 4.4% in the previous quarter. In addition, overall investment remained in a depressed state, with gross domestic fixed capital formation down by 12.6% over a year earlier, although slightly better than the 17.8% contraction in the preceding quarter. Private businesses amid bleak global economic outlook have curtailed their investment plans in machinery and equipment investment and building and construction. Public sector construction work has yet to kick off growth as it usually takes time for the projects to be launched.

In fact, of the −7.8% GDP contraction in the first quarter of 2009, net export contributed −1.2%, government spending 0.1%, investment −3.4% and private consumption −3.3%. The decline in both external and domestic demand has caused unemployment rate to rise in the city. Unemployment climbed to 5.3% in the three months ending in April, the highest level in three years.

In response to the deepening of economic recession in the first quarter of 2009, which registered the worst performance in 10 years, the SAR government on 26 May unveiled new fiscal stimulus efforts in a bid to counter the impact of global economic downturn and financial crisis and particularly to promote growth, assist people's livelihoods and preserve jobs. The new package worth HK$16.8 billion (US$2.17 billion) expands upon those measures announced in February's budget and takes the form of temporary tax cuts and subsidies for public services such as electricity bills and housing rent (Table 3). This new relief package combined with previously announced measures would shore up economic growth by 2%, according to Financial Secretary John Tsang.

The fact that GDP tumbled at its fastest rate in a decade in the first quarter of 2009 had prompted the SAR government to revise downwards its economic forecast to a contraction of 5.5%–6.5% in 2009, notably lower than the prediction in February of a 2–3% contraction.

In April 2009, Hong Kong's exports of goods fell by 18.2% from a year earlier, lower than the decline of 21.1% in March. Although this

Table 3. Hong Kong's new relief measures.

	Main items in the new relief package	Amount (HK$)
Tax relief measures	Income tax rebates increased to HK$8,000 from HK$6,000.	2.0 billion
Subsidies	• Suspending two quarters of property rates.	4.2 billion
	• Waivers on public housing rentals for up to two months.	2 billion
	• One extra month of payment for recipients of Comprehensive Social Security Assistance, Disability Allowance and Old Age Allowance.	1.8 billion
Create more jobs	• Waiving fees for registering businesses.	1.7 billion
	• Stepping up efforts to improve hygiene and prevent swine flu.	300 million
	• Extra funding for Operation Building Bright.[8]	1.0 billion
Subsidise further studies	Injecting additional amount to continuing education fund.	1.2 billion
Promote exports	Injection into SME export marketing fund.	1.0 billion
Guarantees for corporate lending	• Extending a credit loan programme for enterprises until the end of this year.	N/A
	• The government's guarantee under the Special Loan Guarantee Scheme, up to 80% from 70%.	

Source: South China Morning Post, 27 May 2009.

could spell a glimmer of hope, Hong Kong's economy in the rest of year is likely to remain slackened. A swift recovery will hinge on the revival of an external environment when the financial crisis begins to abate.

---

[8] "Operation Building Bright" (the Operation) was first announced in the 2009–2010 Budget and is a two-year programme aimed at providing subsidies and one-stop technical assistance for owners of about 1,000 old buildings in their repair works, including old buildings without owners' corporations. The Operation aims to achieve the dual objectives of creating more job opportunities for the construction sector in the near future and improving building safety and the cityscape.

ECONOMIC INTEGRATION WITH MAINLAND CHINA

Unlike its fellow regional financial centre Singapore, which expects its economy to shrink by as much as 9% in 2009, Hong Kong's economy will be somewhat cushioned by the mainland, whose economy will probably register a growth of 7.2% as forecasted by the World Bank,[9] if not 8% as targeted by its government. Indeed, Hong Kong has over time developed close integration with the mainland economy and stands to benefit from this huge and growing hinterland.

Hong Kong's merchandise trade relationship with the mainland has seen steady increase since 1996, mainly on re-exports which are associated with outward processing activities. Overall, the mainland is getting increasingly important as a partner of Hong Kong's trade in goods, both as an export destination and an import supplier, as shown in Figure 11. Trade in service has seen similar trends where Hong Kong's export of service to the mainland has increased considerably over time (Figure 12).

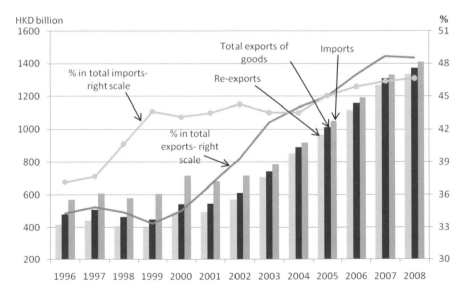

Source: Hong Kong Census and Statistics Department.

Fig. 11.   Hong Kong's merchandise trade with mainland.

---

[9] IMF forecast is 6.7%.

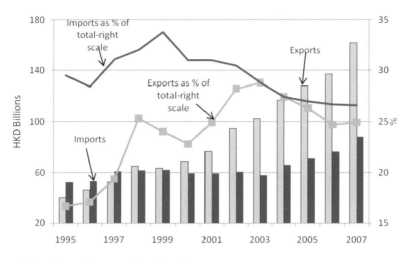

Source: Hong Kong Census and Statistics Department.

Fig. 12. Hong Kong's trade in service with mainland.

To boost Hong Kong's economy, Beijing on 19 December 2008 announced 14 measures from speeding up cross-boundary infrastructure projects to further liberalising *Renminbi* business in Hong Kong (Table 4). Specifically, it includes encouraging and supporting mainland enterprises to use Hong Kong as a financial services platform for offshore capital-raising. In fact, as of December 2008, total market capitalisation of mainland companies listed in Hong Kong accounted for 60% of total, reaching US$790 billion.[10] Beijing's support also included the endorsement of the "Outline of the Plan for the Development of Pearl River Delta (PRD) Region" (hereafter referred to as the "Outline") and another supplement to Closer Economic partnership Arrangement (CEPA[11]). Both plans will foster closer links and cooperation between Hong Kong and the mainland economy.

---

[10] "Annual Economic report: Hong Kong 2008 — 20 Mar. 2009", http://www.sinoptic.ch/hongkong/pdf/eco/2009/2009_rapport.pdf.

[11] CEPA between mainland and Hong Kong was first signed in 2003 and came into effect from January 2004. It covers three broad areas, i.e. trade in goods, trade in services, and trade and investment facilitation. In subsequent years, CEPA receives annual supplements (Supplements II–V) which expanded progressively the scope of market access and liberalisation.

Table 4.   Central government's measures to boost Hong Kong's economy.

1	Allow qualified enterprises to settle trade in *Renminbi* in Hong Kong.
2	Set up a currency swap arrangement between the People's Bank of China and the Hong Kong Monetary Authority.
3	Encourage mainland enterprises to use Hong Kong as a financial services platform to start local and international businesses. Mainland organisations are also encouraged to set up or expand their branches in Hong Kong.
4	Support mainland enterprises to list in Hong Kong.
5	Assist in speeding up the construction of the Hong Kong-Zhuhai-Macao Bridge.
6	Support the speeding up of other selected cross-boundary infrastructure projects.
7	Endorse the "Outline of the Plan for the Development of Pearl River Delta Region" to enhance cooperation among Guangdong, Hong Kong, and Macao with a view to developing the region into a world-class metropolis circle.
8	Support Hong Kong enterprises to participate in the construction of Shenzhen Metro Line 4 with the Build-Operate-Transfer (BOT) mode.
9	Support the development of Shenzhen-Hong Kong border areas.
10	Consolidate Hong Kong's position as an international shipping centre.
11	Introduce policy measures to help SMEs, including Hong Kong-funded SMEs in the mainland.
12	Expand further the Individual Travel Scheme.
13	Study further liberalisation measures with a view to signing the CEPA VI as soon as possible.
14	Ensure the stable supply of food, water, electricity and natural gas to Hong Kong.

The Outline was released on 8 January 2009 by mainland's top economic planning body, National Development and Reform Commission (NDRC). This 12-year development outline marked a major milestone for closer cooperation among Hong Kong, Macau and the PRD region on all fronts. The Outline maps out comprehensive development schemes for the three jurisdictions to take initiatives in areas such as tourism, environmental protection, infrastructural and transport arrangements, regional development and city planning.

In regard to CEPA, on top of the provisions granted in previous phases, Supplement V, signed in July 2008 and effective from January 2009, includes a string of further liberalisation measures covering 17 service sectors such as expanding the business scope allowable for Hong Kong companies and lowering thresholds required to set up business and provide services to the mainland. The supplement allows early and pilot implementation in Guangdong province where greater power of approval of projects is delegated (Table 5).

Both the Outline and Supplement V to CEPA have provided opportunities for the SAR to shore up its ailing economy. An important area with immediate relevance is tourism. Mainland visitors to Hong Kong rose by 8.9% in 2008 while non-mainland arrivals dropped by 0.3%. Accounting for 57% of total, visitors from mainland

Table 5. Cooperation measures with Guangdong under Supplement V to CEPA.

Education	(i) To delegate to Guangdong the authority to approve applications submitted by Hong Kong institutions for setting up schools for the children of Hong Kong residents; and (ii) to set up a joint approval mechanism by the Ministry of Education and the Guangdong authorities to jointly assess and approve education institutions and projects operated jointly by Guangdong and Hong Kong.
Environment	(i) To permit Guangdong to approve the qualification of Hong Kong Service Supplier for setting up enterprises to operate environmental pollution control facilities in Guangdong; and (ii) to support the abatement of atmospheric pollution in the Pearl River Delta region, as well as the prevention and control of water pollution of the Pearl River.
Tourism	(i) To extend the coverage of "simplified entry arrangement for a period of 144 hours" to the whole of Guangdong; (ii) to allow mainland-authorised Hong Kong travel enterprises to organise group tours to Hong Kong Disneyland for non-Guangdong residents who have resided and worked in private enterprises, joint venture enterprises, or foreign enterprises in Shenzhen for over one year; and (iii) to support Guangdong's pilot programme for a wholesale tourism reform, including the strengthening of Guangdong-Hong Kong tourism cooperation.

are getting more important to the SAR's tourism income given their rising spending power. With new facilitation measures under the Individual Visit Scheme, mainland residents especially those from Guangdong can now enjoy enhanced convenience to visit Hong Kong, thus boosting inbound tourism and in turn benefitting retail, hotels, food and beverage, and other related industries in Hong Kong.

Closer cooperation and deeper integration with the bordering PRD and the vast hinterland beyond have many implications. Among others, Hong Kong can raise its competitiveness as a financial centre and business hub, restructuring itself towards higher value-added and knowledge-based activities. However, one of the consequences of this rising integration is the inevitable increasing dependence of Hong Kong's economy on that of the mainland. Yet turning to Beijing as a last resort during this turbulent and difficult period is in line with the pragmatism of the SAR government.

Ranked as the world's freest economy by the Heritage Foundation for 15 straight years, Hong Kong has long followed a "Market Leads, Government Facilitates" principle in forming public policies. During economic hard times like now, the SAR government has deliberately implemented counter-cyclical measures to cope with the financial crisis which also prompted relevant authorities to step up supervisory efforts and strengthen oversight of the financial institutions to ensure resilience. The outcome of these initiatives will have influence over whether Hong Kong's extraordinary commitment to "lassez faire" economic freedom will endure.

At the industry level, Hong Kong's financial market, an integral part of the international nexus, has been seriously hit by the current global financial crisis. Its financial service sector, accounting for 6% of total workforce but 16% of GDP, is bound to be adversely affected. Activities dwindled in a wide spectrum of financial services including fund raising, share trading and asset management. Indeed, financing and insurance activities posted year-on-year declines of -0.8% and -6.0% in the last two quarters of 2008. What is more, due to staff retrenchment by some financial institutions, there was a decrease in sector employment by 11,400 or 5.4% from August 2008 to February 2009.

Over the longer term, the financial crisis, after fully running its course, will bring about reforms in the global financial framework, in which Hong Kong needs to use its freewheeling ability to adjust swiftly and adapt wisely. The question of its long-term pre-eminence as a financial hub resurfaces as the State Council in Beijing outlined new plans to develop Shanghai into an international financial centre by 2020. In the race for financial supremacy, Hong Kong still has advantages that Shanghai cannot match in terms of financial infrastructure and sophistication. However, challenges faced by the SAR's financial sector cannot be underestimated as big investment decisions and big profits are increasingly being made northward in the mainland.

Chapter 8

Financial Crisis Offers Respite for the Macao Economy

ZHANG Yang and Fung KWAN

Since the second half of 2008, Macao's casino revenue growth has come to a halt because of a deteriorating global economy and mainland's imposition of tighter visa restrictions on Chinese visitors to Macao. Gross gaming revenue registered a contraction of 12.7% in the first quarter of 2009 while GDP dipped by 12.9%. Yet the current break in the gambling- and tourism-led boom will give the territory a much-needed respite to re-examine its economic growth pattern. A potential driver of growth could be the rise of more diversified tourism with leisure and business conventions likely to be the focal point.

The tourism and gaming sectors have contributed much to Macao's economy in recent years. Its economy grew approximately 17% annually on average between 2002 and 2008 when new casino resorts and tourist attractions were opened. Since the ending of the monopoly on gambling in 2002, Macao has opened its gaming sector to foreign investment.

It began to rival Las Vegas to become the world's largest gaming centre after overtaking the global gambling capital in earnings in 2006.

The gaming industry in Macao has been thriving since 2002 when the Special Administrative Region (SAR) government liberalised the gaming industry and granted concessions to three gaming operators who in turn signed sub-concessions with other investors. As of March 2009, there are 31 casinos operated by six concessionaires.[1] In 2008, Gross Gaming Revenue (GGR)[2] in the territory reached an all-time high of MOP109.8 billion (US$13.7 billion),[3] up by 31% from a year ago (Figure 1). In the same year, tax revenue on gaming accounted

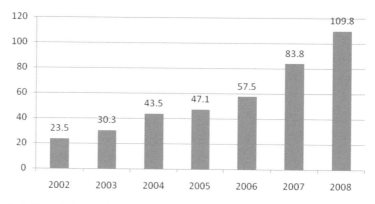

Source: Statistics and Census Service (DSEC), Macao SAR Government.

Fig. 1.   Macao's gross gaming revenue (billion MOP).

---

[1] They are Sociedade de Jogos de Macau (known as SJM; headed by Stanley Ho); Galaxy Casino (a subsidiary of Galaxy Entertainment Group, from Hong Kong); Wynn Resorts (of Steve Wynn); Venetian Macau (Sheldon Adelson); a partnership of MGM with Pansy Ho (daughter of Stanley Ho); and a partnership of Melco and PBL of Australia.

[2] Gross Gaming Revenue is the net win from gaming activities, which is the difference between gaming wins and losses before deducting expenses. GGR excludes betting businesses such as horse and dog races and sports wagering.

[3] Macau adopts the currency board system under which the legal tender, pataca (MOP), is 100% backed by foreign exchange reserves, the Hong Kong dollar (HKD). The pataca is pegged to the HKD at a rate of 1.03 MOP per HKD, and indirectly to USD at 8 MOP per USD approximately.

for 82% of government revenue. The expanding casino sector has re-energised Macao's tourism industry which saw total visitors reaching 22.9 million in 2008, doubled in six years. Exports of gaming services have been the main propeller of economic boom.

However, the gaming industry expansion has come to a phase of adjustment when the SAR government in April 2008 imposed a freeze on gaming licences and new land resources for further casino development. Macao is also not spared in the current global economic meltdown. The pinch of the financial crisis and global economic slump has been felt in the local gaming sector. Indeed, when Wall Street sneezes, Macao is one of the first economies to catch the cold.

The growth of GGR, peaked in the first quarter of 2008, declined in the subsequent two quarters before it eventually plunged into negative zone in the final quarter (Figure 2), the first downturn since the handover of Macao. The collapse of the gaming boom became more evident when GGR registered a contraction of 12.7% in the first quarter of 2009, substantially down from a growth of 61.8% in early 2008.

Specifically, the global financial crisis has led several cash-strapped casino operators to suspend work on their multi-billion-dollar investment projects in Macao, which are unlikely to resume any time soon

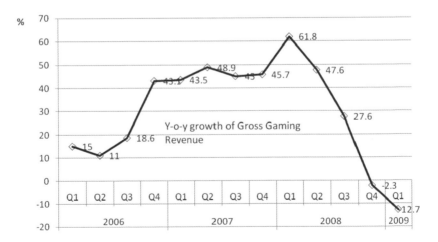

Source: Statistics and Census Service (DSEC), Macao SAR Government.

Fig. 2. Quarterly growth of gross gaming revenue.

until capital markets improve. While casino developers struggled with a cash squeeze, waves of lay-offs began after years of desperately in need of labour.

It is at Venetian Macao, a subsidiary of Las Vegas Sands Corp and a US$2.4 billion project which is unprecedented in scale in Asia, that the slowdown can be seen most keenly. Casino worker numbers were cut, weekly working hours for employees scaled back and most importantly, construction of new hotels, huge shopping centres and several new casinos halted or postponed. In November 2008, Las Vegas Sands dismissed 9,000 non-resident construction workers[4] in Macao and placed an indefinite moratorium on the bulk of its planned US$12 billion investment until its liquidity position improves.

Sands Corp is hardly alone in feeling the pain. Across the enclave, some 10,000 foreign and 2,000 local workers lost their jobs as of January 2009.[5] Thousands of migrant workers from southern China and Hong Kong have been sent back across the border. More recently, Wynn Macau implemented in May a foreign worker repatriation programme to address current business volumes and upcoming quota adjustments. The laying off of at least 25 non-local casino managers will take effect at the end of June. Along the Cotai Strip,[6] the building construction of major casino, shopping centres and hotel projects, including Shangri-La, St Regis and the Sheraton group, has come to a standstill, leading to severe repercussion to the local communities.

Underlying this decline in GGR was the reduction in discretionary income as a result of factory closings in southern China and the downturn in regional business. This was reinforced by Beijing's tightening of travel permits for mainland residents wishing to visit Macao, a policy aimed at keeping Chinese domestic consumption

---

[4] "Macau economy: Unemployment creeps up", *The Economist Intelligence Unit*, 2 Apr. 2009, http://www.eiu.com/index.asp?layout=VWArticleVW3&article_id=1894410174&country_id=330000033&page_title=Latest+analysis&rf=0

[5] "Asia's Las Vegas, Macau, Fights The Economic Crisis", *The Independent*, 14 Jan. 2009, http://www.huffingtonpost.com/2009/01/14/asias-las-vegas-macau-fig_n_157792.html.

[6] Cotai Strip is a finger of reclaimed land which merges the Cotai Island and Coloane of Macao.

high as well as preventing corrupt officials from gambling away public coffers on the dice table. Visas were restricted to single entry from June 2008, down from double entry in a month, and to once every other month from July. Moreover, mainland visitors with travel permits to Hong Kong have been barred from entering Macao since September 2008 unless a separate travel permit is obtained.[7]

These new restrictions significantly reduced the frequency with which individual travellers from the mainland could visit Macao and the duration for which they could stay. Not surprisingly, this has had great impact on the gaming business given GGR is closely associated with tourist arrivals, as evidenced in Figure 3. In fact, Chinese VIP gamblers, or high rollers, make up 70% of overall gaming revenue in Macao.

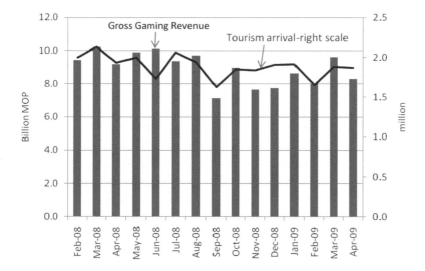

Source: Statistics and Census Service (DSEC), Macao SAR Government.

Fig. 3. Gross gaming revenue and total tourist arrivals.

---

[7] Individual Visit Scheme (IVS), introduced by the central government of China in July 2003, has been the main driver of Macao's tourism and gaming boom. According to the Scheme, mainland Chinese wishing to visit Hong Kong and Macau are allowed to travel as individuals rather than as members of tour groups as previously required. However, restrictions on the IVS were imposed by the central government in June 2008. From July, individual travellers from the mainland were allowed to apply for entry visas to visit Macao only once every two months, down from twice a month previously.

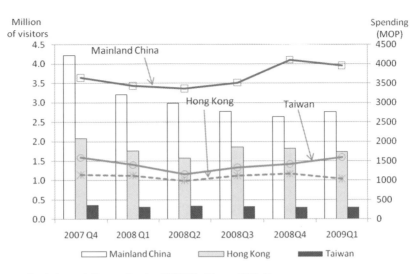

Source: Statistics and Census Service (DSEC), Macao SAR Government.
Note: Bar chart shows number of visitors on left scale, while per capita spending is plotted in lines with right scale.

Fig. 4.   Number of visitors and per capita spending by source markets.

For the whole year of 2008, visitor arrivals totalled 22.9 million, down from 26.9 million in the previous year. Judging by source markets, tourists from the mainland have the highest per capita spending and consist of 50.6% of total arrivals, followed by 30.6% from Hong Kong (Figure 4). Same-day visitors continued to dominate, accounting for 53.7% of the total.

ECONOMIC GROWTH SLOWING SHARPLY

With the gaming and tourism industry, the key driver of Macao's economic prosperity, losing its momentum in the second half of 2008, Macao's overall economy was inevitably adversely affected. Real GDP growth moderated markedly in 2008, registering an annual growth of 13.2%, significantly lower than the 25.3% in 2007 (Figure 5). On closer examination, within the year of 2008, Macao's economy saw a sharp slowing down with growth rate sliding from 32.5% in the first quarter to 22.4% in the second and 10.4% in the third.

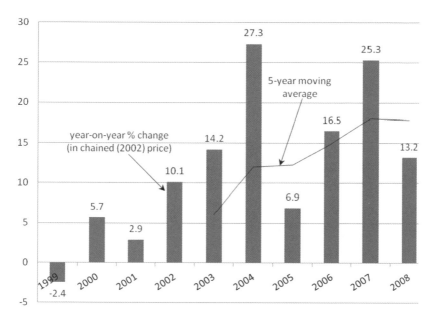

Source: Statistics and Census Service (DSEC), Macao SAR Government.

Fig. 5. Macao's economic growth.[8]

The contraction of 7.6% in the last quarter in 2008 has been the worst since 1999, followed by an even more severe plunge of –12.9% in the first quarter of 2009 (Figure 6). Compared to neighbouring economies that were also battered by the outbreak and ramifications of the global financial crisis, Macao's economy showed a lack of resilience as its GDP plummeted more dramatically than that of Hong Kong, mainland China, Singapore and Taiwan towards the beginning of 2009 (Figure 7).

---

[8] Las Vegas Sands, a world gaming icon, launched the US$240 million Sands Macao in May 2004. This was followed by the opening of Galaxy's Waldo in July. On the back of this boom in the gaming and tourism sector which brought about large amount of investment and massive construction, GDP growth in 2004 registered a stunning 27.3%. Against this astonishing growth rate, performance in the subsequent year moderated, especially so when Macao's exports of goods were adversely affected by the cancellation of the global textile and garment quota system and a weak economy in the Euro Zone.

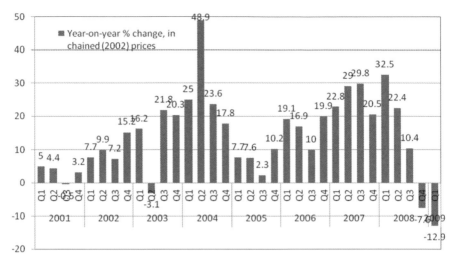

Source: Statistics and Census Service (DSEC), Macao SAR Government.

Fig. 6.   Quarterly GDP growth.

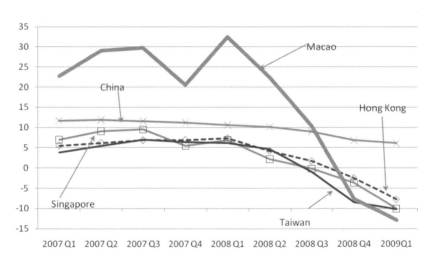

Source: EIU Country Data.

Fig. 7.   Economic performances of selected Asian economies.

The contraction was attributable to a notable drop in merchandise exports, significant cutback in investment and most importantly, marked deterioration of exports of service in the gaming and tourism sectors. In fact, net exports, predominantly driven by exports of

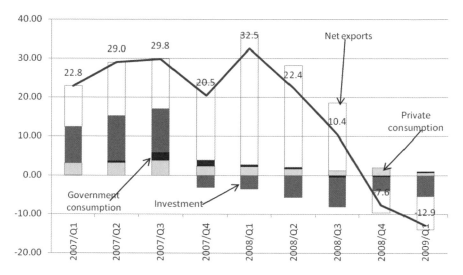

Source: Statistics and Census Service (DSEC), Macao SAR Government.

Fig. 8. Contribution to quarterly GDP growth (percentage point).

services, had been the key propeller of rapid GDP growth in recent years before falling into negative territory in the last quarter of 2008 and the subsequent one (Figure 8), leading to contraction of two consecutive quarters, unseen since 1999.

For the year of 2008, exports of merchandise goods fell by 25.4%. Particularly in the last quarter, exports of goods plunged remarkably by 42.4% with exports to the US, the largest market for Macao's merchandise export, down significantly by 53.4%. Exports to mainland China and EU plummeted by 23.4% and 72.1% respectively. This steady merchandise export decline in the last quarter of 2008 was primarily the result of weakening textile and garment sales abroad which fell by 56.5%. In April 2009, merchandise exports fell by 48.9% (Figure 9).

As the global credit crisis has deprived casino operators of the capital required to carry on with their investment programmes, the second half of 2008 saw an exacerbation of the investment slowdown where overall investment declined by 25% in the third quarter and 15.1% in the last. In the first quarter of 2009, investment registered a deeper fall of 32% against the same period in 2008. In contrast, private consumption held up well thanks largely to rising median employment

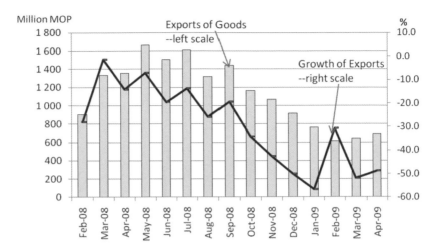

Source: Statistics and Census Service (DSEC), Macao SAR Government.

Fig. 9.   Exports of goods.

earnings. In the last quarter of 2008 retail sales rose by 20.7%, of which sales of watches, clocks and jewellery accounted for 21.7%. Retail growth moderated to 9.3% in the first quarter of 2009, but private consumption and government expenditure accounted for relatively small shares of the economy and hence had little impact on economic growth.

Along with the economic slowdown, the labour market has seen rapid deterioration since the last quarter of 2008. For the three-month period ending March 2009, the unemployment rate registered 3.8%, compared to 2.9% a year earlier. However, the reported unemployment rate underestimated the severity of labour market conditions as it did not account for the repatriation of foreign workers, which are not counted as normal domestic labour and hence not reflected in the official jobless rate. Indeed, employment of nonresident workers has fallen sharply due to the suspension of casino construction. Meanwhile, inflation pressure has receded considerably. The Consumer Price Index increased by 2.5% in March 2009, moderating from the 6.2% at the end of last year (Figure 10).

Thanks to the past spectacular casino boom and soaring gambling tax receipts until recently, Macao's government was armed with over

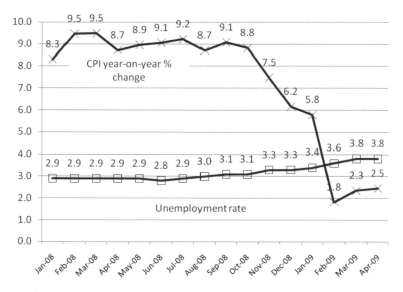

Source: Statistics and Census Service (DSEC), Macao SAR Government.

Fig. 10. Unemployment and inflation (%).

MOP80 billion[9] (US$10 billion) in accumulated fiscal reserves at the end of 2008 and therefore has ample funds to cope with the economic slowdown. In his annual policy address delivered in November 2008, Chief Executive Edmund Ho Hau Wah announced that the government had budgeted MOP10.2 billion (US$1.3 billion) for investment in public work projects including the construction of a light rail transit system, public housing, old neighbourhood reorganisation, and landscape works of the city's World Heritage sites.

To cushion the impact of the global financial crisis especially on small and medium enterprises (SMEs), the government plans to inject MOP1.5 billion (US$0.2 billion) into the Industrial and Commercial Development Fund to provide funding for SMEs. Meanwhile, the SAR authorities have doled out cash to ease people's hardship through tax breaks in various fields, housing subsidies, textbook

---

[9] "Macau's Loses 10 Percent Public Revenue in January 2009", Macau Daily Blog and News, 23 Feb. 2009, http://macaudailyblog.com/macau-business/economy-business/macaus-loses-10-percent-public-revenue-in-january-2009/.

allowances, electricity and medical subsidies and cash handouts to residents.

THE NEED TO DIVERSIFY MACAO'S ECONOMY

An open and vibrant free-market economy, Macao since the opening up of its gaming industry in 2002 has attracted more foreign investment, spurring tourism and overall consumption, transforming this once tranquil place of just half-a-million people into a magnet for gamblers all over the region. The gaming sector contributed to nearly 50% of Macao's GDP in 2007 (Figure 11) and 19.7% of total employment in 2008.

The growth had been astounding and most of the local systems were affected too quickly to have had time to react properly. Macao had been straining under the load of visitor influx and was crippled by labour shortage and infrastructure bottlenecks, especially so when approvals of new projects had slowed dramatically after the high-profile conviction of the former secretary for transport and public works for corruption.

With credit crunch, weakening economic conditions and mainland's tighter visa rules, Macao now has to deal with less money spent

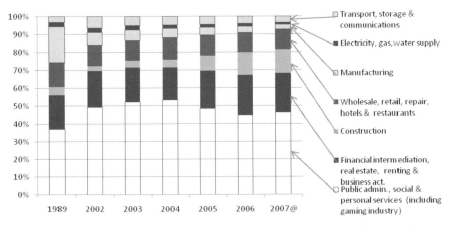

Source: Statistics and Census Service (DSEC), Macao SAR Government; at figures subject to revision.

Fig. 11.   Composition of Macao's GDP by sectors.

on the table and less cash to spend on a dramatic expansion plan that is supposed to transform the enclave into Asia's biggest tourist destination. The changed reality and current break in the gambling- and tourism-led boom, however, will give the territory a much-needed respite to re-examine its economic growth pattern and address the city's infrastructure shortcoming which constitutes one of the biggest potential obstacles to its future development. China's Vice-President Xi Jinping in his visit to the SAR in January 2009 urged the territory to promote long-term economic diversification.

In fact, Macao continues to host a significant but shrinking textile and garment industry, the key component of its manufacturing sector (Figure 11). In 2008, exports of textiles and garments generated only MOP9.1 billion compared to MOP109.8 billion in gross gaming receipts. Macao's textile industry will continue to relocate northward to the mainland for cheaper land and labour, leaving the enclave more dependent on gambling to generate growth. Moreover, local SMEs have been struggling to survive as they have to compete with the rapidly expanding gaming and tourism interests for resources. As such, horizontal diversification of Macao's economy seems hard to realise in the short run.

Nevertheless, the non-gaming side of Macao within its tourism industry has yet to be fully explored; this provides room for vertical diversification while consolidating the advantages of existing industries. Indeed, Macao has identified the MICE[10] industry as a key driver to diversify its economy and become a centre that integrates gaming, shopping, conference and exhibition as well as entertainment and leisure industries.

Being primarily a day-trip market reliant on gambling, recently unveiled non-gaming attractions such as sprawling retail malls, fine dining and entertainment and recreation have generated only weak demand. Hence, a potential driver of growth could be the rise of more diversified tourism in the city, with non-gaming business like leisure and business convention likely to be the focal point.

---

[10] MICE represents meetings, incentives, conventions and exhibitions.

Already, Macao is increasingly becoming a conference destination and a place for trade shows, concerts and sports events.

However, diversification of the economy would not come easily. Unlike Las Vegas whose non-gaming receipt accounts for nearly 60% of total casino resort revenue, the number is merely 20% for Macau.[11] The small enclave lacks the land and more importantly human resource to develop convention centres and an entertainment industry.

Looking ahead, prospects for growth in the short run have deteriorated significantly, primarily owing to falling casino revenue and the halting of construction of some major casino resorts. In addition, investment will stay in the doldrums before the financial crisis begins to abate while private consumption will recede given the uncertain economic prospects. Merchandise exports remain weak amid severe contraction of external demand from EU and the US. The economy of Macao in 2009 is expected to remain sluggish although gambling revenues are expected to recover in the second half of this year.

The opening of the City of Dreams casino on 1 June 2009 was a big vote of confidence in Macao and gave the market a tremendous boost at a time when other casino operators falter and the economy struggles. Moreover, the economy would be cushioned should the central government ease austerity measures on visa for mainland Chinese to visit Macao.

Macao's economic fortunes are tied to the mainland. To boost Macao's economy, Beijing on 26 December 2008 announced a number of measures including speeding up cross-boundary infrastructure projects, promoting financial cooperation, further opening up of mainland's service sector to Macao, and helping SMEs. It also included the endorsement of the "Outline of the Plan for the Development of Pearl River Delta (PRD) Region"

---

[11] "Wooing the high rollers", *The Standard*, 23 May 2008, http://www.thestandard. com.hk/news_detail.asp?we_cat=16&art_id=66219&sid=19050165&con_type=1& d_str=20080523&fc=8.

which will foster closer links and cooperation between Macao and the PRD region.

In January 2009, the central government in Beijing decided to release Hengqin Island, three times the size of Macao lying just off its Coloanes Island, for future joint development by the city of Zhuhai, Guangdong province, and Macao to facilitate closer cooperation and coordination between the two. Although the details of the development scheme have yet to be made public, Hengqin Island is believed to offer Macao great opportunity for territorial expansion and economic diversification.

On top of the provisions granted in previous phases of Closer Economic Partnership Arrangement (CEPA),[12] Supplement V was signed in July 2008 and effective from January 2009 to assist Macao service providers, upon obtaining "service supplier certificates",[13] to tap the mainland market. As of April 2009, 349 certificates[14] had been approved primarily for transport and logistics, conventions and exhibition, management consulting, construction, distribution, telecommunications and advertising. Further, liberalisation measures in Supplement V have expanded the business scope allowable for Macao's companies and lowered thresholds required to set up business and provide services in the mainland (Table 1).

---

[12] The mainland and Macau CEPA is an economic agreement between the Government of the Macau Special Administrative Region and the Central Government signed on 18 October 2003; annual supplements have been added since then. Under the CEPA, all products of Macau origin are exempted from import customs to the mainland.

[13] Criteria to be eligible as Macao service suppliers include incorporation in Macao, three to five years in operation, paid tax in Macao and employs at least 50% of its staff locally.

[14] http://www.cepa.gov.mo/cepaweb/front/eng/itemI_4.htm.

Table 1.   Supplement V to CEPA on liberalisation of trade in services for Macao.

Accounting, auditing and bookkeeping services	The validity period of the "Temporary Performing Auditing Business Permit", applied by Macao auditing firms and auditors for the purpose of conducting auditing business on a temporary basis in the mainland, is extended from two years to five years.
	To agree to the setting up of an examination centre in Macao for the mainland Certified Public Accountants Examination.
Medical and dental services	• To allow Macao service suppliers to set up wholly owned outpatient clinics in the Guangdong province.
	• There is no restriction on the ratio of capital investment between the mainland and Macao partners for the equity joint venture or contractual joint venture outpatient clinics set up by Macao service suppliers in the Guangdong province.
	• There is no requirement on the total amount of capital investment for Macao service suppliers who set up wholly owned, equity joint venture or contractual joint venture outpatient clinics in the Guangdong province.
	• The provincial health administrative department of the Guangdong province is responsible for the proposed establishment and approval procedures for setting up wholly owned, equity joint venture or contractual joint venture outpatient clinics by Macao service suppliers in the Guangdong province.
	• To allow qualified Macao permanent residents with Chinese citizenship to apply for and obtain "Medical Practitioner's Qualification Certificates" of the mainland through accreditation.[15]

(Continued)

---

[15] Details of implementation measures to be promulgated by the Ministry of Health.

Table 1. (*Continued*)

Information technology services	• Effective on the day of signature, when applying for qualification certification of computer information system integration in the mainland, Macao service suppliers are assessed according to the following criteria:
	  • no assessment on professional job title, but assessed by the relevant academic qualifications and working experiences;
	  • projects undertaken in both the mainland and Macao are taken into account for business turnover in system integration qualification;
	  • for enterprises applying for Level 3 qualification certification, personnel involved in software development and system integration should not be less than 25, with no less than 80% of personnel with graduate or post-graduate qualification.
	  • Other assessment criteria will be implemented in accordance with the provisions of the relevant regulations of the mainland.

Services incidental to mining	To allow Macao service suppliers, on a contractual joint venture basis, to provide services of exploitation of oil and natural gas in the mainland.
Placement and supply services of personnel	The minimum registered capital requirement for wholly owned job referral agencies and job intermediaries set up by Macao service suppliers in the Guangdong province will follow the requirements applicable to mainland enterprises in the Guangdong province.
Printing and publishing services	The minimum registered capital requirement for Macao service suppliers who set up printing enterprises in the mainland to provide packaging and ornament services for printed materials will follow the requirements applicable to mainland enterprises.

(*Continued*)

Table 1. *(Continued)*

Convention services and exhibition services	To allow Macao service suppliers to set up wholly owned, equity joint venture or contractual joint venture enterprises in Beijing municipality, Tianjin municipality, Chongqing municipality and Zhejiang province to provide organising overseas exhibition services on a pilot basis.[16] Participating exhibitors should be enterprises registered in that province or municipality correspondingly.
Distribution services	For the same Macao service supplier who opens more than 30 stores accumulatively in the mainland, the Macao service supplier is allowed to run business on a wholly owned basis if the commodities for sale include pharmaceutical products, pesticides, mulching films, chemical fertilisers, vegetable oil, edible sugar and cotton, and if the above commodities are of different brands and come from different suppliers.[17]
Environmental services	To agree that the Guangdong province approve the qualification of Macao service suppliers who set up enterprises engaging in environmental pollution control facilities in Guangdong.
Banking and other financial services (excluding insurance and securities)	• To allow mainland-incorporated banking institutions established by Macao banks to set up data centres in Macao when they meet the following criteria:[18] • incorporated in the mainland on or before 30 June 2008; • data centres have been set up in Macao by parent banks at the time of their incorporation; • data centres with core systems such as customer, account and product information should operate independently;

(Continued)

---

[16] Should be submitted to the China Council for the Promotion of International Trade for approval in accordance with the relevant laws and regulations in the mainland.

[17] If the commodity for sale is processed oil, mainland's commitments to members of the World Trade Organization are still applicable.

[18] Should comply with provisions stipulated in the supervisory cooperation agreement signed by relevant mainland and Macao regulatory authorities relating to data centres of mainland-incorporated banking institutions established by Macao banks located in Macao.

Table 1. (*Continued*)

	• their board of directors and senior management are entitled to the ultimate management authority of the data centres; and • data centres should meet the requirements of relevant regulators and be subject to the approval of relevant authorities of the mainland when setting up the centres.
Social services	To allow Macao service suppliers establish welfare agencies for persons with disabilities in the form of wholly owned private non-enterprises in the Guangdong province on a pilot basis.
Tourism and travel-related services	• To delegate to the Guangdong province the authority of approving Macao service suppliers who set up travel agencies on a wholly owned, equity joint venture or contractual joint venture basis in Guangdong. • To allow Macao permanent residents with Chinese citizenship to sit for the mainland qualification examination for tourist guides. Tourist guide qualification certificates will be awarded to those who have passed the examination in accordance with the relevant regulations.
Transport services	To allow Macao service suppliers to set up wholly owned enterprises and their branches in the Guangdong province to provide shipping agency services to vessel operators who are engaged in shipping routes between the Guangdong province and Hong Kong or Macao on a pilot basis.
Air transport services	To allow Macao service suppliers to submit the economic guarantee provided by mainland-incorporated banks or guarantee companies recommended by China Air Transport Association when applying for setting up wholly owned, equity joint venture or contractual joint venture air transport sales agencies in the mainland.
Road transport services	To delegate to the Guangdong province the authority of approving Macao-invested production enterprises to provide road freight transport services and approving Macao service suppliers who set up repair and driver training enterprises, and passenger and freight transport stations (depots) in Guangdong.

(*Continued*)

Table 1.   *(Continued)*

Individually owned stores	To allow Macao permanent residents with Chinese citizenship to set up, in accordance with the relevant mainland laws, regulations and administrative regulations, individually owned stores in all provinces, autonomous regions, municipalities directly under the Central Government in the mainland, without being subject to the approval procedures applicable to foreign investments. The number of employees for each store shall not exceed eight persons. The scope of business for individually owned stores, excluding franchising, includes building-cleaning services and advertising production services. Additional service sectors for the Guangdong province particularly include trade brokerage and agency services (excluding auction); and renting and leasing services (excluding renting and leasing of housing services).
Services of architectural, engineering, urban planning and landscape architecture	To allow Macao service suppliers to set up construction and engineering design enterprises in the mainland in the form of equity joint venture or contractual joint venture without any restrictions on the proportion of total investment contributed by mainland partners to the registered capital.
Related sscientific and technical consulting services	To allow Macao service suppliers to carry out prospecting and surveying services of iron, manganese and copper in the mainland on a wholly owned, equity joint venture or contractual joint venture basis.

Source: Macao Special Administrative Region Economic Services; http://www.cepa.gov.mo/cepaweb/front/eng/index_en.htm.

Chapter 9

China's Trade Prospects and China-ASEAN Trade Relations

Sarah Y. TONG and CHONG Siew Keng

Since late 2008, China's decade-long surging trade expansion has come to a grinding halt due to the global economy's sharp slow-down. Domestically, this has led to not only a considerable downward moderation in China's economic growth, but also rising concerns about employment and possible social instability. Externally, China's gloomy export outlook has caused significant chain reactions on trade development of its regional trading partners due to the expansion of the highly inter-dependent regional production network. With growing danger of trade protectionism across the world, China and its Asian neighbours, including ASEAN countries, have little choice but to continue their commitment to free trade and economic integration in both intra- and extra-regional perspectives. At the same time, the region as a whole needs to also develop its own consumer market to reduce its reliance on the industrial market.

Trade expansion has been important, if not essential, to China's economic growth in recent decades. With an annual growth rate of 17%

since the reform started in 1978, trade has consistently outstripped the already staggering growth of the overall economy where Gross Domestic Product (GDP) on average grew by 10% a year. Consequently, China has become a leading trader in the world, ranking number two in export and number three in import in 2008, and accounting for 12% and 9% of the world total respectively. In 1978, China's trade to GDP ratio was around 10%. It has since increased significantly, especially since the early 1990s, nearly doubling the 30% in 1990 to reach 58% in 2008.[1]

More importantly, external demand has become an important engine for China's economic growth in recent years. Between 2005 and 2008, net export directly contributed around 20% of China's annual economic growth.[2] Moreover, export is crucial for developing China's industries and generating employment. In 2007, exports constituted about 25% of China's total industrial output.[3] According to the Ministry of Commerce, export-related activities supported over 100 million of employment in 2008.[4]

Unfortunately, this rapid trade expansion has suffered a grinding halt since late 2008 as a result of the rapidly deteriorating external economic conditions generated by the global financial crisis. Economies in the US and European Union (EU) weakened considerably towards the end of 2008, registering a drastic decline in import demand.

---

[1] The percentages are calculated by the authors using data from *China's Customs Statistics* 2009 (for trade figures) and International Monetary Fund's *World Economic Outlook Database*, April 2009.

[2] For 2005, 2006 and 2007, the contribution of net export to GDP growth was 24%, 19% and 22% respectively. (Source: China's Statistical Abstract 2008). For 2008, the contribution is estimated to be around 18% (calculated by the authors based on data from the PR China's National Statistical Bulletin on Economic and Social Development 2008 (中华人民共和国 2008 年国民经济和社会发展统计公报).

[3] The percentage is estimated by the authors with trade and industrial figures from China's Statistical Yearbook 2008.

[4] "Vice Minister Yi Xiaozhun of the Ministry of Commerce: China's overall economy achieved stable development (商务部副部长易小准: 商务运行整体平稳)", 6 Dec. 2008, http://finance.sina.com.cn.

Indeed, the World Trade Organization (WTO) predicted that global trade may decline by 9% in 2009.[5]

In the US, real GDP growth, as compared to the previous year, dropped from 2.1% in the second quarter, to 0.7% in the third quarter of 2008. Worse still, the economy contracted by 0.8% and 2.5% in the fourth quarter of 2008 and the first quarter of 2009 respectively. Since early 2008, before an economic slowdown became apparent in the US, import has already started to contract by 1.6% and 2.4% on a year-to-year basis, in the first and the second quarter of 2008, respectively. The contraction accelerated in the following three quarters to 3.5% and 7.5% in the third and last quarters of 2008, and 16.5% in the first quarter of 2009.[6] For the 27 EU members as a whole, GDP declined by 2.4% in the first quarter of 2009, compared to the previous quarter, while total extra-EU import contracted by 22% in the first four months of 2009, on a yearly basis.[7]

The first sign of a significant slowdown in China's trade came two months after the full eruption of the global financial crisis in September 2008. In November 2008, monthly export contracted by 2% from that a year ago, compared to an annual growth of 19% in October 2008. The change is even more drastic for import, which contracted by 18% in November 2008, a sharp fall from the 15% increase in the previous month. The downward trend continued in

---

[5] WTO: 2009 PRESS RELEASES, "WTO sees 9% global trade decline in 2009 as recession strikes", 23 Mar. 2009, http://www.wto.org/english/news_e/pres09_e/pr554_e.htm.

[6] Bureau of Economic Analysis, "Gross Domestic Product: First Quarter 2009 (Preliminary)", http://www.bea.gov/newsreleases/national/gdp/2009/txt/gdp-109p.txt.

[7] The EU27 includes Belgium, Bulgaria, the Czech Republic, Denmark, Germany, Estonia, Ireland, Greece, Spain, France, Italy, Cyprus, Latvia, Lithuania, Luxembourg, Hungary, Malta, the Netherlands, Austria, Poland, Portugal, Romania, Slovenia, Slovakia, Finland, Sweden and the UK. Source: Eurostat News Release, "April 2009 Euro area external trade surplus 2.7 bn euro", 17 Jun. 2009, "Euro area GDP down by 2.5% and EU27 GDP down by 2.4%", 3 Jun. 2009. http://epp.eurostat.ec.europa.eu.

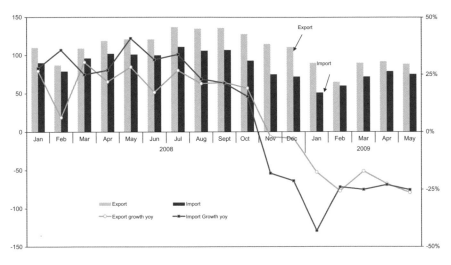

Source: China's Customs Statistics, various issues.

Fig. 1.   China's monthly export and import, January 2008-May 2009 (in bil USD and %).

the following five months as falls in export rapidly caught up with sinking imports (Figure 1). The most serious monthly decline occurred in January (in import) and February (in export) of 2009. When combined, the export and import of the two months contracted by 21% and 34%, respectively, compared to those of the previous year.[8] For the first quarter of 2009 as a whole, export contracted by 20% on a year-to-year basis, while import declined by 31%.[9] Trade statistics since February seem to suggest a moderation in the rapid freefall, as the contraction in trade has been modified and the downward trend

---

[8] The January trade statistics included an important seasonal element: The 2009 Chinese New Year was in late January while the 2008 lunar new year was in early February. It is thus more comparable to combined trade figures of January and February.

[9] Trade data used in this paper are mostly from China's Custom Statistics (various issues) unless specified otherwise.

in monthly trade reversed. Meanwhile, China's trade surplus, which shrank to a mere US$4.8 billion in February, one of the lowest monthly figures since late 2004, returned to US$18 billion in March and US$13 billion in April, a level equivalent to the monthly average of US$15 billion for 2006.

The extent of the downward slide in China's trade has been both broad and deep. This is because over the past decade, China's trade expansion has been accompanied by closer economic ties with major economies in the world. China's rising trade with its Asian neighbours is of particular significance as the country has become the linchpin of an intensifying regional production network.

First, economic recession in the industrial world, notably the US and EU, led to a considerable fall in world trade through import decline. Since 2002, after its WTO accession, China's trade with these two economies has expanded rapidly. Since late 2008, when the shock waves of the crisis spread from the financial sector to the real economy in the US and EU, this upward trend has been reversed abruptly. Export to EU started to decline in December 2008 by 3.5% on a yearly basis. The contraction worsened in the following months, to 17.5% in January, 30.2% in February, and 20.2% in March 2009. Comparatively, export to the US suffered slightly less and only began to decline in 2009, by 8.8% in January, 24.2% in February, and 12.3% in March. In the first quarter of 2009, the fall in exports to the US and EU was about 22% and 15% respectively, from that of the same period in 2008.[10]

The US and EU, the world's largest economies and key markets for the export of final products, together accounted for about 40% of China's total export. The importance of the two markets to China's export would be even higher if re-export through such

---

[10] Export to Hong Kong, within which a considerable portion is re-exported to the US and EU according to Hong Kong official statistics, started to shrink in November 2008 before those to the US and EU. Compared to those a year ago, the mainland's export to Hong Kong has decreased for five months in a row since November 2008 to 10%, 7%, 36%, 12% and 21% respectively.

places like Hong Kong and Singapore is taken into account.[11] Imports from the two economies also declined sharply between late 2008 and early 2009.[12] For the first quarter of 2009, imports from the US fell by 18%, while imports from EU declined by more than a third (36%) from that a year ago.

Within Asia, China's trade with Northeast and Southeast Asia both contracted by significantly more in import. Between November 2008 and March 2009, China's total nominal export and import contracted by 12% and 26% on a yearly basis. During the same period, export to Japan declined by only 8% while import from Japan decreased by 24%. The figures for Taiwan are 28% and 49%, respectively. China-ASEAN trade was affected in much the same pattern; China's export to ASEAN dropped by 15% and import by 32%. Although part of the import decline is attributed to lower commodity prices due to slower global economic growth, it reflects the serious chain reaction on the intense regional production network from a negative shock in external demand.

The heavy inter-dependence across Asia in trade activities is dominated by the trade in goods under the category of equipment and machinery in recent years, especially in trade with China's major Asian trading partners. In 2008, for example, products under a broad category of machinery and appliances[13] made up more than half of

---

[11] According to China's official statistics, export to Hong Kong accounted for 15%–20% of China's total in recent years. Based on official statistics from Hong Kong, at least one-third of re-export originated from mainland China were shipped to the US and EU. Consequently, we estimate an additional 5%–10% of China's export.

[12] Import from EU began to decrease in November 2008, by 8.6% in November, and 6% in December. Import decline from the US started in January 2009.

[13] These include products under Harmonised System (HS) Sections XVI (Machinery and Mechanical Appliances; Electrical Equipment; parts thereof sound recorders and reproducers, television image and sound recorders and reproducers, and parts and accessories of such articles), XVII (Vehicles, Aircraft, Vessels and Associated Transport Equipment), and XVIII (Optical, Photographic, Cinematographic Measuring, Checking, Precision, Medical or Surgical Instruments and Apparatus; Clocks and Watches; Musical Instruments; parts and Accessories thereof).

China's total export and 46% of China's total import, while products of traditional trade items such as textile and clothing[14] accounted for only 15% of total export and 2% of total import.

Indeed, China trades heavily with its regional trading partners on machinery and appliances, especially for import in large part for processing and re-exporting to a third market. For example, products in machinery and appliances made up 43% of China's export to and 63% of China's imports from Japan in 2008 respectively. Similarly, import from South Korea and Taiwan of goods in machinery and appliances accounted for 60% and 67% of China's total imports from these two economies in 2008. For ASEAN-5 countries and Vietnam as a whole, China's import from this group of countries in machinery accounted for 58%[15] of the total in 2008.

Since late 2008, export of such products was hit hard and started to under-perform when compared to China's total export. Between August and October 2008, export of machinery and electronic appliances grew by 18%, 18% and 15% respectively, compared to those a year ago, while China's total export grew by 21%, 21% and 19% during the same period. Since November 2008, when total export has shrunk for five consecutive months, export of machinery and appliances continues to perform badly, contracting by 16% on a yearly comparable basis while total export contracted by 12% for the same period. Even more significantly is the decline in import for machinery and appliances, by 24% in the five months between November 2008 and March 2009[16] (Figure 2).

Within China, firms in process trade were affected first and the most badly. As shown in Figure 3, while ordinary export was still growing towards the end of 2008, albeit at a much lower pace,

---

[14] These include products under HS Sections XI (Textiles and Textile Articles) and XII (Footwear, Headgear, Umbrellas, Sun Umbrellas, Walking-Sticks, Seat-Sticks, Whips, Riding-Crops and Parts thereof; prepared Feathers and Articles made therewith; Artificial Flowers; Articles of Human Hair).

[15] The figures are much higher for the Philippines (91%) and Malaysia (64%).

[16] Total import shrank by 26%, due to sharp contraction in import of minerals, metals and other material contributed to a large part by falling commodity prices.

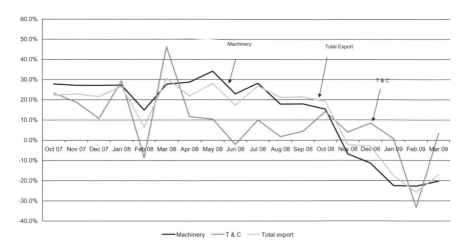

Source: China's Customs Statistics, various issues.

Fig. 2.   China's monthly export growth, October 2007-March 2009 (in %).

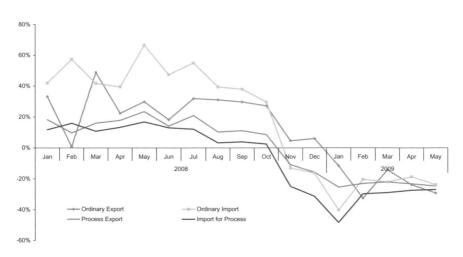

Source: China's Customs Statistics, various issues.

Fig. 3.   Monthly growth in ordinary and process trade January 2008-May 2009.

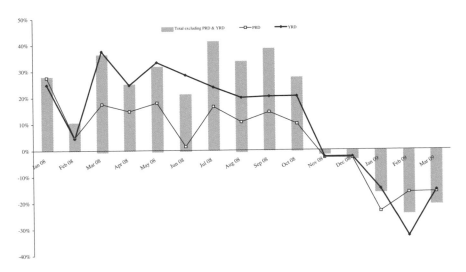

Source: China's Customs Statistics, various issues.

Fig. 4. Monthly growth of export for PRD, YRD and the rest of the country January 2008-March 2009.

process trade started to fall in November 2008, by 11% in export and 25% in import.[17] Into 2009, process trade continues to perform generally badly compared to ordinary trade, especially in import.

Consequently, regions with a higher concentration of trade activities, especially of process trade, suffer more than the rest of China. The Pearl River Delta (PRD) region in Guangdong Province and, to a lesser extent, the Yangtze River Delta (YRD) region, are two such regions. As shown in Figure 4, as early as March 2008, export growth for the PRD region was already much weaker than the rest of the country, while export growth for the YRD started to decline in the second half of 2008. The decline in import of the two regions is even more dismal compared to the rest of the country (Figure 5). Since January 2008, the monthly import growth for both regions has been considerably lower than the rest of the country.

---

[17] Ordinary import also dropped in November and December 2008 by 13% and 16% respectively.

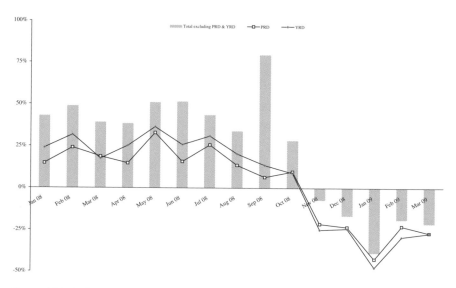

Source: China's Customs Statistics, various issues.

Fig. 5. Monthly growth of import for PRD, YRD and the rest of the country January 2008-March 2009.

Overall, global economic downturn has led to a sharp deterioration in world trade. As one of the world's top exporters relying heavily on the developed market, China is hit directly and severely. Such negative external shocks spread far beyond China's borders to affect all major Asian economies, especially those that are more export-oriented. Intra-Asia trade, which had grown rapidly, to a large extent consists of intra-industry trade and is thus far from adequate to replace extra-regional demand. Therefore, the so-called decoupling between developing Asia and the developed market in trade is still in its early development.

CHINA-ASEAN TRADE AFFECTED CONSIDERABLY

Trade, export in particular, is crucially important for many economies in East and Southeast Asia. In 2007, for example, merchandise trade to GDP ratio for ASEAN members ranged from about 50% for Laos and Indonesia to 349% for Singapore. In part, this is due to growing intra-Asia trade, especially intra-industry trade. More importantly, China has become the centre of this intensifying production network in East and Southeast Asia.

It is thus no surprise that a decrease in China's overall trade has resulted in its declining trade with ASEAN. In March 2009, total trade with ASEAN dropped by 28.5% to US$15.4 billion from US$19.7 billion a year back, where imports suffered a 34.1% decline, considerably worse off than the 22.2% drop for export.[18] Such a gap, between development in export and import, reflects the important characteristic of the China-ASEAN trade. To a large extent, China, especially its foreign invested enterprises, buys materials, parts and components from ASEAN members and then ships the finished products to consumers in the industrial economies.

This pattern of "triangular" trade implies that, as industrial economies experience a serious slowdown, ASEAN's export suffers through two channels. First, export demand from industrial countries drops substantially. Second, export to China also disappears as manufacturers in China cancel or delay their import order from ASEAN due to uncertainty in their export demand. As shown in Figure 6, between August and October 2008, when China's overall import was still growing at 22.9%, 20.8% and 15.4% respectively, growth of China's import from ASEAN already dropped sharply to 8.9%, 2.7% and −0.1% respectively, on a yearly basis. In the following three months, China's import from ASEAN continues decreased by 25.4% (November 2008), 31.4% (December 2008) and 49.7% (January 2009) respectively, considerably larger than its overall import. Among the members, the Philippines has seen the largest decrease in its export to China, which contracted by over 50%, on a yearly basis, for five months in a row since November 2008.

Such major drops in China-ASEAN trade are clearly driven by the intensive intra-industry trade between the two entities shown by the

---

[18] "Briefing of Import and Export for March 2009 (2009 年 3 月进出口简要情况)", Ministry of Commerce of the People's Republic of China, 20 Apr. 2009, http://zhs. mofcom.gov.cn.

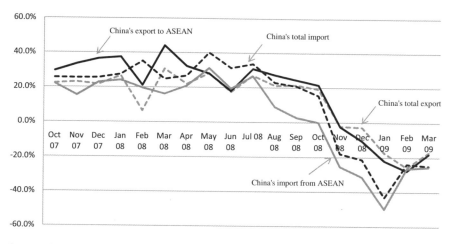

Source: China's Customs Statistics, various issues.

Fig. 6.   Export and import between China and ASEAN.

growing importance of trade in machinery and equipment, especially for some ASEAN members such as the Philippines, Singapore, Thailand and Malaysia where trade in this category accounts for roughly half of China's imports in recent years.[19]

This is reflected in the sharp decline of imports of goods in machinery and equipment from economies, such as Japan, Korea, Taiwan and Singapore which are key suppliers of parts and components to China. As shown in Table 1, for the first quarter of 2009, while China's total export of products in machinery, vehicles and equipment fell by 22%, imports of such products dropped by 27%. The gap between export decline and import reduction is significantly larger for China's trade with its developing Asian neighbours. In the case of South Korea, China's export of goods in this category declined by 11% while import dropped by 28%, on a yearly basis. Similarly, the

---

[19] Sarah Y. Tong & Lim Tin Seng, *Sino-Asian economic integration and its impacts on intra-Asian trade.* EAI Working Paper no. 144.

Table 1. China's trade in machinery, vehicles and equipment (in million USD and %).

	China's import			China's export		
	Jan–Mar 09	Jan–Mar 08	% change	Jan–Mar 09	Jan–Mar 08	% change
China's Total	183,127	264,544	–31	245,639	305,971	–20
China's Trade in Machinery, Vehicles and Equipment	89,638	122,096	–27	127,156	162,378	–22
ASEAN5 + Vietnam						
Indonesia	354	503		1239	1674	
Malaysia	3689	4739		1996	2986	
Philippines	1887	5228		707	851	
Singapore	1949	2718		4002	5073	
Thailand	2548	3506		1353	1915	
Vietnam	123	154		1091	1424	
ASEAN-5 + Vietnam	10,550	16,848	–37	10,388	13,921	–25
US	7850	9112	–14	23,438	27,998	–16
EU	16,882	18,715	–10	26,432	35,871	–26
Japan	15,062	21,587	–30	8952	11,941	–25
S. Korea	11,693	16,330	–28	5844	6531	–11
Taiwan	9118	17,194	–47	2160	3211	–33

mainland's export to Taiwan decreased by 33% while import dropped by 47%. For the ASEAN-5 countries and Vietnam, the reduction was 25% and 37%, respectively.

While China's trade with all ASEAN members has been affected considerably, the impact varies across countries. Since the early 2000s, China has become an increasingly important export designation for most ASEAN countries.[20] In 2007, the shares of export to China in total export were close to or above 10% for all five of ASEAN's original members, including Thailand, Singapore, Indonesia, Malaysia and the Philippines. For the three new members, export to China also accounted for more 6.3%–7.5% of their total export in 2007 (Figures 8.1–8.5).

Moreover, these numbers may under estimate the full impact on ASEAN of a declining demand from China. First, in the last decade, intra-ASEAN trade has grown rapidly, accounting for around 25% of the total (Appendixes 1 and 2). China's 6%–10% market share for ASEAN's export is crucially important. Indeed, China is the third largest export destination for Laos, Myanmar, Singapore and Thailand, and the fourth largest export market for Indonesia, Malaysia, the Philippines and Vietnam.

Moreover, China's importance as an overseas market may also be under estimated as some exports to China via Hong Kong were recorded as exports to Hong Kong. According to Hong Kong statistics, a large portion of import from ASEAN to the territory is re-exported to the mainland, especially for Malaysia, Thailand and the Philippines.[21] As shown, export to Hong Kong made up a

---

[20] The only exceptions are Brunei, Cambodia and Vietnam. For Vietnam, the share of export to China in Vietnam's total export dropped to 7.5% in 2007 from 11% in 2004 when the country's export to the US expanded significantly by over 40%. For Brunei, the share of export to China in the country's total export fluctuated between 1.8% and 6.7%. China is not an import export market for Cambodia.

[21] In 2008, for example, total exports from Malaysia, Thailand, and the Philippines to Hong Kong were HKD 66 billion, 64 billion, and 48 billion, respectively. In the same year, re-export from Hong Kong to the mainland China originated from these three countries amounted to 44 billion, 30 billion and 25 billion Hong Kong dollars.

considerable portion of total export for several ASEAN members, including Singapore (11.5%), the Philippines (7.9%), Thailand (5.7%) and Malaysia (4.6%).

The third possible under estimation is based on the fact that as manufacturers in China often serve as the last point in the production chain and intra-ASEAN trade often forms part of the broader regional production network, a sharp drop in China's import demand would not only directly lead to declining export from individual ASEAN members, but also indirectly cause a severe contraction in intra-industry trade among ASEAN members, especially for the five original ASEAN members. Thus, both China-ASEAN and intra-ASEAN trade will shrink as a result of weaker demand from China.

Different ASEAN members have been affected differently by the on going economic slowdown and the resultant trade decline. The worst affected is the Philippines, which saw its export to China drop by over 60% in the first quarter of 2009. Indonesia, Thailand, Malaysia and Singapore also experience significant decline in their export to China, by 38%, 29%, 25% and 25% respectively. Vietnam is the least affected, where export to China decreased by 14% in the first quarter on a year-to-year basis (Figure 7).

For China-ASEAN trade, as well as intra-ASEAN trade, especially the five original ASEAN members (ASEAN5) and Vietnam, exports from ASEAN-5 to China had already achieved strong progress even before the region was devastated by the 1997 financial crisis since the 1980s. China's accession to the WTO in late 2001 ensures a more open world market for China's products. The implementation of the China-ASEAN tariff reduction plan[22] under the ASEAN-China Free Trade Agreement (ACFTA) further enhanced

---

If we assume a process and profit mark-up for Hong Kong traders of around 10%, we may conclude that more than half of Malaysia's and Thailand's exports were designated for mainland China (or close to half for the Philippines).

[22] Under the ACFTA, ASEAN countries and China will grant each other preferential tariff, and a zero tariff regime is envisioned for trade in goods and services between ASEAN and China by 2010 for the more advanced ASEAN members and 2015 for the less advanced members. From 20 July 2006, preferential rates have been applied to almost 7,000 items.

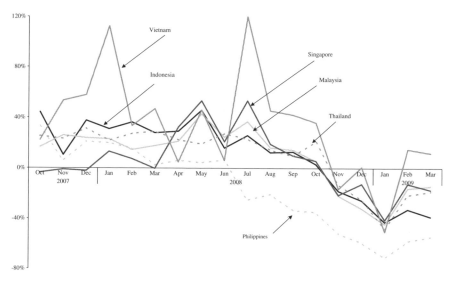

Source: China's Customs Statistics, various issues.

Fig. 7.   ASEAN'S export to China (% change).

trade between ASEAN and China. Thus, ASEAN's export to China accelerated and achieved double-digit export growth while import from China also increased rapidly.

Consequently, China has become a key export market and a principal source of imports for ASEAN countries. Bilateral trade experienced an eight-fold increase from US$22.4 billion in 1998 to US$183.4 billion in 2007. Share of exports to China in ASEAN's total export expanded from 3.2% in 1998 to 9.2% in 2007. More significantly, trade in machinery and related products constituted an important part of the China-ASEAN trade. For example, exports of electrical machinery and apparatus accounted for 54% of Malaysia's exports to China in 2008, and likewise, electrical and electronic equipment and parts plus machinery appliances accounted for 45% of Malaysia's import from China.[23]

As shown in Appendixes 3 and 4, the average annual growth rate of ASEAN's export to China was 24.1% between 1990 and 2007,

---

[23] "China market offers opportunities for exports". *New Straits Times*, 18 May 2009.

which was significantly higher than the 20.8% growth for China's total import during the same period. The share of China's import from ASEAN in China's total import doubled from 4.9% in 1990 to 9.8% in 2007. Likewise, China's export to ASEAN's grew by an average annual rate of 19.6% a year and its contribution to China's total export increased, albeit by a much smaller magnitude, from 7.8% in 1990 to 8.5% in 2007.

While China is becoming increasingly important for ASEAN's trade, the country is not the top trading partner for most ASEAN countries, which trade mostly with either a fellow ASEAN state or a developed country such as the US or Japan. To assess the impact of a sharp drop in China's trade, it is useful to examine China's bilateral trade relations with individual ASEAN members, especially the dynamics of their export to China.

For Indonesia, the top two export markets were Japan and the US in 2007, while Singapore and China ranked third and fourth. The share of export to China in Indonesia's total climbed to 8.8% in 2007 from around 4% in the late 1990s. Since the early 2000s, China's relative importance increased rapidly, while its total export also expanded sharply.[24] The development is similar for import. In 2007, China was the second largest source of import for Indonesia, after Singapore. While import from China made up less than 4% of Indonesia's total import for most of the 1990s, China's relative importance rose rapidly since the late 1990s to reach 5% in 1999 and to over 12% in 2007 (Figure 8.1).

For Malaysia, the top two export markets are the US and Singapore, followed by Japan and China. The share of export to China in Malaysia's total was 8.6% in 2007 from less than 3% in the late 1990s (Figure 8.2). For both Singapore (Figure 8.3) and Thailand (Figure 8.4), China was the fourth largest export market in 2007, accounting for about 10% of the two countries' total export, up from around 4% in the early 1990s. The Philippines (Figure 8.5) has

---

[24] Data for Figures 8.1–8.5 are from Asian Development Bank, "Key Indicators for Asia and the Pacific 2008".

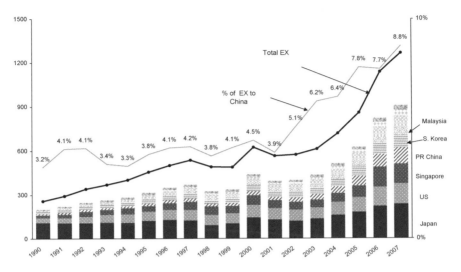

Note: The 7th to 10th largest export markets for Indonesia are India, Australia, Thailand and Germany.

Fig. 8.1.   Major export markets for Indonesia 1990–2007 (Billion US$ and %).

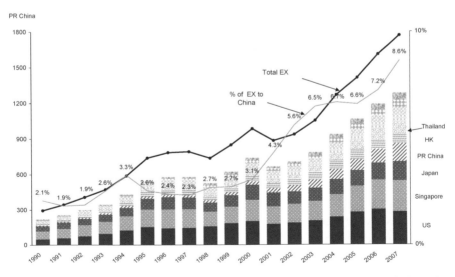

Note: The 7th to 10th largest export markets for Malaysia are S. Korea, the Netherlands, Australia and India.

Fig. 8.2.   Major export markets for Malaysia 1990–2007 (Billion US$ and %).

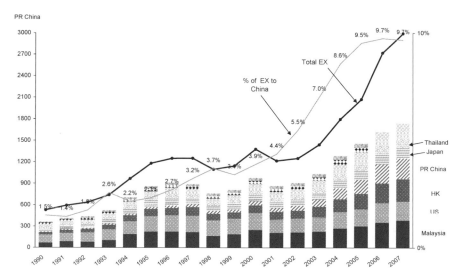

Note: The 7th to 10th largest export markets for Singapore are S. Korea, Australia, Germany and the Netherlands.

Fig. 8.3. Major export markets for Singapore 1990–2007 (Billion US$ and %).

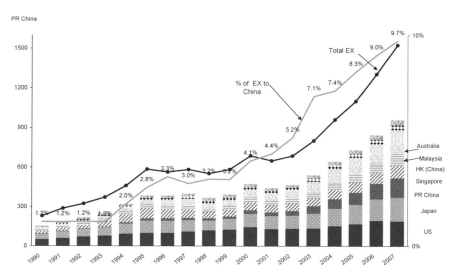

Note: The 8th to 10th largest export markets for Thailand are Indonesia, the United Kingdom and the Netherlands.

Fig. 8.4. Major export markets for Thailand 1990–2007 (Billion US$ and %).

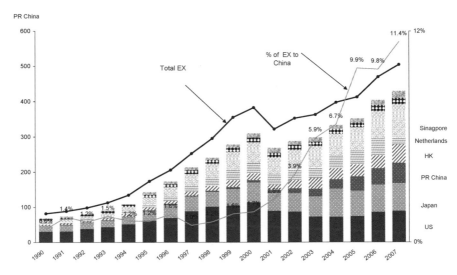

Note: The 7th to 10th largest export markets for the Philippines are Malaysia, Germany, S. Korea and Thailand.

Fig. 8.5.   Major export markets for the Philippines 1990–2007 (Billion US$ and %).

seen by far the most significant increase in exports to China. Up to 2000, export to China accounted for less than 2% of the country's total export. In 2007, the figure was 11.4%, making China the third largest export market, following the US and Japan.

It is evident that trade with China, export in particular, is essential to the recent trade development and growth of ASEAN. As both parties are important elements of a regional production network, China-ASEAN trade has a large portion of intra-industry trade, reflected by the dominance of trade in materials, parts and components. For example, over half of ASEAN's exports to China are products under the category of "machinery and mechanical appliances; electrical equipment; parts thereof sound recorders and reproducers, television image and sound recorders and reproducers, and parts of accessories of such articles" (accounting for 58% of the total in the first quarter of 2009). The shares are especially high for the Philippines (83%) and Malaysia (65%) in the same quarter.

Another 10% or so of China's import from ASEAN is for mineral products.

With declining global demand for Chinese exports, China's import from ASEAN has also decelerated. China's total import from ASEAN suffered a decline of US$3 billion, an 11% dropped since the fourth quarter in 2008. The biggest drop was in machinery, mechanical and electrical appliances and parts, which saw a 65% decrease.[25] With reference to Table 1, China's import of machinery, mechanical and electrical appliances and parts from ASEAN-5 and Vietnam suffered a −37% growth. Japan's trade in machinery with China remained low for 2009 Q1, resulting in a negative growth of 30% of China's import from Japan. Similarly, for South Korea and Taiwan, China's import suffered a negative growth of 28% and 47%, respectively.

As demand from China decreases, trade among ASEAN members are also affected considerably. Within ASEAN, trade flows registered 50% for both intra-regional trade and extra-regional trade. Unlike the EU, a highly integrated single market where intra-EU trade accounts for more than two-thirds of the total, ASEAN continues to depend heavily on extra-regional trade, which accounts for more than three quarters of the region's export. More importantly, even intra-ASEAN trade, which to some extent is part of a wider regional production chain, is vulnerable to the overall business climate outside the region.

In the 1990s, merchandise exports among ASEAN countries grew considerably, from US$29 billion to reach US$104 billion in 2000 (Appendix 1). With an average annual growth of 14% in intra-ASEAN export compared to an 11% annual growth for extra-ASEAN export, the share of intra-ASEAN export in total rose from 20% to 24% (Table 2). Between 2000 and 2007, intra-ASEAN export and extra-ASEAN export grew at about the same pace. This reflects ASEAN's relatively open approach to regionalism, where economic integration within the region has not been achieved at the expense of

---

[25] "China's exports, imports of new- and high-tech products slow down in 2008", Ministry of Commerce of the People's Republic of China, 21 Feb. 2009.

Table 2.   Merchandise exports and imports of ASEAN countries by destination, 1990–2007 (by value and percentage change) (billion dollar and percentage).

Origin	Destination	ASEAN	All other regions	World	Share (%)
Value of export					
ASEAN	1990	29	115	144	20
	2000	104	328	432	24
	2007	216	649	864	25
Annual percentage change					
ASEAN	2000–2007	11	10	10	
	2007	13	12	12	
Value of import					
ASEAN	1990	26	136	162	16
	2000	89	291	381	24
	2007	190	584	774	25
Annual percentage change					
ASEAN	2000–2007	11	10	11	
	2007	10	13	13	

Source: International Trade Statistics 2008, World Trade Organization.

excluding the rest of the world. At the same time, this also implies that ASEAN's trade is not self-sufficient and continues to be closely linked to trade development elsewhere, including the rest of Asia. The situation for intra-ASEAN merchandise import is quite similar, growing at about 13% a year in the 1990s and raising its share in total import from 16% in 1990 to 24% in 2000. Since 2000, intra-ASEAN import and extra-ASEAN import have grown at roughly the same pace.

To strengthen economic integration and enhance the overall competitiveness of the region, an ASEAN Free Trade Area (AFTA) was launched to promote trade by eliminating tariffs and nontariff barriers among ASEAN members. Several sub-regional development schemes were also initiated, such as the Brunei Darussalam-Indonesia-Malaysia-The Philippines East ASEAN Growth Area (BIMP-EAGA), the Mekong Basin Cooperation and the

Indonesia-Malaysia-Thailand Growth Triangle (IMT-GT). These sub-regional cooperation initiatives aim to narrow the development gap among members and increase intra-regional trade. Overall, the goal is to establish an ASEAN Economic Community (AEC) by 2015 to create a single market and production base and integrate ASEAN fully into the global economy.[26]

ASEAN economies have been affected significantly by the global economic downturn. Even in Indonesia, a country which is more dependent on domestic demand, economic growth also slowed down to a five-year low of 4.4% in the first quarter of 2009,[27] as export demand for some commodities, such as coal and chemicals, faltered. For ASEAN countries which are more export-reliant, such as Singapore, Malaysia, Thailand and the Philippines, the results are even gloomier. Singapore's economy contracted by 10.1% in the first quarter of 2009, while its total trade dropped by 28.5% on a yearly basis.[28] The decrease in trade was attributed to the sharp slowdown in global demand for both oil and non-oil trade, with the oil trade dragged down further by low prices. Singapore's key non-oil domestic exports (NODX) decreased by 26% in the first quarter of 2009 over

---

[26] The ASEAN Free Trade Area (AFTA) came into force on 1 Jan. 1993. To eliminate tariffs and nontariff barriers, ASEAN members also signed an agreement on the Common Effective Preferential Tariff (CEPT) Scheme on 28 Jan. 1992, which was subsequently updated on 31 Jan. 2003. AFTA is on track towards achieving its end goal of 2010 for ASEAN-6 and 2015 for the newer members, namely Cambodia, Laos, Myanmar and Vietnam (CLMV). For ASEAN-6, about 99% of tariff lines covered by the AFTA are at 0–5% and more than 60% of these items are already duty-free. For CLMV, about 88% of the products traded in the region are being liberalised under the AFTA. With regards to services, ASEAN signed the ASEAN Framework Agreement on Services (AFAS) in 1995. For details on ASEAN's sub-regional development initiatives and AEC, refer to ASEAN's webpage, http://www.aseansec.org.

[27] "Indonesia's Q1 GDP growth slows to 4.4 percent y/y", CNBC, 15 May 2009. http://www.cnbc.com/id/30757676.

[28] "2009 GDP Growth Forecast Maintained at −9.0 to −6.0 Per Cent" (Press Release), Ministry of Trade and Industry, Singapore, 21 May 2009. http://www.singstat.gov.sg/news/news/gdp1q2009.pdf.

the same period of 2008, due to lower shipments of electronic and non-electronic NODX.[29]

Thailand's GDP contracted by 7.1% in 1Q 2009, as compared to a decrease of 4.2% in 4Q 2008. Export of goods measured in US dollar decreased by 19.9%, whereas import dropped sharply by 38.3%.[30] Thailand's export contraction is mainly due to the decline in its export in gold and goods in high technology category such as vehicles, electrical appliances and computers.[31]

The Malaysian economy contracted by 6.2% (4Q 08: +0.1%) in the first quarter of 2009, largely due to the deterioration in external demand and a large inventory drawdown, particularly in the manufacturing and commodity sectors. Total exports declined by 20%, with a sharp contraction in manufactured exports (−18%) due to lower demand for both electronics and electrical and non-E&E products from major markets. In addition, commodity exports turned negative 23.8% (4Q 08: 6.1%), reflecting the impact of lower prices and weaker demand.[32]

For the Philippines, exports dropped by 30.9% on a year-to-year basis in March 2009. For the first quarter of 2009, export declined by 36.8% compared to that a year ago, with the biggest drop in electronic products and garments. Electronic products, which make up more than half of Philippine exports, fell to US$1.619 billion in March, a decline of 33.9% from the same period in 2008.[33]

---

[29] "Review Of 1Q 2009 Trade Performance and Outlook for 2009", IE Singapore Website, 1 Jun. 2009. http://www.iesingapore.gov.sg.

[30] "Gross Domestic Product: Q1 2009", Office of the National Economic and Social Development Board (Thailand), 25 May 2009, http://www.nesdb.go.th/Portals/0/eco_datas/account/qgdp/data1_09/detail_Eng.pdf.

[31] "Press Release on Economic and Monetary Conditions for March and the First Quarter of 2009", Bank of Thailand News, http://www.bot.or.th/Thai/PressAndSpeeches/Press/News2552/n1652e.pdf.

[32] "Overview of the Economic and Financial development in Malaysia in the first quarter of 2009", Bank Negara Malaysia, 27 May 2009. http://www.bnm.gov.my/view.php?dbIndex=0&website_id=1&id=702.

[33] "Philippine export dropped 30.9% in March", ASEAN Affairs, 13 May 2009. http://www.aseanaffairs.com/philippines_daily_news_updates/trade/philippine_export_drops_30_9_in_march.

In contrast, China's economy expanded by 6.1%[34] in Q1 2009 on a yearly basis, thanks to strong domestic demand. While exports continue to fall, on a yearly basis the pace has modified. As many of China's main trade partners, notably EU, the US and Japan are in recession, prospects of export resurgence remain gloomy. To boost exports, China raised export rebate on 3,800 items, including textiles and garments, iron and steel, nonferrous metals and petrochemicals in May 2009, the sixth increase since August 2008. Additional assistance is also provided including expanding export credit insurance and implementing tax breaks and more financial access for exporters.[35]

With economic stagnation and a gloomy outlook, there is a danger that countries may resort to protectionist measures. For example, Indonesia have called on its civil servants to buy local products to counter the effects of collapsed export demand apart from the import restriction imposed on 500 products in December 2008. Likewise, Malaysia banned the hiring of foreigners and retrenched 100,000 foreign workers in its manufacturing sector.[36]

Under the current gloomy global economic scenario, China is seen as one of the very few bright spots on ASEAN's trade horizon, which the region can tap on for its growth. With a population of 1.3 billion, China has become a magnet for exporters with its great potential market and, together with Japan and South Korea, is looked upon by ASEAN countries as an economic dynamo in the region.[37] China is expected to play a crucial role in addressing various issues confronting East and Southeast Asia, including further trade liberalisation, financial cooperation, and boosting demand within the region.

---

[34] "Gross Domestic Product (GDP) (First Quarter, 2009)", National Bureau of Statistics of China.

[35] "China's State Council rolls out more policy to boost exports", *Xinhua Net*, 27 May 2009. http://news.xinhuanet.com/english/2009-05/27/content_11445880.htm.

[36] Aekapol Chongvilaivan, "APEC's trade policy: Enhance transparency", *The Straits Times*, 19 May 2009.

[37] Ernesto Pernia, "China urged to further liberalizing trade", China Economic Net, 8 Apr. 2009. http://en.ce.cn/Business/Macro-economic/200904/08/t20090408_18740087.shtml.

It is thus necessary to accelerate the ASEAN+3 (China, Japan and South Korea) cooperation, also referred to as "10+1", to expand demand in the region and offset the waning consumption in the US and Western Europe.[38] To work closely with other Asian countries, China is pushing forward 10+1 (ASEAN plus China) and 10+3 co-operation, with the aim of establishing an Asian capital market and a 10+3 foreign exchange reserve pool. By fostering closer regional cooperation, Asian economies are expected to be among the first to walk out from the shadow of the financial crisis and China is an important force.[39]

Although trade between China and ASEAN has been greatly affected by the economic crisis, much has been done to improve their bilateral trade. Regional cooperation and collaboration between ASEAN and China via different engines aim to transform challenges of the economic crisis into opportunities for future growth and development. These include closer cooperation through the China-ASEAN Free Trade Agreement (CAFTA).

With these cooperation efforts, ASEAN is likely to replace Japan as China's third largest trade partner in the future, following the United States and EU. Trade between China and ASEAN rose by 14% to US$231.12 billion in 2008 despite the global economic crisis.[40] Much is attributed to the realisation of the CAFTA by 2010. By 2010, when the ACFTA is established, bilateral trade volume will

---

[38] "Experts: China should lead regional trade liberalization", *China Daily*, 8 Apr. 2009. http://www.chinadaily.com.cn/china/2009-04/08/content_7658043.htm. "Joint Media Statement of the 13th ASEAN Finance Ministers' Meeting", ASEAN website, 9 April 2009. http://www.aseansec.org/22483.htm.

[39] On 12 April 2009, China announced eight-point proposals on strengthening the China-ASEAN cooperation, include the signing of the China-ASEAN Investment Agreement; efforts to vigorously promote China-ASEAN infrastructure and inter-connectivity building; advancing ASEAN integration and regional cooperation; greater financial cooperation among East Asian countries, etc. ("China's Proposal on Enhancing Cooperation with ASEAN Appreciated", Embassy of the PR China in Indonesia, 22 Apr. 2009. http://id.china-embassy.org/eng/sgdt/t558491.htm).

[40] "ASEAN may become China's 3rd largest trade partner", *China Daily*, 10 Apr. 2009, http://www.chinadaily.com.cn/china/2009-04/10/content_7667964.htm.

amount to US$1.2 trillion, transforming the area into the world's third largest FTA by trade volume after those in North America and Europe.

EXTERNAL ENVIRONMENT AND GOVERNMENT POLICY MEASURES

Faced with a worsening external environment, China's trade prospects in 2009 are clouded by gloomy expectations of continued decline. With recessions in the United States and the EU still unfolding, the bulk of China's export is expected to fall further or stagnate. Trade between China and the developing markets is no escape from shocks of economic crisis either, as demand from emerging markets constitutes only a small portion of global demand and the prospects of these emerging economies have also deteriorated.

An emerging concern for China's prospects in trade arises from potential trade conflicts and possible increases in protectionist measures. As economic recession worldwide inevitably causes job losses and income decline, governments in both industrial and developing countries are under increasing pressure to resort to protectionism to safeguard the interest of their domestic industries. Although governments have vowed not to raise trade barriers at the G20 meeting in November 2008 and again in early 2009, many have since either announced or implemented measures that deem to obstruct trade, such as the well-publicised "Buy American" clauses passed by American legislatures, although they were watered down somewhat in February 2009.[41]

Even before Obama was sworn into office, there was growing worries that America might resort to protectionism to save domestic jobs. Indeed, since early 2009, there have been growing signs of protectionism in the United States, often in various obscure ways. For example, in the stimulus package passed by American legislature,

---

[41] David E. Sanger, "Senate Agrees to Dilute 'Buy America' Provisions", *The New York Times*, 4 Feb. 2009, http://www.nytimes.com.

there is a strong sense of "Buy American". On 10 March 2009, American legislature passed a law which in effect forbids all Chinese exports of poultry and meat to American market.[42]

Meanwhile, other major economies have all heightened their protectionist measures. WTO experts predict that new waves of protectionism will rise in global trade, involving practically all major economies. Countries with strong protectionist tradition, notably India, have promptly resorted to protectionism when global trade growth stagnated. Incidences of anti-dumping accusations worldwide have increased by 31%, according to trade expert Chad Brown.[43] The WTO added, however, that the world will avoid "an imminent descent into high-intensity protectionism" such as occurred during the Great Depression of the 1930s, thanks to trade treaties that cap tariffs on imports.

To prevent further fall in trade and especially the labour-intensive process trade, China's government at both the central and local levels have promptly reoriented its economic policy towards boosting trade and controlling unemployment. Take the PRD region, one of the worst hit in China, for example. The provincial government of Guangdong has pledged 200 million RMB in aid of export-process SMEs that are waddling in difficult financial situations.[44] Similarly in the YRD region where there is also a high concentration of export activities, local governments, including those of Shanghai, Jiangsu and Zhejiang, have met promptly and agreed to act in coordination to support export firms.

Almost immediately after the financial crisis made an impact on China's trade, especially of labour-intensive products, the Chinese government adjusted upward tax rebates for these exports, which was first lowered in September 2008 to encourage industrial upgrading.

---

[42] "China blasts 'discriminative' U.S. measure on Chinese poultry imports", *Xinhua News Agency*, 13 Mar. 2009, http://news.xinhuanet.com.

[43] "The nuts and bolts come apart", *The Economist*, 26 Mar. 2009, http://www.economist.com.

[44] http://www.fibre2fashion.com/news/textile-news/newsdetails.aspx?news_id=66796.

For the worst-hit sectors, the government implemented two rounds of additional tax rebates and other measures to ease the difficulties with effect from November 2008 and April 2009 respectively. The first round of export tax rebate was targeted at labour-intensive goods such as textile and some chemical products; the second round was introduced in accordance to the Key Industrial Development Strategy, covering mainly electronic appliances, chemical products and textiles.[45]

Facing a possible rise in protectionism in export markets, the Chinese government has reiterated its willingness and commitment to support free trade and strengthen closer economic ties with China's trading partners. Premier Wen Jiabao stated during his speech at Cambridge University in February 2009 that China would like to seek cooperation and mutual trust with all major world economies to combat global economic recession.[46] This stance is reaffirmed by President Hu Jintao in the G20 summit held in early April through his own speech and the joint agreement in strong support of free trade and international coordination.[47]

China's trade prospects in 2009 allow no room for optimism. This is in part due to the overall gloomy prospect of the global economy. The International Monetary Fund (IMF) recently estimated that the world's economic growth for 2009 to be only about 0.5% and the growth rates for most advanced economies are in the negative.[48] In addition, a recent report by the WTO estimates that world trade will

---

[45] PR China's Ministry of Finance, "Announcement on Raising the Rate of Tax Rebate for Export of Labor-intensive Goods (关于提高劳动密集型产品等商品增值税出口退税率的通知)", 17 Nov. 2008. http://szs.mof.gov.cn.

[46] "Full text of the Chinese Premier's speech at University of Cambridge", *Xinhua News Agency*, 3 Feb. 2009, http://news.xinhuanet.com.

[47] "Hu Jintao: to promote the diversification and the rationalization of the international monetary system (胡锦涛: 促进国际货币体系多元化 合理化)", *China Daily*, 3 Apr. 2009.http://www2.chinadaily.com.cn; "A list of the main outcome of G20 summit in London (G20 伦敦峰会主要成果一览)", 2 Apr. 2009, *China News Service*, http://news.sina.com.

[48] "IMF expects G-7 growth to grind to a halt", *The New York Times*, 8 Feb. 2009, http://www.iht.com.

decline by 9% in 2009, the biggest contraction since the Second World War.[49] This will no doubt put pressure on demand for China's export which in turn depresses China's demand for import, especially materials, parts and equipment for process trade. Such chain reaction will affect significantly trade relations between China and its regional trading partners, including those in Southeast Asia.

APPENDIX 1

Merchandise exports of ASEAN countries by destination, 1990–2007 (billion dollars and percentage).

| Origin | Destination | ASEAN | All other regions | | World |
			Total	Asia	
Value					
Indonesia	1990	3	23	15	26
	2000	11	54	28	65
	2007	23	95	55	118
Malaysia	1990	9	21	10	29
	2000	26	72	33	98
	2007	45	131	66	176
Philippines	1990	1	8	3	8
	2000	5	34	13	40
	2007	8	42	26	50
Singapore[a]	1990	14	39	15	53
	2000	42	96	45	138
	2007	95	204	122	299
Thailand	1990	3	20	7	23
	2000	13	56	23	69
	2007	33	120	59	153
ASEAN	1990	29	115	—	144
	2000	104	328	—	432
	2007	216	649	—	864

(*Continued*)

---

[49] "WTO sees 9% global trade decline in 2009 as recession strikes", WTO, 23 Mar. 2009, http://www.wto.org/english/news_e/pres09_e/pr554_e.htm.

(*Continued*)

Origin	Destination	ASEAN	All other regions		World
			Total	Asia	
Share					
Indonesia	2000	2.7	12.5	6.6	15.1
	2007	2.7	11.0	6.4	13.7
Malaysia	2000	6.0	16.7	7.6	22.7
	2007	5.2	15.1	7.6	20.4
Philippines	2000	1.3	7.9	3.1	9.2
	2007	0.9	4.9	3.0	5.8
Singapore[a]	2000	9.6	22.3	10.4	31.9
	2007	11.0	23.6	14.2	34.6
Thailand	2000	3.1	12.9	5.4	16.0
	2007	3.8	13.9	6.9	17.7
ASEAN	2000	24.0	76.0	—	100.0
	2007	25.0	75.0	—	100.0
Annual percentage change					
Indonesia	2000–2007	11	8	10	9
Malaysia	2000–2007	8	9	10	9
Philippines	2000–2007	6	3	10	3
Singapore[a]	2000–2007	13	11	15	12
Thailand	2000–2007	14	12	14	12
ASEAN	2000–2007	11	10	—	10

[a] Includes significant re-exports.
Source: International Trade Statistics 2008, World Trade Organization.

APPENDIX 2

Merchandise imports of ASEAN countries by origin, 1990–2007 (billion dollars and percentage).

Origin	Destination	ASEAN	All other regions		World
			Total	Asia	
Value					
Indonesia	1990	2	20	10	22
	2000	8	35	12	44
	2007	30	63	20	92

(*Continued*)

(*Continued*)

Origin	Destination	ASEAN	All other regions		World
			Total	Asia	
Malaysia	1990	6	24	12	29
	2000	20	62	34	82
	2007	37	110	64	147
Philippines	1990	1	12	5	13
	2000	5	32	15	37
	2007	13	45	26	58
Singapore[a]	1990	12	48	21	61
	2000	40	95	42	135
	2007	66	197	96	263
Thailand	1990	4	29	16	33
	2000	10	52	27	62
	2007	25	116	67	141
ASEAN	1990	26	136	—	162
	2000	89	291	—	381
	2007	190	584	—	774
Share					
Indonesia	2000	2.2	9.2	3.1	11.5
	2007	3.8	8.1	2.6	11.9
Malaysia	2000	5.2	16.4	8.9	21.5
	2007	4.8	14.2	8.2	19.0
Philippines	2000	1.4	8.3	3.8	9.7
	2007	1.7	5.8	3.3	7.5
Singapore[a]	2000	10.5	24.9	11.0	35.3
	2007	8.5	25.5	12.5	34.0
Thailand	2000	2.7	13.6	7.1	16.3
	2007	3.2	15.0	8.7	18.2
ASEAN	2000	23.5	76.5	—	100.0
	2007	24.5	75.5	—	100.0
Annual percentage change					
Indonesia	2000–2007	20	9	8	11
Malaysia	2000–2007	10	8	9	9
Philippines	2000–2007	14	5	8	7
Singapore[a]	2000–2007	7	11	13	10
Thailand	2000–2007	13	12	14	12
ASEAN	2000–2007	11	10	—	11

[a] Includes significant imports for re-export.
Source: International Trade Statistics 2008, World Trade Organization.

APPENDIX 3

China's export to ASEAN, 1990–2007 (USD million and %).

	Indonesia	Malaysia	Philippines	Singapore	Thailand	Vietnam	Laos	Myanmar	Brunei	China's total export	Share of ASEAN (%)	Growth (%)
1990	653	561	182	2095	1107	5	16	138	27	62,760	7.8	
1991	835	802	243	2227	1149	18	12	315	32	71,967	6.8	17.8
1992	752	975	184	2253	1219	32	31	285	50	85,621	6.6	2.6
1993	936	1096	182	2404	905	86	18	357	38	91,696	6.6	4.2
1994	1369	1363	320	2885	1388	144	20	406	49	120,869	7.5	31.9
1995	1495	1709	660	4042	2096	330	22	680	89	148,959	7.6	40.0
1996	1598	1876	653	4439	1953	329	23	573	92	151,168	7.5	3.7
1997	1518	2232	972	5668	2260	404	5	627	78	182,920	6.4	19.3
1998	906	1849	1199	4851	1822	515	20	586	10	183,746	7.1	−14.6
1999	1242	2139	1040	5697	2495	673	24	447	19	194,936	7.4	17.2
2000	2022	3237	786	7116	3377	1401	38	546	17	249,208	7.4	34.6
2001	1843	3804	975	7195	3711	1606	60	547	19	266,709	8.2	6.6
2002	2427	6157	1252	8869	4928	2159	60	797	23	325,744	7.6	35.0
2003	2957	7300	1798	11,073	6067	3139	108	999	65	438,364	8.0	25.6
2004	4101	10,339	2659	16,211	8182	4595	109	1029	50	593,358	8.0	41.1
2005	5843	13,177	2973	20,526	11,153	5900	116	1028	59	762,337	8.3	28.6
2006	10,403	15,887	3672	27,243	13,801	8215	186	1328	110	969,284	8.5	33.0
2007	13,966	18,746	7813	31,890	16,382	12,384	176	1834	111	1,219,690		27.8
Average annual growth (%) 1990–2007	19.7	22.9	24.8	17.4	17.2	59.1	15.2	16.5	8.7	19.1		19.9

Source: Asian Development Bank, *Key Indicators* 2007 and 2008.

APPENDIX 4

China's import from ASEAN (USD million and %).

	Indonesia	Malaysia	Philippines	Singapore	Thailand	Vietnam	Laos	Myanmar	Brunei	China's total import	China's Share of total ASEAN (%)	Growth (%)
1990	834	619	62	799	269	8	6	33	3	53,810	4.9	
1991	1191	639	128	858	335	19	2	96	4	63,877	5.1	24.2
1992	1396	772	114	1113	386	96	3	119	7	81,872	4.9	22.5
1993	1249	1204	167	1905	430	136	26	150	0	103,628	5.1	31.4
1994	1322	1933	164	2098	930	296	8	130	0	115,706	5.9	30.6
1995	1742	1889	209	2759	1642	362	9	136	0	132,164	6.6	27.1
1996	2057	1882	328	3395	1868	340	1	125	0	138,949	7.2	14.3
1997	2229	1852	244	4053	1744	474	0	67	0	142,163	7.5	6.7
1998	1832	1994	344	4065	1769	440	7	56	0	140,385	7.5	−1.5
1999	2009	2318	575	3920	1861	746	9	92	11	165,718	7.0	9.8
2000	2768	3028	663	5377	2806	1536	6	113	56	225,175	7.3	41.7
2001	2201	3821	793	5329	2863	1417	7	122	135	243,567	6.9	2.0
2002	2903	5253	1356	6863	3553	1518	9	124	220	295,440	7.4	30.6
2003	3803	6810	2145	10,134	5707	1883	10	154	295	412,836	7.5	41.9
2004	4605	8460	2653	15,392	7099	2899	11	188	203	561,422	7.4	34.2
2005	6662	9303	4077	19,752	9105	2916	23	249	189	660,218	7.9	25.9
2006	8746	11,646	14,620	26,513	11,806	2260	45	230	196	791,793	9.6	45.5
2007	11,077	15,263	19,625	28,927	14,834	2850	75	325	170	953,305	9.8	22.5
Annual growth (%) 1990–2007	16.4	20.7	40.3	23.5	26.6	41.5	16.2	14.3	26.3	18.4		23.3

Source: Asian Development Bank, Key Indicators 2007 and 2008.

Chapter 10

Sino-South Korean Bilateral Trade in the Current Economic Crisis

ZHOU Shengqi

Since the normalisation of formal diplomatic relations, China and South Korea have seen a surging development in bilateral trade. However, the increasing competition between "made-in-China" and "made-in-Korea" products both at home and in overseas markets is putting the brakes on the bilateral trade growth. The ongoing global financial and economic crisis makes things worse. From a long term and sustainable development perspective, endorsing a bilateral free trade agreement is probably a preferred choice for China and South Korea to achieve "win-win" results.

China established trade relations with South Korea as early as the mid-1970s. However, due to the lack of formal diplomatic relations, most of the trade was conducted indirectly via Hong Kong, thus limiting the trade volume.

The establishment of formal diplomatic relations in 1992 opened a new chapter for bilateral economic relations between China and South Korea and trade has surged since. In 2008, bilateral trade amounted to US$186 billion, up from only US$5 billion in 1992, reflecting an average annual growth of 28% (Figure 1), which was significantly higher than the 19% average annual growth for the national total over the same period.[1]

Meanwhile, the trade structure has also changed considerably. In the early 1990s, trade from China to South Korea was often in primary goods as well as labour-intensive products, while China imported technology-intensive and capital-intensive manufactured products from South Korea. In recent years, trade between the two countries is mostly in technology- and capital-intensive goods, (Appendix 2). Foreign invested enterprises (FIEs), especially those with investment from South Korea, played a critical role in the structural changes of the bilateral trade.

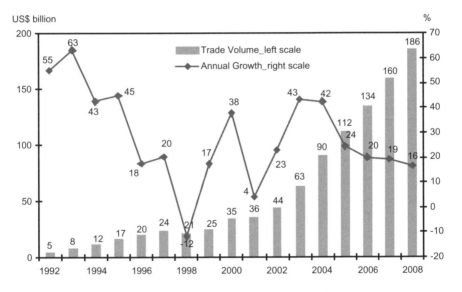

Source: General Administration of Customs of PRC: Customs Statistics.

Fig. 1.   China's trade with South Korea (1992–2008).

---

[1] Due to the lack of official statistics on bilateral trade in services, this chapter will focus on commodity trade between China and South Korea.

However, growth of Sino-South Korean trade has decelerated since 2005 due to a number of reasons, including trade frictions from anti-dumping measures put in place by both sides, food safety concerns, decreasing foreign direct investment (FDI) from South Korea to China and increasing divestment from China, as well as the uncertainty related to the signing of a bilateral agreement on free trade area (FTA) between the countries. The policy shift of the Lee Myung-bak administration to revitalise South Korea's relationships with the US and Japan and its efforts to build the country into a "global Korea" may further decelerate the bilateral trade growth dynamics.

The ongoing global economic crisis that spilled from the financial sector to the real economy in the second half of 2008 led to a rapid increase in unemployment, a steep fall in industrial production and consumer demand, and a sharp decline in world trade. This is especially true for China and South Korea, the two trade-driven economies. Both external and internal demand have weakened for both countries, implying that Sino-South Korean trade has entered its toughest phase since the normalisation of bilateral diplomatic relations. Since July 2008, the downward trend in bilateral trade growth has continued or even exacerbated throughout 2009 (Figure 2).

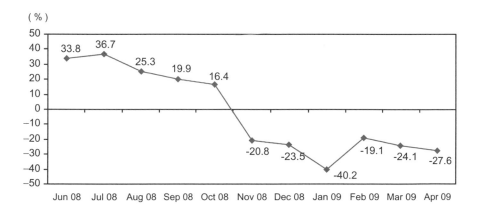

Source: General Administration of Customs of PRC: Customs Statistics.

Fig. 2. China-South Korea monthly trade growth (October 2008–April 2009).

DEVELOPMENT IN BILATERAL TRADE

Since the early 1990s, bilateral trade has grown rapidly in most years except for 1998 and 2001 and reached over 40% in some years. Between 1992 and 2008, China's total export to and import from South Korea grew by average annual rates of 25% and 35% respectively (Figure 3), much higher than those of China's overall export and import during the same period.[2]

In 2008, China's exports to and imports from South Korea amounted to US$73.9 billion and US$112.2 billion, a remarkable increase from US$2.4 billion and US$2.6 billion respectively in 1992 (Table 1). In 2003, China surpassed the US to become South Korea's largest trading partner, only 10 years after the normalisation of bilateral diplomatic ties. Meanwhile, China has consistently incurred trade deficit with South Korea as China's export to South Korea has grown slower than China's import from South Korea on average.

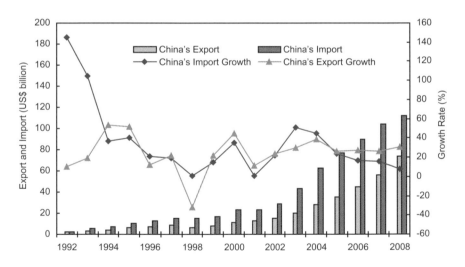

Source: Ministry of Commerce of PRC: Import and Export Statistics (1992–2008).

Fig. 3.   China's export to and import from South Korea (1992–2008).

---

[2] China's average annual increasing rate of export and import trade volume was 20% and 19%, respectively, during the period of 1992–2008 (calculated by the author based on data from the General Administration of Customs of PRC).

Table 1. China and South Korean bilateral trade development (1992–2008).

	1992 (A) (US$ billion)	2008 (B) (US$ billion)	(B)/(A)	Average annual growth rate (%)
China's export to South Korea	2.4	73.9	31	24.5
China's import from South Korea	2.6	112.2	43	35.3
China's trade balance	−0.2	−38.2	182	87.2

Source: Ministry of Commerce of PRC: Import and Export Statistics.

Table 2. Share of China-South Korea bilateral trade in South Korea's total trade (2004–2008).

	2004 (%)	2005 (%)	2006 (%)	2007 (%)	2008 (%)
China-South Korea bilateral trade/ South Korean total foreign trade	18.8	20.5	21.2	22.0	22.1
South Korea's export to China/ South Korea's total export	19.6	21.8	21.3	22.1	23.6
South Korea's import from China/ South Korea's total import	14.2	14.8	15.7	17.7	17.7

Source: KITA (Korea International Trade Association): Statistics — Trade by Country.

China has also been South Korea's largest exporting market since 2004, its number one source of imports since 2007, and its number one source of trade surplus since 2003 followed by the Hong Kong Special Administration Region (HKSAR) and the US. Table 2 shows the share of bilateral trade in South Korea's overall external trade from 2004 to 2008.

South Korea is also an important trading partner for China. Since 2003, South Korea has been China's sixth largest trading partner as well as its sixth largest exporting market after the US, EU, HKSAR, Japan and ASEAN. South Korea is also China's fourth largest source of imports since 2007, behind Japan, EU and ASEAN, and China's

Table 3. Share of China-South Korea bilateral trade in China's total trade (2004–2008).

	2004 (%)	2005 (%)	2006 (%)	2007 (%)	2008 (%)
China-South Korea bilateral trade/ China's total foreign trade	7.8	7.9	7.6	7.4	7.2
China's export to South Korea/ China's total export	4.7	4.6	4.6	4.6	5.1
China's import from South Korea/ China's total import	11.1	11.6	11.3	10.9	9.9

Source: Ministry of Commerce, China: Import and Export Statistics.

second largest source of trade deficit since 2001 after Chinese Taipei. Table 3 shows the share of Sino-South Korean trade in China's total trade.

Several key factors conducive to the rapid growth in bilateral trade include improving bilateral economic and political ties,[3] complementarities in economic structure between a more developed South Korea and a less developed China, as well as the large number of FIEs from Korea. By engaging in processing trade, these FIEs, together with their local affiliates, are crucial to China's recent trade expansion and integration of China into an expanding regional and global production network.[4] Moreover, it is generally acknowledged that proximities between the two societies, geographically and culturally

---

[3] From a "friendship and cooperative relationship" when China-South Korea bilateral diplomatic ties were normalised in 1992 to a "cooperative partnership for the 21 century" under former South Korean president Kim Dae Jung, then to a "comprehensive cooperative partnership" during the Roh Moo-hyun administration, and further to a "strategic cooperative partnership" announced during Lee Myung-bak's inaugural visit to Beijing as the new President of South Korea, political and economic relations between the two countries have not only deepened, but also broadened.

[4] John Wong, "China's Major Economic Challenge: Sustaining High Growth Whilst Fixing Its Growth Problems", in: *Interpreting China's Development*, edited by Wang Gangwu and John Wong, (Singapore: World Scientific, 2007), pp. 83–96.

(e.g. Confucian heritage[5]), as well as increased person-to-person exchanges,[6] are important to promoting bilateral trade.

As bilateral trade expands, the trade structure has also undertaken considerable changes. In the early 1990s, China's principal exports to South Korea were primary goods and labour-intensive products, while its major imports from South Korea centred on manufactured products and capital-intensive products. In 1993, for example, the top three Chinese exports to South Korea were textiles and textile articles (25%), vegetable products (19%) and mineral products (18%) which together accounted for 63% of China's total exports to South Korea. In turn, South Korea's top three exporting items to China were base metals (23%), machinery and electrical equipment (20%) and textiles and textile articles (18%) which made up 62% of South Korea's total export to China (Appendix 2).

The export trends have changed substantially over the past 15 years. While South Korea continues to export capital- and technology-intensive products to China, more of such products are also shipped in the opposite direction. In 2008, export of machinery and electrical equipment accounted for 36% of China's total exports to South Korea, up from 7% in 1993, while export of base metals accounted for 27% of the total, up from 6.5% in 1993. On the other hand, the export shares of textiles and textile articles and mineral products in China's total export to South Korea dipped to only 7% and 6% respectively, while vegetable products were no longer among China's top export items to South Korea (Appendix 2).

The technological level of China's export to South Korea has also increased significantly over the years. For China's export to

---

[5] "South Korea Views the Rise of China", The Woodrow Wilson International Center for Scholars, 9 Mar. 2009, http://www.wilsoncenter.org/ondemand.

[6] According to China's official statistics, nearly 4.8 million South Koreans visited China and more than two million Chinese visited South Korea in 2007. In addition, there are currently over 57,000 South Korean students studying in China, or a third of all foreign students in China. Likewise, more than 34,000 Chinese students are currently studying in South Korea, accounting for over half of all international students in South Korea according to ROK's Ministry of Education.

South Korea in the first quarter of 2008, the share of goods classified as high-tech and medium-tech products accounted for 30% and 16% of the total, up from 23% and 12% respectively in 2000. In turn, during the first quarter of 2008, South Korea's export of high-tech and medium-tech products to China accounted for a respective 31% and 45% of South Korea's total exports to China. Therefore, to a certain extent, the pattern of division of labour between the two countries has been gradually transformed from a pure "vertical division" to a "horizontal division",[7] or from "inter-industry trade" to "intra-industry trade".[8]

FIEs, especially those with investment from South Korea, contributed significantly to the structural changes in bilateral trade. These firms often import parts and components as well as necessary equipment from China's more developed neighbours especially Japan, South Korea and Taiwan, before they export finished, processed or assembled products to the developed markets. In addition, various policy initiatives have also grown in importance, such as higher tax rebate for capital- and technology-intensive exports, subsidy for research and development (R&D) of high-tech and new products, the implementation of "boosting trade with science and technology" (*kejixingmao*) strategy adopted by the Chinese government to encourage industrial upgrading and the adoption of more advanced technologies.

GROWING COMPETITION BETWEEN THE TWO COUNTRIES

More than 16 years of double-digit growth in bilateral trade and investment have resulted in South Korea's increasing dependence on

---

[7] Korea Institute of International Trade Research, China–South Korean Trade Structure Transferring from "vertical division" to "horizontal division", 8 Aug. 2008.
[8] Li Dun, "*Zhonghan chanyenei maoyi shizheng yanjiu*", (An Empirical Study on China-South Korea Intra-industry Trade), *International Trade Journal*, No 4, 2007, pp. 49–54.

exports to China. At the same time, Chinese firms are rapidly closing the technological gap with South Korean firms, including those in IT, electronics, automobile, shipbuilding and other high-tech industries that are crucial to South Korea's export earnings. In an eight-page "reference material" statement, the Ministry of Strategy and Finance of South Korea said that the Chinese industry has emerged as a strong rival in key export markets for products ranging from clothes to consumer electronics and China's rise as a global economic power is most likely to intensify competition between the two countries in domestic and overseas markets.[9]

According to an official report made by the Ministry of Commerce, Industry and Energy of South Korea, based on a survey of 300 South Korean companies in January 2006, 86% of respondents in the survey believed that the pace of technological development was faster in China than in South Korea. The report also believed that South Korea was less than three years ahead of China in developing appliances containing liquid crystal displays (LCDs) and had only a two-year lead in rechargeable batteries. The gap was even narrower with CDMA mobile phones and communication equipment manufacturing, while Korea's automobile parts makers have a three-to-eight year lead in the production of many key parts and systems, and the Korean lead in the shipbuilding sector was about a decade.[10] In addition, the Korea Development Bank (KDB) estimated in 2007 that China's technology had already reached 95% of South Korean levels and could surpass them in almost all areas in five years.[11]

---

[9] Yoo Choonsik, "South Korea Wary as China Rises to Economic Power", *Reuters*, 13 Apr. 2009, http://www.reuters.com/article/ousiv/idUSTRE53C13420090413.
[10] Scott Snyder, "Kim Jong-Il Pays Tribute to Beijing — in His Own Way", *Comparative Connections, A Quarterly E-Journal on East Asian Bilateral Relations*, CSIS (Center for Strategic & International Studies), 12 Apr. 2006, http://www.csis.org/pacfor/ccejournal.html, p. 6.
[11] Bruce Klingner, "South Korea's Uncertainty Path with China", *Korea Times*, 26 May 2008, http://www.koreatimes.co.kr/www/news/nation/.

Table 4.   Growth rate of China's and South Korea's exports to selected markets.

Year	China's exports			South Korea's exports		
	US (%)	Japan (%)	EU (%)	US (%)	Japan (%)	EU (%)
2005	30.4	14.3	34.1	−3.5	10.7	15.3
2006	24.9	9.1	26.6	4.5	10.4	5.0
2007	14.4	11.4	29.2	5.9	−0.6	13.7
2008	8.4	13.8	19.5	1.3	7.1	4.3

Source: Ministry of Commerce, China: Import and Export Statistics and Country Report.

Indeed, China's increasing competitiveness as a low-cost producer has already begun to challenge the leading position of South Korean exports in key markets and sectors. Since 2005, China's exports to the US, Japan and EU, the three most important markets for South Korean exports, have grown much faster than those of South Korea, which greatly eroded South Korea's market shares in these economies (Table 4). A recent survey, conducted by International Trade Research Institute of Korea International Trade Association (KITA), covering 597 South Korean exporters and 647 overseas buyers, revealed that "made-in-China" products are the chief competitor for "made-in-Korea" products (accounting for 60% of respondents) followed by Japanese products (15%), Taiwanese products (11%) and EU products (10%).[12]

Furthermore, South Korea has been increasingly concerned with the acceleration of imports from China, from a 26% increase in 2005 to a 31% increase in 2008, and the deceleration of exports to China, from a 23% increase in 2005 to a mere 8% increase in 2008 (Figure 3). According to a survey by the Hyundai Research Institute in 2007, Chinese goods accounted for over 35% of South Korea's

---

[12] Yonhap News Agency, "Haiwai maijia: hanguo chanpin zhuyao jingzheng duixiang shi zhongguo he dongnanya" (Oversea Buyers: S. Korean Firms' Major Competitors from China and Southeast Asia), 2 Apr. 2009, http://chinese.yonhapnews.co.kr/allheadlines/2009/04/02/.

imported consumer products, up from 10% in 1992. According to the same survey, the market shares of Chinese steel products and electronics increased from 4.03% and 0.92% in 1992, to 26.2% and 26.1% in 2006 respectively. The report concluded that South Korea had lost its competitiveness to Chinese goods since 2004.[13]

In the meantime, South Korea's exports to China have decreased faster than China's overall import demand in recent years. For instance, in 2008, China's import of electronics and machinery from South Korea grew by 6% and 5%, respectively, while China's total imports of the two products grew by 17% and 19%. More significantly, China's imports of automobile and parts from South Korea, South Korea's second largest export item, dropped by 3% in 2008, while total imports grew by 28%.[14]

A 2007 survey showed that half of the South Korean firms operating in China believed that they have lost their comparative advantages to their Chinese counterparts in the Chinese market.[15] These firms are also facing tougher challenges due to the Chinese government's application of much stricter criteria for overseas investments in China. These new criteria encourage projects involved in the transfer of high technology and effective management of environmental issues while restricting investment that focusses on processing or attempts to take advantage of China's low labour costs.

The increasing competitiveness of Chinese exports over South Korean products has led to new trade frictions in bilateral trade development, which is represented by product safety issues (mainly on food products), while trade disputes between the two countries, caused by

---

[13] Scott Snyder, "Teenage Angst: 15th Anniversary of Diplomatic Relations", *Comparative Connections, A Quarterly E-Journal on East Asian Bilateral Relations*, CSIS, 10 Oct. 2007, http://www.csis.org/pacfor/ccejournal.html, p. 2.

[14] KITA, "Impacts and Implication of Chinese Economic Hard Landing on Korean Economy", 2 Mar. 2009, http://www.kita.org/special report/.

[15] Scott Snyder, "Teenage Angst: 15th Anniversary of Diplomatic Relations".

anti-dumping measures on imports, have decreased with South Korea's recognition of China as a full market economy in November 2005.[16]

The rising product safety problem resulting from tainted imports has led to serious public health concerns in the two countries, especially within South Korea. South Korean consumers were concerned with food safety when Korea Food and Drug Administration (KFDA) announced in July 2005 that cancer-causing malachite green was detected in both live and frozen processed eels imported from China.

The problem was later highlighted by the "kimchi war" between the two countries. On 21 and 27 October 2005, KFDA announced twice that Chinese-made kimchi contained parasite eggs in levels higher than permitted, most likely in connection with Chinese use of animal manure as fertilisers for growing cabbage. The products in question were recalled and destroyed. The subsequent national outcry among South Korea consumers dried up kimchi imports and to some extent confirmed Chinese suspicions that the Korean press and protectionist farmers were trying to manipulate Chinese access to the Korea kimchi market. According to a report by the Korea Restaurant Association, over half of Korea's restaurants were serving kimchi made in China in the first half of 2005, as a cost-saving measure.[17]

On 24 October 2005, South Korea's Ministry of Foreign Affairs and Trade (MOFAT) revealed that the Chinese government had warned the South Korea embassy in Beijing that it might retaliate. Indeed, on 31 October 2005, the General Administration of Quality Supervision, Inspection and Quarantine of China (GAQSIQ) announced an import ban on 10 types of food product from major

---

[16] According to China's Ministry of Commerce, till now, China has adopted 30 anti-dumping measures against South Korean exports, mainly on petrochemical goods, iron and steel, among which there was only one case in 2007 and 2008 respectively. South Korea, in turn, has implemented 29 anti-dumping measures on imported Chinese items since 1992, centring on petrochemical goods, paper products, battery and household appliances; in 2008, there were only two cases, 14 Apr. 2009, http://www.cacs.gov.cn/cacs/anjian/searchresult.aspx.

[17] "Six-Party Success and China's Peninsular Diplomacy", Scott Snyder, *Comparative Connections, A Quarterly E-Journal on East Asian Bilateral Relations*, CSIS, 1 Oct. 2005, http://www.csis.org/pacfor/ccejournal.html, p. 6.

Korea manufacturers of kimchi, chili paste and meat barbeque sauces, claiming that the above Korea-made products contained parasite eggs.

Neither Beijing nor Seoul wanted the "kimchi war" to escalate. After several rounds of talk and consultation between government agencies, a mutual understanding was reached and the import bans on relevant products were removed by the end of 2005. However, the concern over product safety remains and the two countries further tightened their inspection of imported products, especially on food and cosmetics. In consequence, more imports were detected as containing harmful chemicals, heavy metals or parasites (Appendix 3).

China's tainted milk powder scandal in early 2008 further pushed for more stringent inspection of Chinese food product exports to South Korea. The KFDA conducted a nationwide inspection of imported foods, announcing in October 2008 of the detection of melamine in 10 Chinese dairy products. These findings prompted the immediate banning, recalling, or destroying of Chinese-made products suspected of containing melamine, the tightening of regulatory measures and the introduction of new standards for other substances such as heavy metals.[18]

While product safety issues have remained manageable, the undercurrents of negative public sentiments aroused in the recent bilateral trade frictions should not be ignored. Nationalistic sentiments connected to issues of national pride (such as the Olympic torch relay incident in Seoul[19]) and historical and territorial spats between the two countries may be stimulated (Appendix 4).

---

[18] Scott Snyder, "Sweet and Sour Aftertaste", *Comparative Connections, A Quarterly E-Journal on East Asian Bilateral Relations*, CSIS, 15 Jan. 2009, http://www.csis.org/pacfor/ccejournal.html, p. 6.

[19] The Olympic torch passed through Seoul on 27 April 2008 with the same tension and protests that accompanied torch relays in other cities around the world following the March riots in Tibet. A unique and controversial feature of the torch relay in Seoul was the simultaneous demonstrations by both pro-Tibet demonstrators and overseas Chinese students in South Korean universities. Reports that the Chinese students sparked violent clashes with other demonstrators enraged both the Chinese and the South Koreans.

Whether South Korea and China will resort to anti-dumping measures to protect home industries from competition remains to be seen.

BILATERAL TRADE IN ECONOMIC CRISIS

The US sub-prime-induced financial crisis has hit the real economy to become a global economic crisis. Trade-dependent economies like China and South Korea were hard hit by the contraction in trade finance and a slowdown in demand.

As a consequence of the deficit in credit and trade finance, the regional and global production has been experiencing a significant reduction, leading further to a contraction in the demand for exports. Since China and South Korea are closely linked to each other by regional and global production and supply chains, the contraction in production has negatively impacted on the bilateral trade.

Although China's export to and import from South Korea in 2008 rose 31% and 8% to US$74 billion and US$112 billion, respectively, the monthly export and import growth has already started to decline from July 2008. In November, the two countries began to see negative growth both in export and import. Into 2009, this downward slide has continued (Figure 4).

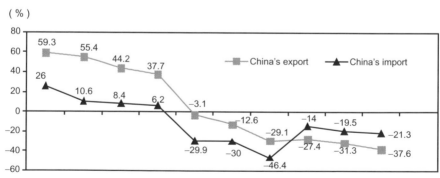

Source: General Administration of Customs of PRC: Monthly Statistics.

Fig. 4. Sino-South Korean monthly export and import growth (July 2008–April 2009).

To minimise the adverse impact of the economic crisis on bilateral trade, the two countries have adopted several proactive policies and measures. In November 2008, Beijing and Seoul agreed to strengthen bilateral cooperation on food safety amid escalating concerns about tainted imports by expanding information-sharing facilities between Chinese and South Korean health-related agencies. In December 2008, the central banks of China and South Korea, the People's Bank of China, and the Bank of Korea, signed a bilateral *yuan-won* swap deal (RMB 180 billion vs. 38 trillion *won*, or about US$ 27.2 billion).

Since November 2008, China has successively raised its export tax rebate for textiles and clothes from 11% to 16%, mechanical and electrical products from 11% and 13% to 17%, light industrial products from 5% to between 11% and 13%, and electronics and IT products from 14% to 17%. To stabilise processing trade, China has also relaxed limitations on restricted and prohibited products from January 2009, and further simplified import customs clearance for used mechanical and electronic equipment since April 2009.[20]

In the case of South Korea, to boost exports to China, the Ministry of Knowledge Economy has formulated various measures that do away with the reliance on China-based South Korean subsidiaries and multinational firms engaged in final assembling. These include expanding short-term export insurance by 30% to 20 trillion *won* (US$14.4 billion), increasing export credit guarantee from 8.2 billion *won* to 100 billion *won* (about US$700 million), holding a large-scale South Korean commodity fair in Beijing in September 2009, supporting South Korean participation in various exhibitions and fairs in China, organising four purchasing parties to China in 2009 and inviting Chinese enterprises to take part in the imports exhibition in May 2009, Seoul.[21]

---

[20] Ministry of Commerce of PRC, *Policy Release*, Nov. 2008–Apr. 2009, http://english.mofcom.gov.cn/policyrelease/policyrelease.html.

[21] Yonhap News Agency, *Measures to boost exports to China*, 18 Mar. 2009, http://english.yonhapnews.co.kr/business/.

In spite of the trade stimulative measures taken by the two countries, there is still no sign of improvement in bilateral trade development. It is most likely that China and South Korea will experience a big drop in bilateral trade in 2009 over the previous year. KITA predicted in a report in February 2009 that South Korean export to China will probably drop by 10% to 38% compared to that of last year.[22] The KDB also projected that Korean exports to China will decrease by 15% to 30% in 2009 year on year.[23] Beijing and Seoul will thus have to do a lot more in terms of reformulating more comprehensive and coordinative trade initiatives.

BILATERAL FTA: A PREFERRED CHOICE

Due in part to the slow progress in global multilateral trade talks such as the World Trade Organization (WTO)'s Doha Round, Regional Trade Arrangements (RTAs) have been increasingly favoured in recent years to promote trade and investment, strengthen industrial and technological cooperation, as well as settle disputes between trade partners. According to the WTO, by December 2008, some 421 RTAs have been formed and notified to the WTO, with Free Trade Agreements accounting for over 90%.[24]

As early as March 2005, China and South Korea had already launched a non-governmental joint feasibility study on a bilateral FTA based on the agreement reached between Chinese President Hu Jintao and former South Korean President, Roh Moo-hyun in APEC Leaders' Meetings in Chile in November 2004. After the completion of the non-governmental joint study in end 2006, the two countries

---

[22] KITA, "*Impacts and Implication of Chinese Economic Hard Landing on Korean Economy*", 2 Mar. 2009, http://www.kita.org/special report/.

[23] Yonhap News Agency, "*Chanye yinhang cheng jinnian dui zhongguo chukou zuiduo jiang jianshao 30%*" (KDB said exports to China will drop by 30% at most this year), 17 Feb. 2009, http://chinese.yonhapnews.co.kr/allheadlines/2009/02/17/.

[24] WTO, *Regional trade agreements*, 04 March 2009, http://www.wto.org/english/tratop_e/region_e/region_e.htm.

proceeded with another University-Industry-Government joint research on the bilateral FTA in 2007.

The joint research was reported to have a smooth run with nearly a dozen meetings and a series of special workshops being held in 2007 and 2008.[25] The initial findings show that the establishment of a China-Korean bilateral FTA would bring considerable mutual benefits to the two countries.[26]

Based on findings of the two joint studies, China has repeatedly called for initiating formal negotiations on the bilateral FTA and seems eager to further deepen its trade, investment and technology cooperation with South Korea. South Korea, on the other hand, seems increasingly uncomfortable with its growing trade dependence on Chinese market. It has expressed growing concerns that its agricultural, fishery, labour-intensive textile, and leather industries would be hit once the bilateral FTA is set up due to cut-rate competition from Chinese products.

However, the challenges of increasing competition and weak domestic as well as external demand necessitate a rethink of bilateral trade relations. To establish bilateral FTA is perhaps the best way forward for China and South Korea to achieve "win-win" results from a long term and sustainable trade development perspective for not only trade but also investment, technology and social comprehensive cooperation. To realise such a goal, much determination and efforts are required from the Beijing and Seoul governments.

---

[25] China Ministry of Commerce, "Zhonghan ziyoumaoyiqu shi gongying de xuanze", (Sino-South Korean FTA is a Win-Win Choice), 5 Jun. 2008, http://chinawto. mofcom.gov.cn/aarticle/.

[26] Scott Snyder, "Six-Party Success and China's Peninsular Diplomacy", *Comparative Connections, A Quarterly E-Journal on East Asian Bilateral Relations*, CSIS, 1 Oct. 2005, http://www.csis.org/pacfor/ccejournal.html, p. 6.

APPENDIX 1

A chronology of Sino-South Korean trade-related events (since 1990).

1990:

15 September | PRC and ROK open the first direct ferry line linking Weihai, China and Inchon, South Korea.

1991:

30 January | KOTRA (Korea Trade-Investment Promotion Agency) establishes representative office in Beijing, and CCOIC (China Chamber of International Commerce) opens representative office in Seoul.

1992:

24 August | PRC and ROK establish formal diplomatic relations. China opens its embassy in Seoul, and South Korea sets up its embassy in Beijing.

30 September | China and South Korea sign "PRC-ROK Trade Agreement", "PRC-ROK Mutual Investment Protection Agreement" and "Agreement on Establishing PRC-ROK Joint Committee for Economic, Trade and Technological Cooperation".

1993:

14 July | ROK establishes Consulate-General in Shanghai.

6 September | PRC sets up Consulate-General in Pusan.

1994:

26–29 March | ROK President Kim Young-sam visits China and holds summit meeting with PRC President Jiang Zemin. The two countries sign bilateral "Air Service Agreement" and "Agreement on Establishing PRC-ROK Industrial Cooperation Committee".

12 September | ROK sets up Consulate-General in Qingdao, China.

1995:

17 November | PRC President Jiang Zemin visits South Korea and holds summit meeting with ROK President Kim Young-sam in Seoul. Both countries sign "PRC-ROK Agreement on Economic Development and Cooperation Fund Loan".

1996:

24 November | PRC President Jiang Zemin meets ROK President Kim Young-sam on the sideline of the APEC informal summit meeting in Manila, the Philippines.

(Continued)

(Continued)

1997:

October	South Korea in financial crisis. China promises not to devalue RMB and provides financial help to the South Korean government.
24 November	PRC President Jiang Zemin meets ROC President Kim Young-sam on the sideline of the APEC informal summit meeting in Vancouver, Canada.

1998:

14 November	ROK President Kim Dae-jung visits China and holds talks with PRC President Jiang Zemin in Beijing. The two countries pledge to build a "Sino-South Korean cooperative partnership for the 21 century".

1999:

8 July	South Korean Consulate opens in Shenyang, China.
28 November	ROK President Kim Dae-jung holds talks on economic issues with PRC Premier Zhu Rongji on the sideline of ASEAN+3 meeting in Manila, the Philippines.

2000:

31 July	China and South Korea sign "Agreement on Garlic Trade".
3 August	ROK and PRC governments sign a fishing pact designed to clarify limits of commercial fishing areas.
22–17 October	China Premier Zhu Rongji arrives in Seoul for a state visit and attends the Asia-Europe Meeting (ASEM) in Seoul.

2001:

21 April	China and South Korea sign "Memorandum of Agreement on Garlic Trade", ending the garlic dispute between the two countries.
24 April	China and South Korea sign "Agreement on Establishing PRC-ROK Investment Cooperative Committee".
31 April	South Korean consulate-general opens in Guangzhou to assist Korean companies operating in the region and help to arrange personnel exchanges.
5 November	ROK President Kim, PRC Premier Zhu Rongji and Japanese Prime Minister Koizumi Junichiro agree to establish a trilateral forum among economic ministers to strengthen economic cooperation at the ASEAN+3 meeting in Brunei.

(Continued)

(*Continued*)

2002:

28–29 March	China and South Korea celebrate the 10th anniversary of establishing diplomatic relations and announce 2002 as the PRC-ROK national exchange year.
30 March	The Korea-China Investment Cooperation Committee is launched in Seoul under the chairmanship of the Korean and Chinese finance ministers.
24 August	PRC President Jiang Zemin and ROK President Kim Dae-jung exchange congratulations on the 10th anniversary of the normalisation of China-ROK relations.

2003:

24 March	KOTRA launches a special "China Business School" course designed to educate Korean businesses on specialised topics regarding trade and investment with China.
7–10 July	ROK President Roh Moo-hyun visits Beijing and Shanghai for his first set of meetings with China's President Hu Jintao, announcing plans to build "full-scale cooperative partnership".
5 October	The ROK Commerce Ministry announces that China has officially become Korea's No. 1 export destination, surpassing the US for the first time.

2004:

12 May	ROK and PRC begin bilateral negotiations on South Korea's opening of its rice market as required under the WTO's Uruguay Round.
15 May	Finance ministers of Japan, China, and South Korea meet on the sidelines of the Asian Development Bank meeting in Seoul to discuss enhanced regional financial cooperation measures, including establishment of currency swaps.
19 November	PRC President Hu Jintao meets with ROK President Roh Moo-hyun at the APEC meeting in Santiago, Chile to announce initiating nongovernmental possibility study on PRC-ROK bilateral FTA.
31 December	China becomes South Korean top trading partner.

(*Continued*)

(Continued)

2005:

16 March	PRC and ROK launch nongovernmental joint feasibility study on a bilateral Free Trade Area (FTA).
21–23 June	ROK PM Lee Hae-chan meets with PRC PM Wen Jiabao during a three-day visit to Beijing and signs a memorandum of understanding to jointly develop cutting-edge technology and facilitate cooperation in the field of neon-technology.
10 August	The People's Bank of China announces that the South Korean *won* is one of the components of the currency basket created as part of a new "managed float" mechanism for revaluing the *Yuan*.
17 November	PRC President Hu and ROK President Roh Moo-hyun hold summit meeting and address ROK National Assembly in Seoul. South Korea grants China market economy status. The two countries sign the Joint Research Report on Planning Medium- and Long-term Development of Economic and Trade Cooperation.

2006:

25–27 May	PRC Commerce Minister Bo Xilai meets counterpart ROK Commerce and Industry Minister Chung Sye-kyun to discuss trade issues.
28 August	South Korea and China agree to strengthen cooperation on technology development, standard settings, and device manufacturing at the sixth Korea-China economic ministerial meeting held in Seoul.
17 November	Chinese Minister of Commerce Bo Xilai and ROK Trade Minister Kim Hyun-chong agree to update a feasibility study on a China–South Korea FTA at government-industry-university level in early 2007.

2007:

7 February	China and South Korea sign an agreement to actively cooperate on establishing electronic governance systems.
13–16 June	The first Korea-China-Japan Industrial fair is held in Seoul to foster industrial and commercial exchange.

(Continued)

(Continued)

24 August	China and South Korea celebrate the 15th anniversary of the normalisation of relations between the ROK and the PRC.
7 September	PRC and ROK sign a revised Investment Promotion and Protection Agreement.
20 September	ROK opens new consulate general in Xi'an, China.

2008:

19 February	South Korea's Ministry of Commerce, Industry and Energy announces that the government has decided to implement measures to support South Korean investors in China who are planning to withdraw from the country.
27–30 May	ROK President Lee Myung-bak visits China and talks with PRC President Hu Jintao. They agree to forge a "strategic cooperative partnership" between the two countries.
25–26 August	PRC President Hu Jintao makes his second state visit to Seoul and holds talks with ROK President Lee Myung-bak. The two parties agree to further intensify cooperation in trade, investment, environment, IT, finance, logistics, energy and intellectual property, etc. and initiate employment licence labour service cooperation. The two parties also decide to open a bilateral economic cooperation website.
12 December	The People's Bank of China and the Bank of Korea finalise a US$27.2 billion *won-yuan* swap agreement.

2009:

7 March	Chinese Foreign Minister Yang Jiechi at China's annual parliamentary session calls for enhanced China-Japan-ROK cooperation on the financial crisis and says FTA negotiations with ROK should begin as early as possible.
1 April	PRC President Hu Jintao holds talks with ROK President Lee Myung-bak at the G-20 summit meeting in London, UK.

Source: Compiled by the author with information from Xinhua News Agency, China and Yonhap News Agency, South Korea.

APPENDIX 2

Top 10 trading items between China and South Korea (1993, 2008). (By the category of H.S code).

No.	1993 China's export	%	1993 S. Korea's export	%	2008 China's export	%	2008 S. Korea's export	%
1	Textiles and textile articles	25.3	Base metals and articles of base metal	23.4	Machinery, electrical equipment, television image and sound recorders	35.9	Machinery, electrical equipment, television image and sound recorders	38.9
2	Vegetable products	18.6	Machinery, electrical equipment, television image and sound recorders	20.2	Base metals and articles of base metal	26.6	Optical, photographic, and medical or surgery instruments	13.5
3	Mineral products	18.3	Textiles and textile articles	18.4	Textiles and textile articles	6.7	Products of the chemical or industries allied	12.3
4	Machinery, electrical equipment, television image and sound recorders	7.3	Plastics, rubber, and articles thereof	11.4	Mineral products	6.3	Mineral products	9.9

(*Continued*)

(Continued)

No.	1993 China's export	%	1993 S. Korea's export	%	2008 China's export	%	2008 S. Korea's export	%
5	Products of the chemical or industries allied	6.5	Leather, fur skins, and articles thereof	6.6	Products of the chemical or industries allied	6.0	Base metals and articles of base metal	8.4
6	Base metals and articles of base metal	6.5	Mineral products	6.4	Optical, photographic, and medical or surgery instruments	2.8	Plastics, rubber, and articles thereof	7.9
7	Prepared food stuffs, beverages, and tobacco	4.5	Products of the chemical or industries allied	6.3	Miscellaneous manufactured article	2.5	Transport equipment	3.8
8	Leather, fur skins, and articles thereof	2.8	Paper and articles thereof	3.0	Glassware and ceramic products	2.4	Textiles and textile articles	2.8
9	Wood and articles of wood	1.9	Transport equipments	1.2	Transport equipment	2.0	Paper and articles thereof	0.5
10	Footwear and headgear	1.9	Miscellaneous manufactured articles	0.9	Plastics, rubber, and articles thereof	1.8	Leather, fur skins, and articles thereof	0.4
Total		93.6		97.8		93.0		98.4

Source: Ministry of Commerce, China: Country Report.

APPENDIX 3

List of tainted products detected by South Korea or China (since 2005).

Date	Product	Contaminant	Producer
July 2005	Ginseng	Insecticide	South Korea
August 2005	Eel, carp, and goldfish	Malachite green	China
October 2005	Kimchi	Parasite eggs	China
October 2005	Kimchi, chili paste, and meat barbeque	Parasite	South Korea
February 2006	Sea sedge	Arsenic	South Korea
April 2006	Dried Hizikia fusiformis	Arsenic	South Korea
December 2006	Cultivated flatfish	Nitrofuran	China
July 2007	"QUA" brand T-shirt, dress	Azo dyes	South Korea
July 2007	Confectionary	Aluminium	China
August 2007	Oriental medicine	Lead, mercury, cadmium, and arsenic	China
September 2007	Sauces	Di-phthalate	China
October 2007	Seaweed meal	Lead	South Korea
February 2008	Infant formulas	Excessive copper	South Korea
March 2008	Dried purple seaweed	Arsenic	South Korea
April 2008	Pickled garlic	Sorbic acid	China
May 2008	Kimchi	Foreign matter	China
June 2008	Batatas decaisme	SO_2	China
September 2008	Béchamel	Excessive sorbic acid	South Korea
September 2008	Cracker sandwiches Tasty rice snack Rice soft cakes	Chemical melamine	China
October 2008	Dairy products	Chemical melamine	China
October 2008	Feed additives	Chemical melamine	China
October 2008	Kidney beans	Pesticide	China
November 2008	Cooked duck meat	Antibiotic	China
November 2008	Cod fillet	Parasite	South Korea
December 2008	Rice wine	Excessive manganese	South Korea
January 2009	Dried persimmon	Parasite	China
February 2009	"Laneige" brand eye cream "Dae Jang Geum" face pack	Excessive bacteria	South Korea

(Continued)

(Continued)

Date	Product	Contaminant	Producer
February 2009	"Nongshim" brand noodle	Excessive bacteria	South Korea
April 2009	"Lucean" brand cosmetics	Asbestos	South Korea
April 2009	Sanitary pad	Excessive bacteria	South Korea
April 2009	Beef products	Clenbuterol	China

Source: Compiled by the author based on inspection reports made by KFDA and GAQSIQ (General Administration of Quality Supervision, Inspection and Quarantine of China).

APPENDIX 4

Historical and Territorial Spats Between China and South Korea

The historical dispute between China and South Korea involves the conflict over the origins and legacy of the Goguryeo, an ancient kingdom (37 BC–668 AD) located mostly in the present day northeast China and North Korea. PRC claims that Goguryeo is part of China's history and a decision by the PRC Ministry of Foreign Affairs to delete all references to the history of Korea prior to 1948 caused a huge public backlash in ROK in 2004, and led for the first time to a harsh reassessment of China's rise and its implications for the Korean peninsula. After intensive negotiations, the two sides announced a five-point verbal agreement to prevent the Goguryeo issue from affecting other aspects of the bilateral relationship. The agreement includes a pledge by China to remove its claim to Goguryeo from Chinese history; however, this did not lead to an immediate restoration of Korean historical information on the Chinese Foreign Ministry website. The agreement was criticised by many South Koreans as a stopgap measure; as it is not binding on both sides, it has therefore limited capacity to prevent a recurrence of the issue. As expected, the conflict over the issue emerged again in 2006 when a report by the Chinese government-sponsored Centre of China's Borderland and

History and Geography Research claims that the Goguryeo kingdom is part of Chinese history. This claim was considered by Seoul as a violation of the 2004 agreement in which China has agreed to refrain from making public claims to the kingdom. Beijing on the other hand argued that the report was academic work and was unrelated to government claims. The recurrence of this issue illustrates ongoing sensitivities to China's and South Korea's activities regarding historical claims.

The territorial spat refers to the dispute over a submerged rock 4.6 m below sea level (at low tide) located in the East China Sea between South Korea and China, which South Korea considers the rock as lying within her Exclusive Economic Zone (EEZ) and China also declares it to lie within her EEZ. The territory was referred to by South Korea as "Ieodo" or "Parangdo", and as "Suyan" Rock by China. The rock is located 149 km to the southwest of Korea's Mara island and is 245 km from China's Tongdao island. The rock remains submerged at all times, but South Korea has built maritime scientific facilities and a helicopter landing pad on it to serve as a foundation for the Korean Ieodo Ocean Research Station. On 7 September 2006, China's State Oceanic Administration announced that Chinese planes had conducted surveillance activities of the Suyan Rock.

Source: Edited by the author with information from Chinese and South Korean media.

Chapter 11

Ascendance of China's New Left Amidst the Global Financial Crisis

BO Zhiyue and CHEN Gang

The tug of war between the two main schools of thought in China is tilted slightly in favour of the "New Left" (*xinzuopai*) instead of its rival, the neoliberals, due to the global financial and economic crisis triggered by the US subprime crisis. A strong advocate of the "state capacity" theory, the New Left attempts to use the state power to redress the problems of injustice, inequality, pollution and other negative effects of privatisation, marketisation and globalisation. As a result, there is a shift in the Chinese government's policy from the growth-above-all-else mantra towards a more European-style social-market paradigm that stresses social security, equity and environment protection.

GLOBAL FINANCIAL CRISIS AND NEOLIBERALISM IN CHINA

The global financial crisis has given the New Left in China another reason to celebrate. The US subprime-induced financial crisis has undermined the discourse dominance of the pro-market and efficiency-first Neoliberalism in China and provided an avenue for the "New Left"[1] (*xinzuopai*) to voice their concerns on social inequality, social security issues and market excesses. Shortly after its establishment in 1949, the People's Republic of China identified itself as a member of the socialist camp and included Marxism in the Constitution as the guidance for the socialist construction of the country. Twenty-eight years thereafter, in 1978, China bid farewell to socialism without completely abandoning socialist ideology in name, but few would have believed in its relevance in this increasingly capitalistic world. "Socialism as the real-life alternative to capitalism", as John Bellamy Foster, an editor of a socialist journal and an American professor, observed, "was pronounced eternally dead by the victors since it has been tried and had failed".[2]

Anglo-Saxon neoliberal thinking came into vogue in China's academia after Deng Xiaoping's "southern tour" (*nanxun*) in 1992 when he urged people to get rich. Sharing similar views with their peers in the Western world especially the United States, the Chinese neoliberal scholars and policy makers stress the economic benefit of unfettered markets, privatised state enterprises and a minimalist state role.

Nevertheless, in less than two decades since the fall of the Berlin Wall, the Wall Street collapsed. Beginning with the bursting of the housing bubble in the United States, the subprime mortgage crisis quickly spread to other developed and developing countries before evolving into the worst global economic crisis since the Great Depression (1929–1933). *"The U.S. financial system"*, a *Wall Street Journal* article, *vividly described the spread of the "American disease"* as resembling a patient in intensive care. In its fight with a disease that

---

[1] For a detailed discussion of the term, please refer to Li He: "China's New Left and Its Impact on Political Liberalization", (*EAI Background Brief No. 401*), 26 Aug. 2008.

[2] John Bellamy Foster, "The Renewing of Socialism: An Introduction", *Monthly Review* 57, no. 3 (July–August 2005), http://www.monthlyreview.org/0705jbf.htm.

is spreading, the body convulses, settles for a time and then convulses again. The illness seems to be overwhelming the self-healing tendencies of markets. The doctors in charge are resorting to ever-more invasive treatments and experimenting with remedies that have never before been applied.[3]

First, it was Bear Stearns, which was sold on 16 March 2008 to JP Morgan Chase for US$10 a share, sharply lower than its peak stock price of US$172; then it was Fannie Mae and Freddie Mac, which were both placed under the conservatorship of the Federal Housing Finance Agency (FHFA) on 7 September 2008; next it was Lehman Brothers, which filed on 15 September 2008 for Chapter 11 bankruptcy protection, marking the largest bankruptcy in the US history, followed by AIG (American International Group, Inc.), which on 22 September 2008 surrendered 79.9% of its equity for an injection of US$85 billion from the Federal Reserve of the United States.[4] Having enthusiastically advocated free market, free capital flow, free trade, and minimised governmental intervention that together, has commonly been denoted as "Washington Consensus",[5] the United States finally found that its hands-off model could cause disastrous consequences such as bursting of bubbles in property and securities markets as well as giving a big blow to the financial market and the real economy.

Is neoliberal capitalism coming to its end? Capitalism, Marx argued, like previous socio-economic systems, will produce internal tensions that will lead to its destruction. Who would have thought

---

[3] John Hilsentrath, Serena Ng, and Damian Paletta, "Worst Crisis Since '30s, With No End Yet In Sight", *Wall Street Journal*, 18 Sep. 2008, http://online.wsj.com/article/SB122169431617549947.html.

[4] Some of these companies had record earnings not long ago, in 2006 for instance. See Bradley Keoun and Yalman Onaran, "Record profits at Bear Stearns and Lehman Brothers", Bloomberg News, 15 Dec. 2006, http://www.iht.com/articles/2006/12/14/bloomberg/bxbank.php.

[5] For a detailed discussion of the term, see http://en.wikipedia.org/wiki/Washington_Consensus.

that Lehman Brothers, an American investment bank that had survived the American civil war, two world wars and the Cold War, would go broke in September 2008 after a history of 158 glorious years? Yet even the fiercest critic of capitalism drastically underestimated the self-destructive nature of the system. Marx envisioned that capitalism would be overthrown by the proletariat — the grave-diggers of capitalism. He did not expect, however, that some of the grave-diggers would turn out to be the bourgeoisie themselves.

A key architect of the US financial system who had used neoliberal ideology to manage interest rate policies, Alan Greenspan, former chairman of the United States Federal Reserve for more than 18 years, publicly admitted that the current financial crisis has uncovered a flaw in the way the free market system works and that has shocked him.[6] The largest-ever bailout actions taken by the US government to rescue major financial institutions undermined neoliberal beliefs in governmental nonintervention in the market.

The large-scale state interventions in the birthplace of neoliberalism make both the public and policy makers in China to rethink the neoliberal argument that China should complete its economic and social evolution that began under Deng Xiaoping by selling off state companies, shrinking the government, strictly enforcing property rights, and letting the market work its magic. The pro-market neoliberals in China in some ways tend to echo Ronald Reagan and Margaret Thatcher, though some also share the antidemocratic tendencies of Augusto Pinochet, the Chilean dictator who governed with an iron fist but also pushed the development of a vibrant market economy in the 1970s and 1980s.[7] As the crisis has forced the United States to resume the Keynesian path, Chinese

---

[6] Martin Crutsinger, "Greenspan says flaw in market system", AP News, 23 Oct. 2008, http://ap.google.com/article/ALeqM5jSSJzC1UNusL4eW21xsZ7HJcM8 WQD9409R0O4.

[7] Joseph Kahn, "Some Chinese See the Future, and It's Capitalist", *The New York Times*, 4 May 2002, http://query.nytimes.com/gst/fullpage.html?res=9E07EEDF 1E31F937A35756C0A9649C8B63&sec=&spon=&pagewanted=all.

pro-market neoliberals are expected to lose their credibility to some extent in both the government and academia.

Neoliberals have enthusiastically embraced China's integration with the world economy, especially after its accession to the World Trade Organization (WTO) in 2001. The global financial crisis has made Chinese decision makers and intellectuals pay more attention to the negative impacts of globalisation and privatisation, as well as the limits of the free market mechanism.

Although Marxism has been retained in the Constitution of the People's Republic of China as the guidance for socialist construction, few have believed in its relevance in this increasingly capitalistic country. After Deng Xiaoping advocated the establishment of a market economy after his 1992 "southern tour", the market-centric and efficiency-first-equity-second (效率优先，兼顾公平) "neoliberalism"[8] started to get a *de facto* upper hand in political and economic ideology.

Chinese neoliberals, featured by publicly active scholars such as Zhang Weiying (张维迎), Lin Yifu (林毅夫), Zhou Qiren (周其仁), He Weidong (贺卫东), Zhang Wenkui (张文魁), Zhao Xiao (赵晓), and Zhang Jun (张军), strongly advocated the shrinking of the state to facilitate a growing market economy. Such voices in favour of an unfettered and omnipotent market became more and more influential not only in the academia, but also in the government and media. Some neoliberals have become advisers to Chinese leaders, including Premier Zhu Rongji who supported a faster pace of reform and steered the country into the WTO in 2001. During Zhu's tenure as Chinese Premier, tens of millions of workers in the state-owned enterprises (SOEs) were laid off as a result of privatisation.

---

[8] China's neoliberalism is greatly influenced by its Anglo-Saxon cousin. Chinese neoliberals are reform advocators that support efficient market hypothesis, privatisation of state-owned enterprises and trade liberalisation. Deng Xiaoping's "let some get rich first, so others can get rich later" (让一部分人先富起来) is similar to Ronald Reagan's neo-liberal "trickle-down economics".

Neoliberalism had made significant impact upon the party-state's political ideology. In 2002, the "Three Represents",[9] a socio-political ideology credited to former CCP General Secretary Jiang Zemin, became a guiding ideology of the CCP at its 16th Party Congress. The ideology is important as it attempts to transform the CCP from a vanguard revolutionary party led by the proletariat to a ruling party representing the majority of the people. Neoliberals claimed it as a victory because it legitimised the inclusion of members of the business class, i.e. capitalists, into the Party.

Neoliberal thinking continues to influence China's reform even after Hu Jintao and Wen Jiabao replaced Jiang and Zhu as top leaders. Even Hu-Wen's left-leaning plan on the construction of "Harmonious Society" does not mean the neglect of the wealthy or the abandoning of pro-market and pro-business approaches. A significant political development in the neoliberal direction was the passage of a controversial law guaranteeing private property rights in 2007. It enshrines the rights of private individuals to property ownership in the PRC, taking an important step in the country's slow metamorphosis from Leninist monolith into a uniquely Chinese amalgam of socialist ideology and neoliberal capitalism.

To further liberalise the rural land market, the CCP in a high-profile document in 2008 underscored the once-ignored legal rights of farmers to lease their contracted farmland or transfer their land-use right. After a four-day meeting from 9 to 12 October 2008, the Third Plenum of the Seventeenth Central Committee of the CCP introduced the boldest reform measure in 30 years. Hailed as the third land reform in the Chinese media,[10] the Third Plenum's resolution, "The Decision on Major Issues Concerning the Advancement of Rural Reform and Development", stipulated that farmers are allowed

---

[9] The official statement of the "Three Represents" ideology stipulates that the Party must always represent the requirements of the development of China's advanced productive forces, the orientation of the development of China's advanced culture and the fundamental interests of the overwhelming majority of the people in China.

[10] http://news.xinhuanet.com/politics/2008-10/13/content_10184754.htm.

to sublease, rent, swap, transfer or use as shares their contracted land-use rights as long as it is done in accordance with the law and in accordance with the principle of valuntarism and of farmers being appropriately compensated.[11] For the first time since the agricultural collectivisation of the 1950s, the CCP has allowed farmers to transfer their land-use rights. "Transfer" (流转) is the *de facto* substitution for the more sensitive term "trade" (买卖, buy and sell) in the "land problem"[12] faced by the Chinese authorities because they still deny private land ownership.

The CCP document, therefore, obviously is an encouragement and a clear signal by the Party to boost the land-right trade. Apparently, under the guidance of "Marxism", China has taken a solid step down the path of liberal capitalism. Put it in a Chinese saying, this is "flashing the left-turn signal and actually making a right-turn" ("打左灯, 向右转") — a typical Chinese characteristic.

Land policy has been an essential part of China's overall economic policy since the establishment of the People's Republic of China in 1949. Land policies before 1978 were influenced deeply by the socialist ideology while policy initiatives thereafter have largely been guided by economic and development considerations. Indeed, "China's changing land policies are a mirror image of the changing ideological orientation of the CCP itself".[13]

For Chinese policy makers influenced by Neoliberalism, one central task is to reconcile the need to protect the new wealth of the few from the demand for equality from the masses. The state goes from

---

[11] http://news.xinhuanet.com/newscenter/2008-10/19/content_10218932_1.htm.

[12] The authorities were having a "land problem" or 土地问题 when the lack of clear-cut property rights provisions and effective land use regulations and controls together with ineffectual policy implementation, particularly at local levels, contributed to a lot of "misuse of land". For details of the problem, please refer to John Wong and Liang Ruobing, "Changing Land Policies: Ideology and Realities", in *China into the Hu-Wen Era: Policy Initiatives and Challenges,* edited by John Wong and Lai Hongyi, (Singapore: World Scientific, 2006), pp. 301–303.

[13] John Wong and Liang Ruobing, "Changing Land Policies: Ideology and Realities", in Wong and Lai (eds) 2006.

owning assets on behalf of the people to insisting that bureaucrats and well-connected entrepreneurs have a right to profit from those assets.[14] Chinese neoliberals argue that the state should enforce political unity, but protect economic opportunism.

Neoliberals attributed China's years of double-digit economic growth rates and inflow of tremendous foreign investment to their advocacy of free markets and free trade. Neoliberal officials and scholars nonetheless have begun to encounter sustained opposition from fellow reformers on issues like the expanding income gap, environmental degradation and when the over-speculation in property and stock market becomes too serious.

Chinese neoliberals are heavily influenced by the right-wing political and economic philosophy of Ronald Reagan and Margaret Thatcher that emphasised minimum state intervention and maximum free market in Britain and the United States in the 1980s. Works by thinkers closely associated with Thatcherism such as Keith Joseph and Enoch Powell and by liberal economists such as Friedrich Hayek and Milton Friedman have a large Chinese following.

NEW LEFT IN CHINA

Like in other industrialising countries, intellectuals in China have focussed on issues similar to their counterparts in Europe and the United States. Their concern is not whether China should become capitalist, but what kind of capitalism it should have. Like the neoliberals, many of those in the New Left are Western-educated, and they reject communism. But the loose grouping of intellectuals questions the dogma of capitalism. They agree that there is no sure formula for development but disagree on the kind of bureaucratic capitalism that dominates the country today.

---

[14] Joseph Kahn, "Some Chinese See the Future, and It's Capitalist", *The New York Times*, 4 May 2002.

The New Left emphasises state power as the authority to redress the problems of injustice and other negative effects of privatisation, marketisation and globalisation.[15] Xudong Zhang, an associate professor of comparative literature at New York University, compiled a volume of essays, *Whither China? Intellectual Politics in Contemporary China*[16] that explored the conflict between the two camps. Zhang and several of the scholars who contributed essays, including Cui Zhiyuan (崔之元), Wang Hui (汪晖), Wang Shaoguang (王绍光), and Gan Yang (甘阳),[17] were later recognised as representatives of the New Left camp.

The "state capacity" theory, formulated by Wang Shaoguang, then a political scientist at Yale University, and his China-based collaborator, Hu Angang (胡鞍钢), argued for a strong central government to regulate the market and curb its tendency towards regional protectionism and fragmentation and monopoly and unequal competition.[18] More importantly, Wang and Hu's argument maintained that a capable state should maintain credible national defence, a socially just distribution of wealth and the nation's moral and political unity.[18]

As one of the first systematic considerations of the state-market interrelationship in the Chinese context and one of the early responses to the negative impact of neoliberal policies, Wang and Hu's argument received intensive attention not only from intellectuals, but also from top decision makers in Beijing. An economics professor at Tsinghua University, Hu Angang became an influential advisor to former Premier Zhu Rongji and other leaders in

---

[15] Li He, "China's New Left and Its Impact on Political Liberalization", (*EAI Background Brief No. 401*), 26 Aug. 2008, p. 1.

[16] Xudong Zhang (ed.) *Whither China? Intellectual Politics in Contemporary China* (Durham: Duke University Press), 2001.

[17] For details of these key figures of China's New Left, please refer to Li He: "China's New Left and Its Impact on Political Liberalization", (*EAI Background Brief No. 401*), 26 Aug. 2008, p. 4.

[18] Xudong Zhang (ed.) *Whither China?: Intellectual Politics in Contemporary China* (Durham: Duke University Press), 2001, p. 56.

Zhongnanhai, and his policy reports have often been circulated among senior CCP officials for decision-making reference.[19]

Unlike the neoliberal argument that it is in the Chinese interests to embrace "globalisation" in spite of some negative effects, the New Left holds that China's involvement in globalisation has resulted in an unchecked spread of capitalism in China, and China's social problems are nothing but "Western epidemic" or "market epidemic" as experienced by the capitalist countries.[20]

While emphasising economic justice, not economic growth at any price, the New Left launched heated debates with neoliberals over property ownership reform. Questioning the legitimacy of privatising medium- and large-sized SOEs such as Haier, TCL and Kelon, Lang Xianping (郎咸平), Professor of Finance at the Chinese University of Hong Kong, provided accounting evidences to the public to show the huge losses and drain on state assets during the management buyout (MBO) process.

Due to Lang's public exposure of privatisation details of Guangdong Kelon Electrical Holding Co, the country's biggest refrigerator maker, Gu Chujun (顾雏军), former chairman of Kelon, was sentenced to 12 years in jail for embezzlement and making false statements about the registered capital of his Greencool company in order to acquire Kelon. The State-owned Assets Supervision and Administration Commission (SASAC) and China Security Regulatory Commission since then have started to take a much more cautious stance in approving MBO applications.

One major difference between the New Left and neoliberals lies on the priority of equality or efficiency. Neoliberals believe even if privatisation may lead to social inequality, such economic transition would promote efficiency and entrepreneurship. The New Left

---

[19] Wang and Hu's report on state capacity prompted the taxation reform of January 1994, which split revenues and responsibility between the central and provincial authorities.

[20] Li He: "China's New Left and Its Impact on Political Liberalization", (*EAI Background Brief No. 401*), 26 Aug. 2008, p. 7.

school, however, refuses to sacrifice equality for efficiency, fearing that the expanding income gap might sooner or later cause social turmoil and wipe out all the economic gains of the reform.

What is embarrassing to the New Left is that although they advocate the enhancement of state power, the government itself has been leaning to the neoliberals in terms of reform and open-door policies. Another inconvenient truth for the New Left is that despite the recent expansion of state power due to soaring government revenue and frequent macro-control policies, many problems such as income gap, pollution, housing, medical care and education have not been effectively solved. Neoliberals are criticising the New Left for beefing up state power under current Chinese political and cultural circumstances which could only end up with more corruption and waste.

DEBATE ON "UNIVERSAL VALUES"

For neoliberals in China, the breakout of the global financial crisis was ill-timed. Less than half a year after Premier Wen Jiabao (温家宝) published an article in the *People's Daily* (人民日报) championing democracy, human rights, rule of law and freedom as universal values, the subprime mortgage crisis began with the European Central Bank and the United States Federal Reserve injecting US$90 billion into jittery financial markets.[21] A native of Tianjin, Wen (September 15, 1942) became part of the inner circle of the Party in 1985 when he was appointed deputy director of the General Office of the Central Committee of the CCP at the age of 43. Seven months later, he moved on to become the director of the General Office and in that capacity worked with three general secretaries of the CCP (Hu Yaobang (胡耀邦), Zhao Ziyang (赵紫阳), and Jiang Zemin (江泽民)).[22]

---

[21] Larry Elliott, "Credit crisis — how it all began", *The Guardian*, 5 Aug. 2008, http://www.guardian.co.uk/business/2008/aug/05/northernrock.banking.

[22] For Wen Jiabao's bio, see http://www.gov.cn/gjjg/2008-03/16/content_784746.htm.

Wen is considered one of the liberal leaders in China because of his prior association with Zhao Ziyang, the reformist premier and general secretary of the CCP. When Zhao went to the Tiananmen Square on 19 May 1989 to see students on hunger strike, Wen Jiabao was at his side. But when Zhao was purged, Wen stayed on in the CCP leadership. The third-ranking Politburo Standing Committee member since November 2002, Wen was made China's premier in March 2003. In 2007, he published an article in the 27 February issue of the *People's Daily*, the mouthpiece of the CCP, using his own name, something extraordinary in Chinese politics.

In the article, titled "On a few issues concerning the historical task of the primary stage of socialism and our foreign policy", Wen espoused democracy, rule of law, freedom and human rights as universal values of mankind. He said, "Science, democracy, rule of law, freedom and human rights are not unique to capitalism. Instead, they are values that human beings have commonly pursued and civilisation achievements that human beings collectively created in their long history".[23] The difference, as Wen put it, lies in the way these values are realised. "But in different historical periods", Wen continued, "different countries may adopt different forms and take different paths to realise these values; there is no uniform model. The diversity of world civilisation is an objective reality, which is not dependent on the subjective will of the people".[23]

Four months earlier, on 23 October 2006, *Beijing Daily* published an article, "Democracy is a good thing", by Yu Keping (俞可平) (born in July 1959), the deputy director of the Central Translation Bureau and a liberal scholar. Yu argued that democracy is a good thing not just for specific persons or certain officials, but for the entire nation and its broad masses of people.

"Simply put", he said, "for those officials who care more about their own interests, democracy is not a good thing; in fact, it is a troublesome thing, even a bad thing. Just think, under conditions of democratic rule, officials must be elected by the citizens and they

---

[23] *Remin Ribao*, 27 Feb. 2007, p. 2.

must gain the endorsement and support of the majority of the people; their powers will be curtailed by the citizens, they cannot do whatever they want, they have to sit down across the people and negotiate. Just these two points alone already make many people dislike it. Therefore, democratic politics will not operate on their own; they require the people themselves and the government officials who represent the interests of the people to promote and implement".[24]

For China, a modernising developing country, democratisation is even more important in Yu's view. "For us", he said, "democracy is all the more so a good thing, and it is all the more so essential".[24] This is because there is no socialism without democracy and there is no modernisation without democracy. Although Yu's article only represented a scholarly opinion, Wen's piece was an indication of the rise of liberalism in Chinese politics. It was hopeful that the Seventeenth Party Congress would accelerate the pace of democratisation in China.

Most recently, the New Left waged fresh attacks on "universal values" that US neoliberals have been advocating for years. Chen Kuiyuan (陈奎元), the head of the Chinese Academy of Social Sciences (CASS) (中国社会科学院), is the most prominent. In an internal speech at a seminar of the CASS on 26 July 2008, Chen pointed out that in less than 20 years since the end of the Cold War, the myth that the United States is the only superpower in the world has evaporated in economic, political and military areas. Its ideological and cultural hegemony cannot be sustained indefinitely. "We need to establish our national self-esteem and self-confidence", he said. "We should not have any blind worship and should not enshrine the West's values as so-called universal values. In other words, we should not relegate the values of our Party and nation to the status of inferior values".[25]

---

[24] Yu Keping, "Minzhu Shige Haodongxi" ("Democracy is a good thing"), 28 Dec. 2006, http://theory.people.com.cn/GB/49150/49152/5224247.html.
[25] http://www.cass.net.cn/file/20080902197040.html.

Chen charged that some people were dancing to the tune of the West by championing the "universal values" in China. "In the past, Christianity promoted its doctrines as universal values. At present, the West is dominant in discourse, claiming their values such as 'democracy', 'human rights', and free market economic theory as universal values. Some people in our country have also danced to their tunes, advocating adopting these 'universal values' for China".[25]

After Chen's speech was published in the journal of the CASS (中国社会科学院院报) on 2 September 2008, two more articles attacking universal values were released. One was written by Feng Yuzhang (冯虞章), a professor of Qinghua University, and the other was written by Zhang Weiwei (张维为), Senior Research Fellow at Modern China Research Centre, Geneva, Switzerland and Guest Professor at Fudan University and Tsinghua University, China.

Feng's article was originally published in the *Studies of Marxism* (马克思主义研究).[26] It appeared in the *People's Daily* on 10 September 2008. Titled "How to see through the theory of so-called universal values", the article argued that the universal values were simply a ploy of the West to overthrow China's socialist system.[27] What is quite remarkable about the article is that it employed the class analysis method, common among Marxist scholars in the heyday of the Cultural Revolution. Originally published in his personal blog on 10 July 2008,[28] Zhang's article titled "the origins of 'universal values'" was printed in the 15 September 2008 issue of *Study Times* (学习时报), a publication of the Central Party School (中共中央党校).

POLICY AND IDEOLOGICAL IMPLICATIONS

The US-originated global financial crisis provides a good opportunity for the New Left to counterattack neoliberalism. The large-scale

---

[26] http://chinaps.cass.cn/readcontent.asp?id=8680.

[27] *Renmin Ribao*, 10 Sep. 2008, p. 9.

[28] http://blog.tianya.cn/blogger/post_show.asp?idWriter=0&Key=0&BlogID=1137332&PostID=14521753.

bailout actions taken by the US and other Western governments echo the New Left's demand for enhanced state capacity and more intervention and supervision over the market. Neoliberals in China have advocated that the government should take a hands-off stance towards the market, be it bullish or bearish. This argument, however, has lost credibility due to the largest-ever state intervention in the Western world.

There has been an obvious shift in the Chinese government's policy making from the growth-above-all-else mantra towards a more European-style paradigm that stresses social security, equity and environment protection, with huge spending on pension, medical care, education and environment in the coming years. To expand domestic demand, the Chinese government not only announced a four trillion *yuan* Keynesian-style stimulus programme but also approved a long-awaited plan to provide universal health care in three years. According to the health care reform plan, the government will spend 850 billion *yuan* (US$124.26 billion) in the next three years to provide accessible and affordable health care to the country's 1.3 billion people. With this reform, the government is the main bearer of medical expenses by the people by 2011. Though modest by comparison, China's health care plan goes in the direction of what has long been considered a fundamental right in Europe.[29] According to a blueprint for health care over the next decade unveiled by the Chinese government in April 2009, by 2020 the world's most populous country will have a basic health care system that can provide "safe, effective, convenient and affordable" health services to urban and rural residents. The core principle of the reform is to provide basic health care as a "public service" to the people which requires much more government funding and supervision. The document said the government's role in "formulating policies and plans, raising funds, providing service and supervising" must be strengthened in order to ensure the fairness and equity of the service. The reform is aimed at "solving

---

[29] Katrin Bennhold, "Is Europe's welfare system a model for the 21st century?" *The International Herald Tribune*, 27 Jan. 2009.

pressing problems that have caused strong complaints from the public", the document said, referring to long-standing criticism that medical services are difficult to access and increasingly unaffordable.[30]

After the founding of the People's Republic of China in 1949, the government covered more than 90% of medical expenses for urban residents, while rural people enjoyed simple but essentially free health care. When China began its economic reforms in the early 1980s, the system was dismantled as the country attempted to switch to a market-oriented health care system. Due to low government funding and a *de facto* marketisation process in medical services, doctors at state-run hospitals were forced to "generate" income for the hospitals through prescribing highly profitable, sometimes unnecessary drugs and treatment. In many places, this could account for 90% of a hospital's income. Soaring fees plunged many into poverty and made medical services less affordable to ordinary citizens.

Through huge governmental spending in medical care, pension, housing and compulsory education, China hopes to achieve fairer wealth redistribution and increase consumption levels of ordinary folks. As an effort to close the pension gap between corporations and administrative organs, most localities raised the basic pension for enterprise retirees by about 10% at the beginning of 2009. The government is mulling plans for free senior high school education. Through raising the minimum purchasing price of farm produces and granting farmers a 13% subsidy for home appliance purchase, the government is making efforts to stimulate consumption of the 800 million rural residents.

The Hu-Wen leadership seemed to recognise problems of the neoliberal ideology when they took power in 2003. Unlike their pro-market predecessors, Hu and Wen paid more attention to the negative impact of the market upon the society and ecological environment under the new guidelines of "Harmonious Society" and "Scientific Outlook of Development". Despite his adherence to "universal values", Chinese Premier Wen Jiabao himself is a market interventionist, insistently pursuing his controversial macro-control

---

[30] "China unveils health-care reform guidelines", *Xinhua News Agency*, 6 Apr. 2009.

(宏观调控) policy to cool down the overheated property, stock and credit markets. With fast-growing fiscal revenue, the Hu-Wen government vows to increase spending on public social welfare in medical care, pension, housing and education.

New Left scholars have suggested that policy makers slow down the further market liberalisation process of various areas especially the financial, energy and property sectors, change their previous preference for market and privatisation reforms to rectify the unreasonable health care and education system, and reemphasise SOE's role in safeguarding national economic security, but continue to have a firm control over them.

Many Chinese policy makers used to take the United States as the best development model to follow, but the US economic crisis is making them question the value of such blind faith. When China celebrated its 30th anniversary of reform and open-door policy in 2008, the Chinese government began to adjust its attitude towards a balance between the market and the state. As the free market is still the most efficient mechanism to promote the economy, the government is unlikely to return to the mode of command economy, and such ideological debate is likely to reorient the leadership towards stricter state regulations, more state interventions in the market, and a faster pace of building a social security net.

Chapter 12

Will Social Stability in China be Undermined in the Financial Crisis?

ZHAO Litao and HUANG Yanjie

Chinese senior officials expected the year 2009 to be a tough year for the Chinese economy and society. For one thing, about 10 million migrant workers will be unemployed and more than six million college graduates will find it difficult to find a desirable job. However, analysis suggests that it is unlikely that they will pose serious threats to social order and stability. While migrant workers are too disorganised and segregated to launch large-scale protests in urban areas, college students, with the resources to organise protests, will be more likely to lower their expectations rather than resorting to collective action. On the other hand, the government is also acting to pre-empt a potential crisis by increasing employment and appeasing the grievances of disgruntled social groups.

The year 2009 has been regarded as the "toughest" year for China since the turn of the century. Chinese leaders are concerned with the impact of the domestic economic downturn on social stability. Will it

259

push the number of social protests to a new level unseen in the reform period?[1]

Like other economies hard hit by the global financial crisis, unemployment is the top concern in China. Rural migrant workers and university graduates are the two largest groups at risk of unemployment. Unemployment among the educated has become a problem since 2003 despite double-digit economic growth until 2008. The problem worsens in 2009 as the economy continues to slide. Meanwhile, the scale of unemployment for migrant workers — 15.3% of the total of 130 million — is unprecedented, in part because there have never been so many migrant workers in Chinese history.

Most recent unemployment data suggest somewhat optimistic development. In the province of Henan, the largest province of origin for migrant workers, 8.4 million of the 9.5 million migrant workers who have returned before the Chinese New Year have found work.[2] The optimism was further boosted when another inland province, Jiangxi, reports that 2.7 million of the three million returning migrant workers have found work. A cross-provincial survey conducted by the Chinese Academy of Social Science (CASS) shows that about 85% of returning migrant workers from major labour-supplying provinces have found jobs by end April.[3] However, since the base is very large, the unemployment problem of migrant workers is still a challenge to social stability and governance.

Chinese leaders believe that serious and chronic unemployment can trigger social instability. The same conviction is widely shared

---

[1] For instance, Chen Jiping warned of "unprecedented challenges" in 2009 in maintaining law and order in an interview by the state-run *Outlook Weekly*. Chen is deputy secretary-general of the Party's Central Political and Legislative Affairs Committee, a top official in charge of coordinating the courts, public prosecutions, and regional justice departments. See http://news.xinhuanet.com/legal/2009-01/12/content_10643958.htm.

[2] "Henan: 90% of migrant workers have found new work", http://news.xinhuanet.com/society/2009-05/24/content_11426939.htm, 3 Jun. 2009.

[3] Li Peilin, "Present employment situation is better than expected", http://www.cnwnews.com/html/biz/cn_sypl/20090411/95116.html, 3 Jun. 2009.

among the media, the public and the academia. Thus, the issue is not whether the number of social protests will rise, but whether it will rise to a level that the Chinese economy will suffer and the Chinese Communist Party (CCP)'s rule will be undermined.

Over the years, there have been talks of social protests spilling over to become political challenges. Up till 2009, there has been no strong empirical support for this thesis. Although China had difficult moments many times in the past three decades, social protests were largely localised and short-lived, except for the 1989 Tiananmen incident. People are now waiting to see whether 2009 will be different.

At least for now, there lacks any clear sign that China's social stability is in grave danger. The two major groups of losers in the job market, migrant workers and college graduates, are unlikely to stage large-scale protests and other forms of destabilising collective actions in urban areas if they can fulfill basic material needs and retain the hope of a better life. While migrant workers lack organisational powers for collective action in cities, the better organised college graduates are likely to adjust their expectations than resort to more radical means.

More importantly, the current government has found ways to convince people that it is taking quick and adequate actions to tackle the problem of unemployment and economic downturn. In a newly released policy directive from the State Council, governments at all levels are asked to focus on preserving and creating jobs in the economy, via generous fiscal packages and other policy measures to promote all forms of employment. Both migrant workers and college graduates receive special attention in policy formulation.[4]

The CCP is therefore in a very different situation from that of 20 years ago. In the natural course of events, it is unlikely that 2009 will become another 1989, at least for the first several months. However, unexpected events and major policy blunders may provoke a social crisis with politically destabilising implications. It is essential

---

[4] The State Department's notice on "managing well the employment issue under current economic circumstances", 10 Feb. 2009, http://www.gov.cn/zwgk/2009-02/10/content_1226243.htm, 9 Mar. 2009.

that the government address the underlying social and economic problems of the day to soothe tensions and pre-empt future crises.

THE PROBLEM OF UNEMPLOYMENT

Migrant Workers

The global financial crisis has hit China's labour-intensive export sectors hard. Over the last three months, trade experienced sharp contraction on a yearly comparative basis. The direct result of this sharp fall is substantial job losses in export-related sectors employing mostly migrant workers as their labour force. It is estimated that about 20 million migrant workers or 15.3% of the migrant worker population in coastal areas have lost their jobs.[5]

However, the latest survey indicates that the unemployment problem of migrant workers may not be as serious as earlier estimates suggest. The present estimates by the CASS and provincial statistical bureaus seem to suggest a significantly lower rate of unemployment for migrant workers. The present total unemployment is probably below 11 million, as provided in the latest estimate by Yin Weimin, Minister of Labour and Social Security, in mid-March. Experts list the flexibility of work contracts and the adaptability of migrant workers as chief cushioning factors in the process.[6]

Large-scale retrenchment often induces social unrest. In 2008, when the biggest toy factory in China, Smart Union toy factory, closed down and laid off 7000 workers, thousands of workers staged a highly publicised protest outside the factory, forcing the local government to pay their wages and make compensations.[7] Other sporadic protests and demonstrations are frequent scenes in the media.

---

[5] Chen Xiwen, "Facing the social problems arising from 20 million jobless migrant workers", http://www.caijing.com.cn/2009-02-02/110051988.html, 10 Mar. 2009.
[6] Yin Weipin, "11 million returning migrant workers are still jobless", http://nc. people.com.cn/GB/8942373.html, 9 Mar. 2009.
[7] "7000 people lost jobs as toy factory close down in Dongguan", http://www.gd. xinhuanet. com/newscenter/2008-10/18/content_14671959.htm, 9 Mar. 2009.

Nevertheless, there were hardly any large-scale protests or other collective actions with targets other than specific business enterprises.

Since migrant workers are generally under short-term contracts with high turnover rates, and highly differentiated in terms of their origin, age and educational background, they are not as well organised and ideologically inspired as laid-off workers in state-owned enterprises (SOEs) in the late 1990s, especially those who used to serve in the People's Liberation Army (PLA) and who tend to act collectively to protect their rights. Compared with these organised groups, migrant workers lack the power base to launch destabilising collective actions on a large scale in the cities. They are also unlikely to become troublemakers in the urban areas because they are most likely to move on to find another job unlike state enterprise workers who see employment as a taken-for-granted right.

However, there are certain elements of social instability inherent in the massive increase in unemployment in the migrant worker group. First, while migrant workers have weak organisations in the cities, they have very strong kinship ties in the rural areas. Since most migrant workers have either rented out their allotted agricultural land or given up agriculture totally, they are bound to experience hard times making ends meet when they are back in the rural area. Common experiences and grievances may effectively move them to demand direct assistance from the government at the grassroots level or even launch protests against county and township governments. Given the relatively weak control of the party in rural grassroots, it hardly augurs well for social stability in rural communities and townships.

Another potential factor of social instability comes from the disgruntled second generation migrant workers. Second generation migrant workers spent at least part of their childhood and adolescence in the city. Unlike the generation of their fathers, they usually have received some education in the city, have a modern, urban outlook and high expectations of integrating with the urban environment and lifestyle.[8] When their jobs become untenable, they are less willing to

---

[8] "Two generation of migrant workers have different dreams", http://www.nan-fangdaily.com.cn/sd/200901220054.asp, 10 Mar. 2009.

return to their hometowns in the rural area. They are often better educated and well adapted to modern means of communication, with a stronger sense of personal rights and interests. Thus, they are likely to become a source of more effective social protest in the urban area.

Finally, a large "floating population" without fixed work and income is a breeding ground for criminal activities. The problem is particularly acute with regard to disillusioned groups of second generation migrant workers who fail to integrate with urban life due to the lack of education and job opportunities. Today, they already account for more than three quarters of all juvenile delinquencies committed by non-residents in Beijing.[9] With increasing unemployment threatening their lawful livelihood and the lack of material and psychological support for this group of "secondary citizens", it comes as no surprise that major Chinese cities are likely to see a rise in the crime rate in this group of migrant workers. The criminal activities committed by these underprivileged social groups will in turn stigmatise the migrant workers as a group and raise social tensions in the urban area.

College Graduates

Apart from migrant workers, another major victim of the worsening economic situation is China's new entrants to the labour market. A large part of the new entrants are college graduates, amounting to about 6.6 million, the largest batch ever recorded in China. This unprecedented huge inflow of educated labour force is heading for an untimely clash with the worst global economic recession in decades.

Four months ahead of their graduation, polls in major cities in China indicate that by late February 2009, only less than 20% of all prospective college graduates are able to secure a work contract. This is in sharp contrast to the last two years when typically 50–60% students were able to secure work by late February.[10] The figure

---

[9] "Second generation migrant workers account for 70% of juvenile delinquencies in Beijing", *Beijing Youth News*, 12 Dec. 2008.

[10] "Employment rate down 20% from previous year", http://sh.eastday.com/qtmt/20090301/u1a542838.html.

merely increased to 38% at national level at the end of May when the graduating ceremony is only a month away.[11] There are also some significant regional variations, as inland provinces typically enjoy higher rates than the coastal regions. Since the economic crisis has yet to reach the trough, which will eventually come later in 2009 according to many economists, the employment prospects for university graduates are gloomy indeed.

In most cases, unemployment of college graduates is attributable to job mismatch rather than to absolute shortage in the supply of jobs. In China, college graduates often have high expectations of salary and career prospects. However, with the onslaught of the financial tsunami, a lot of highly paid jobs in the service sectors such as IT, banking and Chinese branches of multinational corporations (MNCs) open mainly to college students have been withdrawn or left vacant. College graduates need to sharply lower their expectations in order to find a job, most likely in the industrial sector, which demands technical training often not taught in academic-oriented college curriculum.

College graduates thus become losers in the current job markets — those unable to find jobs join the group of unemployed and those who are lucky enough to find a job but end up with jobs that demand skills and qualifications that are lower than theirs. The resultant unemployment and "underemployment" is likely to become a perpetual source of frustration, discontent and financial and social strain.

Unlike migrant workers, college students belong to the "politically strategic groups" by virtue of their educational background, organisational skills and sometimes radical mindset. It is worth noting that they constitute the most active group within the 300 million "netizens" in China, itself being the most politically active class in today's Chinese society.

Fortunately, college graduates usually have much more resources to weather the crisis since most college students nowadays come

---

[11] "Contract Signing Rate for College Graduates is Going Low". http://www.caijing.com.cn/2009-06-01/110173893.html, 5 Jun. 2009.

from the urban middle class, a background that makes them economically better off and politically more vocal than migrant workers. Hence, they receive more attention from the top leadership and are able to have their voice heard by higher authorities.[12] When the Chinese economy recovers, they will be the first to reap the benefits. Consequently, the possibility of social unrest among college graduates will gradually decrease as the short-run shocks dissipate.

GOVERNMENT INITIATIVES FOR 2009

All the potential sources of instability boil down to the lack of employment and income for these two groups: migrant workers and college graduates. For the migrant workers, since the problem is mainly cyclical shocks and immediate financial strains, the top priority of Chinese leaders in ensuring social stability is job creation and welfare support.

On the one hand, the government has to create as many employment opportunities as possible to make up for the shortfall in export. Much of the four trillion fiscal pump priming has the potential of generating employment: infrastructure, road building and housing projects. Experts' estimates put expected job creation in two years to six million. However, taking the time of implementation and effectiveness of fund allocation into consideration, it remains to be seen whether this gigantic fiscal project alone can solve the bulk of the unemployment problem.

Another approach to employment creation is the structural approach, namely transferring laid-off workers from certain contracting industrial sectors to expanding industrial sectors or the service sector. Compared to developed economies, the service sector in China is very small and in need of huge expansion to meet sweeping social and economic changes. For example, domestic service is one of

---

[12] As an indication of the government's keen concern about the employment problems of college graduates, top leaders like Hu Jintao and Wen Jiabao paid several high-profile and highly publicised visits to university campuses and human resource fairs in December 2008 and January 2009.

the expanding sectors that still has large potential of absorbing excess labour despite falling average wages. Interestingly, this sector not only provides jobs for retrenched migrant female workers, but also attracts educated female college graduates or retrenched female white collar workers to take this opportunity to earn higher-than-average wages as senior household workers, or housekeepers.[13]

Private entrepreneurial activities are also important sources of job creation for rural-based migrant workers. Early in the first phase of economic reform, township and village enterprises have played an essential role in employment creation in the rural sector. Thanks to the new Company Law and other legal and institutional framework, migrant workers have plenty of opportunity to take part in various entrepreneurial activities in their homeland. In this area, the government can play an active role by introducing favourable tax schemes, subsidies, and cheap sources of finance. According to this year's No. 1 Document of Central Committee CCP on agriculture, migrant workers' entrepreneurship has been ranked as a high priority in the government's comprehensive approach towards returning migrant workers and rural development.[14] Armed with better connections, technical knowledge and work experiences, returned migrant workers may well start successful small enterprises in regions where there is a potential market but a shortage of supply. Such enterprises could cover a broad range of consumer goods, such as processed grain, meat products, detergents, textiles and household utensils.

On the other hand, the government needs to reach out directly to laid-off migrant workers with financial constraints and living on the verge of poverty in the cities by offering various forms of transfer payment, subsidy and insurance to fulfill their basic needs, and sustain their trust in the government and society. The year 2008 saw an increasingly active role played by non-governmental organisation in organising social events and responding to social crisis, largely in the

---

[13] "Reshuffling of the domestic service sector". http://edu.sina.com.cn/j/2009-01-07/1523163189.shtml, 5 Jun. 2009.

[14] Gu Shengzu on the No.1 document: http://theory.people.com.cn/GB/49154/49155/8790230.html, 5 Jun. 2009.

interest and as a complement of the state. From 2009, the government could also encourage and rely on them for providing social
support to migrant workers as well.

In addition, the government could encourage migrant workers to
move back to their homeland on the provision that local governments
have effective plans to accommodate them. In fact, the rural area is
in need of the skills, expertise and knowledge acquired by migrant
workers from the cities. Returned migrant workers can act as agents
of transformation in the countryside by helping to commercialise and
industrialise the traditionally farming rural economy.[15]

Like the unemployment problem for migrant workers, "educated
unemployment" needs to be addressed from its root causes: lack of
employment in the economy. However, it is not easy to tackle the
problem directly since this "educated unemployment" is a structural,
psychological as well as economic problem. A practical strategy of the
government is to keep college graduates preoccupied while at the
same time helping them to adjust their expectations. Three major
policies for tackling the problem of educated unemployment have
been adopted.

First, some local governments are prepared to set up trainee programmes for college graduates who are unable to match their
qualifications with the technical requirements of the job market. In
Shanghai, the municipal government is ready to provide over 30,000
trainee positions for a period of six months to one year to incoming
college graduates, which are expected to reach 158,000 in 2009.[16]

Second, the Ministry of Education has allowed an expansion of
50,000 in this year's graduate programme enrollment. This is another
delay strategy to help students enter the job market later with higher
educational qualifications.

---

[15] Zhao Litao, "Return rural migration in China: a source of social instability or a
force for rural transformation"? *EAI Background Brief* No. 424, East Asian Institute,
National University of Singapore.

[16] Press interview with Director of Shanghai Education Bureau, http://www.sh.xin-
huanet.com/zhuanti2009/2009-03/01/content_15826098.htm, 10 Mar. 2009.

Third, the top agency of personnel management in China, the Central Organisation Department of the CCP will increase its recruitment of college graduates to the positions of village head, community leader and staff in other grassroots units of the CCP. This programme was launched in March 2008 to absorb about 100,000 college graduates to fill the need for educated human resources in the CCP grassroots units and the rural areas.[17]

Fourth, some regional governments are experimenting with incentive packages tailored to encourage college graduate entrepreneurship. For example, in early March, the provincial government of Liaoning implemented a policy to exempt graduate entrepreneurs from tax for a period of two years. Scholars also suggest that local governments across China support graduate entrepreneurship by setting up entrepreneur incubators and implementing favourable tax policies. However, in reality, only one percent of all graduates opt for entrepreneurial activities for their first job according to a survey in the economically more developed province of Guangdong.[18]

Fifth, the Chinese government encourages the 147 central-managed SOEs to expand their recruitment of fresh graduates. Most of these large enterprises are in strategic industries; as large recipients of generous government subsidies, they are obliged to implement the government's anti-crisis policies, such as employment creation and industrial restructuring. These large SOEs will be expected to increase their recruitment by 7%. China Aerospace in particular is scheduled to recruit about 12,000 graduates in 2009, a 100% increase over the previous recruitment.[19] However, despite their overwhelming size and capital, these SOEs can only provide up to 20,000 work positions, mostly reserved for graduates from top universities in Beijing.

---

[17] Li Yuanchao, "College graduates as village head, a national talents strategy", http://news.xinhuanet.com/misc/2008-03/07/content_7735377.htm, 5 Jun. 2009.

[18] http://news.xinhuanet.com/politics/2009-06/09/content_11513811.htm, 5 Jun. 2009.

[19] http://finance.ifeng.com/topic/dxsjy/job/zcyw/20090528/717145.shtml, 5 Jun. 2009.

The soothing effect on the whole unemployment problem is expected to be limited.

Sixth, the government is also prepared to enlist graduates as junior officers in the PLA. From 2008, the enlistment policy of the PLA has undergone important changes. The army will provide favourable job conditions to incoming graduates with a view to raising the educational profile of junior army officers in general and the army's capability in conducting knowledge and information-based warfare. The year 2008 already saw a doubling of enlistment of incoming graduates as junior officers. In 2009, the PLA is expected to further increase the enlistment of college graduates. College graduates with long-term career plans are now regarding the PLA as viable choice to improve their career profile.[20]

As short-term solutions, the first and second strategies only serve to delay the entrance of a limited number of college graduates to the job market. The third strategy has the potential of becoming a major policy innovation with transformative and lasting impact on the countryside. However, it is also likely to degenerate into an empty political campaign that could hardly elicit positive response from the increasingly practical and pragmatic college graduates. The entrepreneurial solution is a hotly debated topic, featured prominently in different media, but its effects on employment creation are at best indeterminate. The fifth solution, as argued, only provides limited extra work positions for elite graduates. The enlistment solution seems the most plausible one, but it is also unlikely that the PLA could absorb a large share of the college graduates in the job market.

From a long-run perspective, the unemployment problem of college graduates is deeply rooted in China's distorted economic and institutional structure. The foremost factor hindering full employment of educated labour force is the relatively backward industrial structure that lays too much weight on the manufacturing sector which requires primarily skilled labour, while the modern service sector requires an

---

[20] http://finance.ifeng.com/topic/dxsjy/job/zcyw/20090602/733086.shtml, 6 Jun. 2009.

educated graduate labor force. The second factor has a lot to do with work positions that are closed to the competitive labour markets and follows a rigid system of state management as in the majority of positions in the public service, social sector and the SOEs. Finally, the underdeveloped and weakly integrated labour market is another major source of inefficient labour allocation. More specifically, there is no effective institutional channel to collect, analyse and disseminate information about employment opportunities to the education community and vice versa from potential employees to the enterprises.[21]

Furthermore, it is argued that the over-expansion of tertiary education sector initiated 10 years ago is also a major culprit behind the employment problem; tertiary institutions aimlessly expanded their size and capacity without any regard for quality education and long-term implication on employment. Experts estimate that it may take 5–10 years to reform and perfect these institutional rigidities, especially the imperfect labour sector and tertiary education system.[22] Since all present strategies are only short-run measures without effective means to address these fundamental problems, their effects on employment creation are limited.

A most recent survey by the CASS indicates that the majority of 2008's college graduates have managed to adjust their expectations and come to a compromise with current market conditions in the face of the severe economic slowdown. According to the survey, 86% of the 2008 batch has found work so far, albeit at a 20% lower starting pay. Of the graduating class of 2009, only 45% has found work in late May.[23] Although these figures indicate less-than-expected fall in employment rate for college graduates, they still suggest that over four million college graduates of the 2008 and 2009 batches are still in search of jobs that match their expectations.

[21] Feng Yanshou, "Analysis on the Sources of Graduate's Employment Problem", *Liberation Daily*, 17 Feb. 2009.
[22] Zhou Daping, "New Perspective on Graduate Employment Problem", *The Observer Newsweekly*, 8 Apr. 2009.
[23] http://news.mingpao.com/20090616/cca1.htm, 16 Jun. 2009.

It is still too early to tell how effective these strategies are, but it is important for the government to be seen taking measures when it is supposed to. So far the Chinese government has scored with its quick action in announcing the four trillion stimulus package. For the time being there is a fair amount of confidence in China that it will be the first major economy to recover and rebound. As long as the confidence remains strong, the CCP should not be in a too difficult position to deal with the rising social tension.

RISING PROTESTS, BUT POLITICALLY MANAGEABLE

Since the late 1990s, Chinese officials have begun to realise that rising social protests are a reality, and that grievers often have legitimate complaints about unemployment, illegal taxes, forced evictions, loss of farmland and numerous other developmental problems that China could not solve anytime soon.[24]

Along this line, the CCP now focusses on containment and management of social protests rather than suppression and deterrence. In anticipation of rising social unrest in 2009, it reiterated this point to county party secretaries and security chiefs through group training programmes in Beijing and warned against any relentless use of sheer force in quenching social protests.[25]

The containment and management strategy has worked well thus far. Chinese grievers have not been able to launch broad-based protests that cut across occupations and regions. The same pattern is likely to continue for migrant workers in 2009. Migrant workers' low

---

[24] See Murray Scott Tanner, "Challenges to China's Internal Security Strategy", testimony presented to the US-China Economic and Security Review Commission on 3 Feb. 2006.

[25] County party secretaries are trained in the CCP's Central Party School. The latest round of training focussed on maintaining social stability. See http://news.xin-huanet.com/local/2008-11/15/content_10361613.htm. Meanwhile, the Ministry of Public Security is organising training sessions for county security chiefs with the same focus. See http://news sohu.com/20090218/n262316803.shtml, 28 Feb.

socioeconomic status and *de facto* "secondary citizenship" have prevented urban residents from joining the protests. Urbanites are more likely to side with the government if the protests in urban centres turn violent and confrontational.

Moreover, recent surveys indicate that migrant workers have adapted rather well to the changing economic circumstances as most returned migrant workers have found work since February. The original forecasts of unprecedented unemployment rate have been radically cut back. Thus, the overall risk of mass protests and social stability by migrant workers is quite limited.

Up till now, college graduate unemployment appears to feature more prominently in the overall economic picture. Even if the economy is to recover in the following two quarters of 2009, significant educated unemployment is inevitable, since unemployment is more of enduring structural sources than cyclical in nature.

Furthermore, the chance of finding a satisfactory job is always intertwined with social factors like family origin and background of college graduates, a social group that is much more differentiated from migrant workers. The odds are always in favour of those from rich middle class families and against students from poor rural families. As prospects of employment worsen for all graduates, this enduring source of inequality is becoming ever more prominent. Hard pressed by the harsh economic conditions of the job market and the social reality of inequality based on family origins, social grievances from the less well-placed college graduates are bound to remain high. Despite affirmative action in terms of preferential job provision for graduates from poor households in several provinces, it is generally considered too weak to change powerful social forces geared towards the rich and privileged. Thus, college graduates, especially the unprivileged group, may be a latent source of social protest as well.

However, college graduates are also constrained in mobilising wider support for their protests over unemployment. Job prospects vary with the reputation and location of the university as well as the qualification and performance of the student. College graduates with job offers tend to be more resourceful and come from better universities. They are unlikely to join jobless fellow students in protest over unemployment. College graduates are therefore divided along various lines, which prevent them from becoming a homogenous group.

The cleavage becomes meaningless, however, if the majority of college graduates cannot find a job. If the report is true that less than 20% of prospective college graduates had found a job by late February 2009, China will have a serious problem looming large on the horizon. It would be the first time ever that millions of college graduates share the same problem with an even larger number of migrant workers. The CCP has to hope that either the report is not true or the situation improves substantially in the coming months.

The CCP, however, cannot take popular confidence for granted. It will face the real test in the second half of this year. If the promise that China's economy will be the first to rebound is not delivered, and if the job market does not improve, the current government will be perceived as incompetent and ineffective, and its legitimacy will be questioned. In such a scenario, any seemingly minor issues can be easily politicised to become a powerful mobilising force in collective actions. While this scenario does not look very likely given the state capacity, the CCP has to work hard to prevent the popular perception of government failure.

Chapter 13

The International Financial Crisis and China's External Response

ZHENG Yongnian and LYE Liang Fook

China has been inadvertently thrust into the political limelight as the global financial crisis unfolded in the fourth quarter of 2008. With the world's largest foreign reserves, China has been perceived as a "white knight" or "saviour" to stabilise the international financial system. Despite such inflated expectations, China's external response has so far been cautious and calibrated. China has stated that getting its own house in order is its primary preoccupation. Arising from this premise, China is ready to work with other countries and international institutions to explore ways and means of restoring growth. China wants to be regarded as a responsible and constructive player. It has eschewed a leadership role in bringing the world out of its economic doldrums as it is not in its interests to do so.

The financial crisis that originated from the US and subsequently developed into a world-wide phenomenon has unwittingly thrust China into the political limelight. With the world's largest foreign exchange reserves of US$1.95 trillion,[1] and with roughly two-thirds of this amount believed to be held in US-denominated assets, China is being seen as a possible "white knight" or "saviour" to stabilise the international financial system or to simply bail out the US economy.[2]

The calls for China to do more came mainly from Europe and the US. Jose Manuel Barraso, European Commission President, reportedly called on Beijing just before the Seventh Asia-Europe Meeting (ASEM) Summit in October 2008 to help resolve the global financial crisis in return for Beijing being granted more say in international financial bodies.[3] Less explicitly, John Lipsky, International Monetary Fund (IMF) first deputy Managing Director, reportedly commented in November 2008 that "it is absolutely natural that China will play an increasingly important role in the world economic affairs".[4]

This chapter argues that China's response to calls for it to do more has been cautious and calibrated. In dealing with a crisis affecting the entire world, China has consistently sought to portray itself as a responsible and constructive player on the world as well as regional stage. In particular, China has demonstrated a willingness to work with other countries and institutions to address the challenges at hand. It is also ready to do its part to render assistance to other countries, especially the developing ones, to help them mitigate the negative impact of the crisis. China has further pushed for a retooling of the international financial system to allow a greater voice for developing countries, itself included.

Most noticeably, China does not seek a leadership role in tackling the present crisis. It has stated that its foremost priority is to put its own economic house in order. There are reasons for such an

---

[1] "China's foreign reserves hit $1.95 trillion at end of March", *China Daily*, 11 Apr. 2009.

[2] "Will China bail out the West?", *BBC*, 15 Oct. 2008 and "China seen as savior in global financial crisis", *Herald Sun*, 9 Oct. 2008.

[3] "EU presses China to show leadership in crisis", *Reuters*, 23 Oct. 2008.

[4] "IMF: China to play more important role in world economic affairs", *China Daily*, 6 Nov. 2008.

orientation. The most important reason is that China itself is faced with daunting domestic challenges such as slowing economic growth, massive layoffs, rising unemployment and widening income disparities. There are calls within China for the leaders to do more to tackle domestic problems rather than take on additional external responsibilities. The financial crisis has further triggered an internal ideological debate on the applicability of certain values which are perceived to have originated from the West. Hence, the Chinese leaders have to tread carefully so as not to appear as pandering too much to the West at the expense of China's interests.

To better appreciate China's external response to the international financial crisis, this chapter is divided into four sections. The first section will examine China's response to the crisis. It will highlight some of the key actions taken by China at the national, regional and multilateral levels. The second section will outline some of the key internal challenges that China faces with particular focus on the political front. The third section will look at how China is prudently chalking up political mileage with other countries and institutions by portraying a responsible and constructive image in the present crisis. The fourth and final section will suggest possible ways where China may move forward from current developments.

CHINA'S CALIBRATED EXTERNAL RESPONSE

China has faced much external pressures to shoulder a heavier burden to help the affected economies. Yet, China has cleverly deflected such pressures by not only displaying an open attitude, but also working with all concerned to find solutions at the bilateral, regional and multilateral levels. These approaches, however, have had differing results given the difficulty of coordinating responses across borders.

At the bilateral level, China has been in touch with the key affected countries and working with them to address the challenges. In a telephone conversation with President George Bush in September 2008, President Hu Jintao reportedly expressed the hope that the package of measures contemplated by the US would lead to a gradual recovery of the financial market.[5] Wen Jiabao apparently went further by expressing China's willingness to cooperate with the US to address the crisis.[6] At the working level, the People's Bank of China (China's Central Bank) has stated China's willingness to enhance coordination and cooperation with the US and other markets to overcome current difficulties.[7] In early October 2008, China also joined other G7 central banks in a rare coordinated interest rate cut.

In particular, US Treasury Secretary Hank Paulson has praised China's cooperation in taming the global financial turmoil and acknowledged his useful and constructive discussions with Chinese Vice Premier Wang Qishan on the issue.[8] At the Fifth Strategic Economic Dialogue in Beijing in December 2008, both countries agree to provide an additional US$20 billion to finance trade between China and the US, and between them and other developing economies. Besides the US, Chinese leaders and their officials have also been in touch and held discussions with their respective European counterparts on steps to take to address the crisis.

At the multilateral level, China has attempted to facilitate a broader response to address the crisis but with mixed results. For instance, at the ASEM attended by 45 European and Asian partners in Beijing in October 2008, the focus was on restoring calm to jittery markets and ensuring future growth.[9] The summit called on all

---

[5] "Chinese, US Presidents talk over phone about ties, US financial turmoil", *Xinhuanet*, 22 Sept. 2008.

[6] "FM: Premier Wen elaborates China's policies of reform, development during UN visit", *Xinhuanet*, 26 Sept. 2008.

[7] "China's central bank welcomes US bailout plan, willing to cooperate on financial issue", *People's Daily*, 4 Oct. 2008.

[8] Paulson made these remarks at the National Committee on US–China Relations in New York. See "Paulson lauds China cooperation amid market turmoil", *Reuters*, 21 Oct. 2008.

[9] This is the largest turnout of Asian and European leaders since ASEM was established in 1996. The large turnout was partly due to the admission of new partners after ASEM's second round of expansion in 2007. Members brought in were India, Pakistan, Mongolia, Romania, Bulgaria and the ASEAN Secretariat.

countries to take "firm, decisive, and effective measures" as well as strengthen "coordination and cooperation" to deal with the crisis.[10] The leaders also pledged to undertake effective and comprehensive reform of the international monetary and financial systems. At the APEC Economic Leaders' Meeting in Peru in November 2008, President Hu joined other world leaders to pledge not to implement protectionist measures for the next 12 months — no matter how punishing the global downturn got.[11]

At the first G-20 Leaders' Summit in Washington in November 2008, President Hu Jintao together with other leaders who represent 85% of the world economy endorsed an action plan to deal with the challenges ahead.[12] Key issues agreed included reforming international financial institutions (such as the World Bank and IMF), strengthening financial market transparency and accountability, ensuring banks and financial institutions' incentives "prevent excessive risk taking" and drawing up a list of financial institutions whose collapse would endanger the global economic system.[13]

Subsequently, at the more recent G-20 Summit in London in April 2009, President Hu Jintao reiterated China's willingness to work with other countries to deal with the crisis as a "responsible member of the international society". Hu further drew the analogy that "All countries are on board the huge boat of the world economy. When this boat is riding into the storm, all members on it must work together to steer it out of turmoil".[14]

---

[10] "Full text of statement of the Seventh Asia-Europe Meeting on the International Financial Situation", *Xinhuanet*, 24 Oct. 2008.

[11] In his speech at the APEC Economic Leaders' Meeting, President Hu Jintao reportedly said that "a fair and open multilateral trading regime is conducive to the steady growth of regional and global trade, to the sound growth of the world economy and to the benefit of all parties". See "Leaders stand by free trade, vow to revive Doha", *China Daily*, 24 Nov. 2008.

[12] The G-20 members are Argentina, Australia, Brazil, Canada, China, France, Germany, India, Indonesia, Italy, Japan, Mexico, Russia, Saudi Arabia, South Africa, South Korea, Turkey, the UK, the US and the European Union.

[13] "Leaders welcome G-20 action plan", *BBC News*, 16 Nov. 2008.

[14] "China: G-20 Summit boost confidence", *China Daily*, 4 Apr. 2009.

Some observers have commented that such international gatherings of world leaders are more usually known for their rhetoric rather than concrete outcomes such as coordinated action.[15] It is the view of the authors that such comments have to be put in perspective given the difficulty of coordinating action across borders. More importantly, such comments should not distract us from the reality of China's willingness to work with like-minded countries and institutions to deal with the world economic crisis.

China's effort to play a responsible and constructive role appears to be more pronounced and effective at the regional level. This is primarily due to China's willingness to do more to help its neighbours as well as its growing clout in the region. In May 2009, for instance, the 10 ASEAN countries plus China, Japan and South Korea agreed to set up a US$120 billion emergency currency pool to boost liquidity and help the region overcome the global crisis. China and Japan will provide the bulk of this amount at US$38.4 billion each, followed by South Korea at US$19.2 billion with the remaining amount coming from ASEAN.[16]

Separately, China has announced measures to foster China-ASEAN cooperation and help ASEAN better cope with present difficulties. In April 2009, Chinese Foreign Minister Yang Jiechi met with the envoys of the 10 ASEAN countries in Beijing to inform them of several initiatives. The first was China's establishment of a China-ASEAN investment cooperation fund totalling US$10 billion for cooperation on infrastructure construction, energy and resources, information and communications. The second was China's offer of credit amounting to US$15 billion over the next three to five years to ASEAN countries for various cooperation projects. Third, not forgetting the least developed members of ASEAN was China's extension of US$39.7 million in special aid to Cambodia, Laos and Myanmar to meet their urgent needs. Fourth, China would inject an additional

---

[15] "G-20 Summit: An easy guide to judge its success or failure", *Telegraph*, 2 Apr. 2009.

[16] "ASEAN, China, Japan, South Korea finalize crisis fund pact", *Channelnewsasia*, 3 May 2009.

US\$5 million into the China-ASEAN Cooperation Fund and donate US\$900,000 to the cooperation fund of ASEAN plus China, Japan and South Korea.[17]

China has particularly championed the interest of developing countries at various international and regional forums. As the largest developing country, China is best qualified to assume this role, thereby enhancing its legitimacy in the eyes of the developing world. At the first G-20 Summit in November 2008, President Hu Jintao called on the international community to pay "particular attention to the damage of the crisis on developing countries", especially the least developed ones, and do all it can "to minimize the damage".[18] In particular, the African Union had earlier expressed disappointment over its exclusion from the summit.[19]

At the second G-20 Summit in April 2009, China made a further pitch to take the interest of developing nations into consideration. It made two specific demands concerning developing countries. First, China called on the international financial institutions (i.e. the IMF and the World Bank) to "increase assistance to the developing countries". Second, it called on the IMF and World Bank to improve their governance structure to "enhance the representativeness and voice of the developing countries".[20] While standing up for the interests of the developing countries, China is also subtly and gradually positioning itself to play a bigger role in the international financial institutions.

China is neither willing nor ready (or financially capable) at the moment to over-commit itself externally to deal with the global economic crisis. The main reason is China's need to grapple with urgent domestic challenges, foremost of which is to sustain the growth

---

[17] "China rolls out assistance blueprint for ASEAN", *Xinhuanet*, 12 Apr. 2009.

[18] "Hu urges help for developing nations to cope with financial crisis", *China Daily*, 16 Nov. 2008.

[19] "Leaders urge Africa focus at G-20", *AFP*, 12 Nov. 2008.

[20] News Article at the Chinese Foreign Ministry's Website titled "The second financial summit of G-20 leaders takes place in London" dated 3 Apr. 2009 at http://www.fmprc.gov.cn/eng/zxxx/t556209.htm.

momentum of its economy which had earlier shown signs of slowing down.[21] The decline in export orders and weak domestic demand led to layoffs and factory closures. Domestic investment had also cooled as companies cut back or put off spending on real estate, factories and other assets. The property market had hit a low plateau and stock prices were off 60% compared to a year ago.[22]

At the national level, China has introduced the most concrete of steps to fight the negative impact of the financial crisis. It repeatedly stressed that its priority was to keep its own economic house in order. In ascribing to itself this limited role, China adroitly deflected pressures for it to bail out other economies. President Hu Jintao set the tone when he said at the Seventh ASEM Summit in October 2008 that China's "sound economic growth is in itself a major contribution to global financial stability and economic growth".[23]

Most significantly, on 9 November 2008, China unveiled a comprehensive economic stimulus package of four trillion *RMB* (US$586 billion) to bolster its slowing economy. This amount would be spent by 2010 on a wide array of national infrastructure and social welfare projects, including constructing new railways, subways, airports and rebuilding communities devastated by the earthquake in Sichuan in May 2008. This package comes on top of earlier measures to loosen credit and encourage lending as well as increase tax rebates for exporters.[24]

The announcement of this package was timed just days before the convening of the G-20 Leaders' Summit in Washington on 15 November 2008. The unequivocal message to the world was that Beijing's foremost duty was to its people. President Hu further said in his address to G-20 leaders at the same summit that major developed countries "should undertake their due responsibilities and obligations" by implementing the necessary policies and measures to

---

[21] "Bowring: China can't help", *IHT*, 25 Nov. 2008.

[22] "China's economy sputters", *Businessweek*, 2 Oct. 2008.

[23] "ASEM starts with financial crisis as top agenda", *China Daily*, 24 Oct. 2008.

[24] "Economy gets $586 b power dose", *China Daily*, 10 Nov. 2008.

stabilise their own and international financial markets.[25] This was a veiled call primarily to the US to do more to resolve the crisis.

PRESSING INTERNAL PREOCCUPATIONS

There are strong reasons behind China's measured external response. The most important is the Chinese leaders' concern that the slow-down in China's economy will engender further socio-economic hardships that may threaten China's social and political stability. China's economic growth slipped to 9% in the third quarter of 2008, down from 10.1% in the second quarter. This is the first time in five years that growth has fallen to single digit.[26] The slowdown is partly due to shrinking demand from abroad and partly to worsening down-ward pressure from weak domestic demand.

The falling demand exacerbated layoffs and factory closures. The most hard-hit were the manufacturing and labour-intensive textile, garment and toy sectors. According to official statistics, 67,000 pre-viously profitable SMEs collapsed during the first half of 2008.[27] Also, a total of 3,631 toy exporters or around 53% of the industry's busi-nesses shut down in the first seven months of 2008.[28] The brunt of such collapse was borne by migrant workers who worked for these enterprises.

Finding jobs for the millions of unemployed and more than 20 million new entrants into the workforce in 2009 has been identi-fied as one of the Chinese leadership's biggest challenges.[29] To sustain growth, the government has also recognised the importance of pump priming the economy, stimulating domestic consumption, bolstering

---

[25] "Hu calls for concerted efforts to tide over financial crisis", *China Daily*, 16 Nov. 2008.

[26] China's GDP growth in 2007 was 11.4%.

[27] China's registered SMEs exceeded 4.3 million and contributed almost 60% of GDP, 50% of tax revenue, 68% of exports, and 75% of new jobs every year. See "China's small companies warned of hard times ahead", *China Daily*, 20 Oct. 2008.

[28] "Half of China's toy exporters out of business", *Xinhuanet*, 14 Oct. 2008.

[29] "China's worse nightmare: Unemployment", *Time*, 31 Oct. 2008.

and restructuring the export sector, and restoring confidence to China's stock and property markets. Improving social welfare such as education, health care and extending the pension scheme to rural areas have been given much attention as well.[30]

Besides economics, there is also a political dimension to China's reluctance to play a more active external role. This is related to the pro-people orientation of the Hu-Wen leadership, of which a major tenet is to be responsive to the needs of the people. At a time when China is experiencing an economic slowdown with its attendant problems, the people would expect the government to put their needs first. By responding to this need, the government and, more importantly, the Party are renewing their social contract and in the process reaffirming their legitimacy.

The Chinese leadership also has to take into account the surge in criticism among certain quarters within China of the excesses of the US financial system and to some extent the limits of capitalism. Some of these are constructive criticisms which have placed China's interests in priority. For instance, Wu Jinglian, an economist with the Development Research Centre of the State Council, was quoted as saying that the US financial model, based on excessive expenditure, was in need of a review.[31] Others have suggested that China should seize

---

[30] In January 2009, China's State Council, or Cabinet, passed a long awaited medical reform plan which promised to spend 850 billion *yuan* (US$123 billion) by 2011 to provide universal medical service to the country's 1.3 billion population. Some of the key elements of the plan include (i) expanding the coverage of medical insurance to at least 90% of the rural and urban population by 2011; (ii) building a basic medicine system that includes a catalogue of drugs mostly needed by the public; (iii) improving medical service systems (particularly at the grassroots level). This would include building another 5,000 clinics at township level, 2,000 hospitals at county level and 2,400 urban community clinics in three years; (iv) gradually providing equal public health services in both rural and urban areas in the country; (v) reforming public hospitals. See "China's health care reform aims at public interest, Premier Wen says", *Xinhuanet*, 28 Feb. 2009.

[31] "Zhongguo ying zhuazhu jiyu baituo mei niuqu jingji" (China should seize the opportunity to break free from the US distortion of economics), *Ming Pao News*, 20 Oct. 2008.

the opening provided by the crisis to secure a bigger say in the global political and economic order.[32]

Other criticisms are more extreme in that they discredit what the West stands for and attack those in China perceived to be pandering too much to the West. The opening salvo appeared to be fired by Chen Kuiyuan, President of the Chinese Academy of Social Science (CASS), who reportedly said at a forum in July 2008 that there were some in China who ardently talked about following universal values. Chen cautioned that China should not blindly elevate the values of the West as universal values and denigrate the values of the Party and country as belonging to a different category.[33] Chen's comments seemed to be directed at Premier Wen Jiabao who had previously spoken about universal values such as democracy, rule of law, freedom, human rights and equality and how China should work towards these ideals.[34] Chen's remarks were subsequently published in the 2 September 2008 issue of the CASS newsletter.[35]

Thereafter, renowned publications such as the *People's Daily* (the Party's Central Committee newspaper), *Study Times* (the Central Party School newsletter), and *Guangming Daily* (the Department of Propaganda newspaper) carried articles that variously questioned the existence of universal values, their applicability to China, and the ulterior motives of those who purportedly subscribe to such values.[35]

The exact individual or persons behind these series of articles remain unknown. However, it is reasonable to conclude that the

---

[32] "Zhongguo ying zhuazhu jiyu baituo mei niuqu jingji" (China should seize the opportunity to break free from the US distortion of economics), *Ming Pao News*, 20 Oct. 2008. In particular, these scholars have suggested that China should push for an international financial order where a few major currencies could be readily used instead of only the US dollar. China should also seek a bigger say and participation rights in the area of international financial supervision.

[33] Chen Kuiyuan is also Vice Chairman of the Chinese People's Political Consultative Conference. See http://chinausnews.com/html/46/n-1046.html.

[34] "Hardliners in bid to oust China's PM", *The Sunday Times* (UK), 19 Oct. 2008.

[35] "Yuyong lilun jia weigong Wen Jiabao" (Going through theoreticians to attack Wen Jiabao), *Kai Fang*, Oct. 2008.

views contained in these articles enjoy some degree of currency within the establishment and are even being backed by senior Party members. They also indicate that there are differences in opinion within the leadership on the path to take to perfect socialism in China. While they are unlikely to derail the present course that China has set for itself, the Hu-Wen leadership needs to tread carefully and take into account these voices in charting the way forward.

CHALKING UP POLITICAL MILEAGE

In line with its interests, China has made a conscious effort at portraying itself as a responsible and constructive player in the present crisis. China overtook Germany to become the world's third-largest economy in 2007, sooner than predicted. Its GDP in 2007 was US$3.38 trillion compared to Germany's US$3.32 trillion, but still behind the US at US$13.8 trillion and Japan at US$4.38 trillion.[36] Some analysts expect China to even top Japan as the world's second largest economy by 2009 or 2010.[37] Given its increasing stake in the world economy, China has displayed a certain degree of proactiveness to work with like-minded countries and institutions to deal with the global financial instability and economic woes. It has also taken bold steps to bolster its own economy as an indirect way of contributing to the health of the world economy.

China has further stressed its "responsible and steady attitude" in the investment of its foreign reserves. Yi Gang, China's Central Bank Vice Governor, has stated that China was not about to panic and sell its enormous US-denominated assets.[38] Going further to press the US to do more to bolster confidence in its own economy,

---

[36] "China Passes Germany With 3rd-Highest GDP", *Washington Post*, 15 Jan. 2009. China accounted for around 6% of the world's total GDP by 2007. Its share of the world's total GDP was only 1.8% in 1978. See "NBS: China accounts for 6% of world's GDP in 2007", *China Daily*, 27 Oct. 2008.

[37] "China may top Japan as world's second-largest economy", *China Daily*, 10 Mar. 2009.

[38] "China says its economic fundamentals are good", *AFP*, 14 Nov. 2008.

Premier Wen Jiabao even expressed concern about the safety of Chinese assets in the US.[39] This prompted a quick response from US President Barrack Obama that "China and other nations can be assured of the health of their US investments".[40] The reality is that it is not in China's interests to draw down significantly on its investments in the US as this would not only trigger another bout of financial battering but also, more importantly, lead to a significant depreciation of any remaining US-denominated assets held by China.

China is aware that there is a limit to how much it can do to help the rest of the world as its economy is presently only a fraction of the US and European economies. It is also acutely aware that there remains much concern in the US and some quarters in Europe over China's rising international stature and its intentions. To avoid ruffling such feathers, China has opted to let the US (where the crisis first originated) and key European countries to lead the effort to forge an international response to deal with the crisis.

China has astutely participated in this effort as a concerned and active player willing to do its part to alleviate the negative impact of the financial meltdown. The discussions on the financial crisis at the Seventh ASEM Summit in Beijing in October 2008 was presented as a logical lead-up to the first G-20 Leaders' Summit in Washington in November 2008 that would discuss critical issues such as the "principles of reform of the international financial system as well as the stability and development of the world economy".[41] At the second G-20 Summit in London in April 2009, China reaffirmed its commitment to play a role as a responsible member of the international community. China was careful not to appear to be upstaging the role of the US or any other key European country at the various summits.

---

[39] "Premier worries about safety of Chinese assets in US", *Xinhuanet*, 13 Mar. 2009.
[40] "Obama assures nations on US investments", *Reuters*, 14 Mar. 2009. President Obama's Treasury Secretary Timothy Geithner conveyed the same message of assurance when he visited China in June 2009. See "Geithner tells China its dollar assets are safe", *Reuters*, 1 Jun. 2009.
[41] "Full text of statement of the Seventh Asia-Europe Meeting on the International Financial Situation", *Xinhuanet*, 24 Oct. 2008.

China's current approach harks back to a similar constructive and responsible role it played during the 1997 Asian financial crisis. Then, China gained a great deal of political mileage, particularly *vis-à-vis* ASEAN, when it refrained from devaluing the *Renminbi*. It also made a contribution to a standby credit programme for Thailand, where the crisis first started. This time round China is adopting a similar helpful stance. In fact, it seemed to have played a relatively more active and effective role *vis-à-vis* countries in the vicinity, particularly, the ASEAN member states, by agreeing to provide the necessary funding, credit, and aid to foster China-ASEAN cooperation and help ASEAN tide over current difficulties. By strengthening relations with its smaller and neighbours, China hopes that they will not only view China in a more positive light, but also recognise its claim of peaceful rise or peaceful development as non-threatening and mutually beneficial to countries of the region.

China's positive role in the present economic crisis has not gone unnoticed. For instance, key officials and economists from the World Bank, the US and European countries have complimented China for its economic stimulus package, calling it "timely" and "very wise".[42] Most recently, US Treasury Secretary Timothy Geithner praised Beijing for implementing aggressive stimulus policies to combat the downturn during his visit to China in June 2009. He also expressed the belief that China understands and has "confidence in the Fed's capacity to keep inflation low and stable over time, and in our capacity to — once we get this recovery back in place — bring our fiscal deficits down over time".[43]

Separately, Singapore's Senior Minister Goh Chok Tong was impressed with China's response to the financial crisis. He observed

---

[42] "China's stimulus package timely 'right step' — expert", *China Daily*, 15 Nov. 2008 and "WB, US, Brazil hail China's economic stimulus plan", *China Daily*, 10 Nov. 2008.

[43] "Geithner says Beijing has confidence in US", *The Wall Street Journal*, 3 Jun. 2009. Earlier, US Secretary of State Hillary Clinton also praised China for its timely stimulus package. See "Clinton Praises China Stimulus, Has Hope for North Korea Relationship", *The Wall Street Journal*, 17 Feb. 2009.

that China has, together with Europe and the US, lowered its interest rates to prevent some competitive leakages of funds to the *Renminbi*. He added that China has shown its commitment to keep its economy humming through a series of monetary and fiscal measures.[44]

POSSIBLE NEXT STEPS FOR CHINA

At the moment, China has delineated for itself a modest external role in dealing with the world financial and economic crisis. Its primary preoccupation will continue to be geared towards maintaining the growth momentum of the domestic economy and other prevailing domestic challenges. To be sure, there are optimistic signs that China has weathered the crisis rather well compared to other countries. Yet, this positive development is unlikely to detract China from its daunting domestic challenges in the foreseeable future.

While opting to let the major developed economies take the lead to address the current crisis and its negative impact, China has not neglected to capitalise on the situation to further its foreign policy objectives. Most significantly, it has begun to angle itself to assume a bigger role in any future financial order. Already, President Hu Jintao has called for a new international financial order that is "fair, just, inclusive and orderly".[45] This can be taken to mean more say for the developing countries with China as a key player. Such an approach is also less likely to raise the concerns in some influential quarters in the West that remain fearful of China's intentions and actions.

The current crisis may also hasten the power shift in global politics towards the Asia-Pacific. The US will still emerge from the crisis as the leading economic superpower, but politically chastened

---

[44] "SM impressed by China's response to financial crisis", *Asiaone*, 17 Oct. 2008 http://www.asiaone.com/Business/News/Story/A1Story20081017-94516.html.
[45] "Hu calls for concerted efforts to tide over financial crisis", *China Daily*, 16 Nov. 2008 and "Hu seeks trade boost to fight crisis", *China Daily*, 24 Nov. 2008.

and economically much weakened (because of its bulging external debt). This will provide emerging powers like China and India with more international space in the future. These two growing giants will want more say especially on issues that directly affect their interests.

The calls to reform the international financial institutions will mean that the US and European countries will have to share power with China. The calls to improve the international currency system may result in an outcome where other currencies, other than the US dollar, are also readily accepted. These two processes will be wrought with political wrangling given their sensitive nature. Even if China is eventually given a greater say in these international financial institutions, the US and Europe can be expected to retain influential roles. On the possibility of an alternative reserve currency, this will depend to a great extent on whether other countries are comfortable with this idea. The reality is that the US dollar remains the dominant currency in international finance and trade due to confidence in not only the dollar, but also the rather open and transparent US political system that underpins the dollar.

The present crisis appears to have temporarily put on the back-burner issues that used to hobble relations between China and the West. These include disagreements over human rights, democracy, treatment of dissidents, trade, Tibet and the Dalai Lama. Added to these is that China's ascendency has generated some trepidation in the West that the Washington consensus is losing traction. These differences may come to the fore again especially when the current crisis subsides or when China and the West disagree on the shape of the future financial order.[46]

China may yet have another card up its sleeve. It has so far only set for itself the minimum base position of keeping its own economic

---

[46] China's decision to postpone the China-EU Summit in December 2008 appeared to be primarily directed at France alone and did not appear to have damaged its relations with other European countries. Nevertheless, China and France seemed to have patched things up when President Hu Jintao met French President Sarkozy met at the sidelines of the G-20 Summit in London in April 2009.

house in order. There is sufficient room for China to decide whether it wants to do more on the external front in the future. China's current limited external role underscores the political astuteness of the Chinese leadership to the urgency of addressing pressing domestic issues at home as well as the need for China to refrain from pushing its interests too aggressively abroad.

Index